f
8 .11.06

The Translator as Communicator

Adopting an integrated approach to the practice of translation, Hatim and Mason provide a refreshingly unprejudiced contribution to translation theory.

The authors argue that the division of the subject into literary and non-literary, technical and non-technical is unhelpful and misleading. Instead of dwelling on these differentials, the authors focus on what common ground exists between these distinctions. Through their investigation into how, for example, the 'Bible' translator and the simultaneous interpreter can learn from each other, sets of parameters begin to evolve. The proposed model is presented through a series of case studies, ranging from legal texts to poems, each of which focuses on one particular feature of text constitution, while not losing sight of how this contributes to the whole analytic apparatus.

Their approach is durable and meaningful, especially in view of recent developments in the study of translation and communication, and their book will be of immense interest both to aspiring students of translation and to professionals already working in the field.

Basil Hatim and **Ian Mason** are both based at the Centre for Translation and Interpreting Studies in Scotland at Heriot-Watt University, Edinburgh. Both have published extensively in the area of translation and co-wrote *Discourse and the Translator* (1990).

The Translator as Communicator

Basil Hatim and Ian Mason

London and New York

First published 1997
by Routledge
2 Park Square, Milton Park, Abingdon, Oxon, OX14 4RN

Simultaneously published in the USA and Canada
by Routledge
270 Madison Ave, New York NY 10016

Transferred to Digital Printing 2005

Typeset in Baskerville by Florencetype Limited, Stoodleigh, Devon.

British Library Cataloguing in Publication Data
A catalogue record for this book is available from the British Library

Library of Congress Cataloguing in Publication Data
Hatim, B. (Basil)
    The translator as communicator/Basil Hatim and Ian Mason.
    Includes bibliographical references (p.) and index.
    1. Translating and interpreting. I. Mason, I. (Ian), 1944–
II. Title.
P.306.H38   1996
418'.02-dc20   96–15699

ISBN 0–415–11736–4 (hbk)
ISBN 0–415–11737–2 (pbk)

Contents

Figures

Preface

As the title of this book suggests, we look upon all kinds of acts of translating as essentially acts of communication in the same sense as that which applies to other kinds of verbal interaction. Even apparent exceptions, such as legal texts which constitute an official record of decisions made, or poems which are purely self-expressive, are nevertheless texts composed in the full knowledge that they are likely to be read and to elicit a response. They provide evidence on the basis of which people construct meaning. It is this characteristic which defines the common ground of a wide variety of translation activities: literary translating, religious translating, technical translating, interpreting, subtitling and dubbing, selectively reducing a text in a different language, and so on. Typically, a translator operates on the verbal record of an act of communication between source language speaker/writer and hearers/readers and seeks to relay perceived meaning values to a (group of) target language receiver(s) as a separate act of communication. (In some situations, for example liaison interpreting, the source language act of communication is intended directly and only for a target language receiver.) This is then the essential core, the common ground which we take as the point of departure for our study. Instead of dwelling on what differentiates the literary from the non-literary, the interpreter from the translator, and so on – distinctions which are well documented already – this book focuses on text features which serve as clues to an underlying textual strategy. For it is the case that all texts must satisfy basic standards of textuality before acquiring the additional characteristics of being literary, technical, oral, etc. And characteristics which come to the fore in particular fields of activity may be seen to be present in others where they are not so readily noticed. For example, an idiolectal feature which is conspicuous as a characteristic of someone's casual speech style may also play an important part in literary character portrayal. Features of politeness which are the common currency of face-to-face interaction may also be perceived in semi-technical, literary or sacred written texts. And ability to draw inferences is a universal of human verbal communication.

Approaching texts (as written or spoken records of verbal communication) in terms of an overall, context-sensitive strategy is, we believe, both durable and meaningful as a way of developing translation competence and this study has a pedagogical angle in addition to its aim of investigating the nature of translation. It is perhaps worth stating our view that, if translator training is limited to those superficial characteristics of text which are most typical of what the technical or administrative translator is likely to encounter most of the time (specialized terminology, formulaic text conventions and so on), then the trainee will be singularly ill-equipped to deal with, say, metaphor, allusion, implicature when these occur – as they do – in technical texts. It is also true to say that the nature of communication itself has changed. The communication explosion has brought with it more flexibility, more creativity in the way people use language. Genres of writing and speaking are no longer static entities but are evolving and influencing each other. The stiffly formulaic use of language in official texts has diminished and there are departures from norms – which are all the more significant for being unexpected. Prominent among the themes, concepts and procedures used in our discussions of texts will be the distinction between what we shall refer to as **static** and **dynamic** uses of language. While the static provides the translator with a stable world in which text conventions can be learned and applied, the dynamic poses a greater challenge to the translator's concern to retrieve and relay intended meanings. In our attempt to get to the root of what is going on in texts as records of communicative acts, this distinction is crucial and is closely bound up with approaches to the pragmatics and semiotics of translating.

In Chapters 1 and 2, we set the scene for what is to follow. Chapter 1 provides some examples of similarities of underlying textual strategies in texts of very different provenance and in widely varying translator situations. Chapter 2, which is necessarily more theoretical, proposes a basic model of textuality and discusses the implications it has for our understanding of translation. Key issues are then explored in the following chapters through a series of case studies, each of which focuses on a particular aspect of text constitution in a particular field of translating. Chapter 3 presents an hypothesis about the role of context, structure and texture in various modes of interpreting and Chapter 4 applies this hypothesis to an investigation of the performance of simultaneous interpreters. Chapter 5 investigates politeness phenomena in screen subtitling, while Chapter 6 discusses the discoursal role of idiolect and how it is to be handled in literary translating. The tension between relaying form and function, a traditional area of debate in translation studies, is studied from a discourse-linguistic perspective in Chapter 7, with reference to the translation of the sacred or 'sensitive' text. The cross-cultural competence of the translator is the subject of Chapter 8, in which the structure of argumentation in texts is studied from an intercultural perspective and found to be related to pragmatic factors such as politeness and to socio-cultural attitudes. This chapter provides the grounds for an understanding of ideology in translation, the subject of Chapter 9. Our final three chapters (10 to 12) explore training-related issues: the nature of beyond-the-sentence or text-level 'errors' in translating; an original approach to curriculum design based on a typology of texts; and approaches to the issue of translator performance assessment, all of which have been relatively neglected issues hitherto.

In our text, we have adopted the following typographical conventions. Items highlighted in bold print are included in the glossary at the end of the book; we have generally restricted this procedure to first mention of such items. Square brackets enclose our own deliberately literal translations of text samples in languages other than English.

Our thanks are due to generations of students who willingly took part in the experiments we conducted and often helped with their insights. Many friends and colleagues have helped us with their comments on earlier versions of the chapters in this book. Particular thanks are due to Ron Buckley, Charlene Constable, Ted Hope, John Laffling, Yvonne McLaren, Miranda Stewart and Gavin Watterson. Parts of the text were prepared during a period of study leave spent at the Faculty of Translation and Interpreting, Universitat Autònoma de Barcelona, and we are indebted to Allison Beeby, Sean Golden, Amparo Hurtado and Francesc Parcerisas for their generous help and support, as also to Mercè Tricàs and Patrick Zabalbeascoa of the Universitat Pompeu Fabra. Last but not least, thanks to Eugene Boyle for his patience in sorting out the software. All this support has been of inestimable value. As always, responsibility for any shortcomings which remain is ours alone.

Basil Hatim, Ian Mason February 1996.

Sources of samples

1.1   T. Kenneally (1982) *Schindler's Ark*. London: Hodder and Stoughton.

1.2   T. Kenneally (1994) *La Lista de Schindler* (trans. Carlos Peralta). Barcelona: RBA Proyectos Editoriales.

1.3–5   C. Bédard (1986) *La Traduction technique: principes et pratique.* Montreal: Linguatech.

1.6   S. Berk-Seligson (1990) *The Bilingual Courtroom. Court Interpreters in the Judicial Process.* Chicago: University of Chicago Press, © 1990 University of Chicago.

1.7   A. Camus (1942) *L'Etranger*. Paris: Gallimard, © Editions Gallimard.

1.8   A. Camus (1946) *The Outsider* (trans. Stuart Gilbert). London: Hamish Hamilton.

2.1   Reprinted from the UNESCO *Courier*, April 1990.

2.2   George Orwell (1954) *1984*. Harmondsworth: Penguin.

2.3   Woman interviewed in a BBC television documentary.

2.4   A. Kertesz (1979) 'Visual agnosia: the dual deficit of perception and recognition', *Cortex* 15: 403–19 (cited in Francis and Kramer-Dahl 1992).

2.5   O. Sacks (1985) *The Man Who Mistook his Wife for a Hat.* London: Picador (cited in Francis and Kramer-Dahl 1992).

2.6   Charles Dickens *A Tale of Two Cities* (cited in Gutt 1991).

2.7   S. P. Bobrov and M. P. Bogoslovskaja (1957) *Povest' o dvukh gorodakh*. Moscow: Sobranie sochenennii (cited in Gutt 1991).

2.8   Abdul Rahman Munif (1973) *Al-Ashjaar wa Ightiyal al-Shaykh Marzuuq* (The Trees and the Assassination of Sheikh Marzuq). Beirut: The Arab Establishment for Research and Publishing.

2.9   Abdul Rahman Munif *The Trees* (trans. the Iraqi Cultural Centre 1982).

Bedouin in the Formation of the Saudi State (trans. B. Hatim and R. Buckley). London: Al-Saqi Books.

8.8 Edward Said (1987) *Orientalism*. Harmondsworth: Penguin, p. 33.

8.9 Suggested translation of sentence from Said's *Orientalism*.

9.1 Ayatollah Khomeini (1991); address to instructors and students of religious seminaries, transcribed and translated by BBC Monitoring Service, *Guardian*, 6 March 1989, © the *Guardian*.

9.2 M. Léon-Portilla 'Tiene la historia un destino'/'History or destiny', reprinted from *Correo de la UNESCO/UNESCO Courier*, April 1990.

9.3–6 E. Le Roy Ladurie (1975) *Montaillou, village occitan de 1294 à 1324*. Paris: Gallimard, © Editions Gallimard.

9.3–6 E. Le Roy Ladurie (1980) *Montaillou* (trans. B. Bray) Harmondsworth: Penguin.

10.1 *The Economist*, 10 November 1990.

10.2 Watergate hearing (cited in Fairclough 1989).

10.3 John Ashbery (1979) 'Metamorphosis', in *As We Know*. New York: Viking (cited in McHale 1992).

10.4–5 *Al-Sharq Al-Awasat* 1992.

10.6 Concocted data.

10.7 Muhammed Shuqri (1995) *Zaman al-Akhta'*. Rabat.

10.8 Muhammed Shuqri (1996) *Streetwise* (trans. E. Emery). London: Al-Saqi Books.

11.1 A. Kertesz (1979) 'Visual agnosia: the dual deficit of perception and recognition', *Cortex*, 15: 403–19 (cited in Francis and Kramer-Dahl 1992).

11.2 O. Sacks (1985) *The Man Who Mistook his Wife for a Hat*. London: Picador (cited in Francis and Kramer-Dahl 1992).

11.3 Enoch Powell (cited in Sykes 1985).

11.4 The Woolwich Building Society; reproduced with permission, from an old advertisement used here for illustration only.

11.5 *World Health Forum* vol. 5, no. 2, 1984. Reproduced by permission of the Office of Publications, World Health Organization.

11.6 *UN Official Record of the Diplomatic Conference* (1974–7).

12.1 EU directive.

While the authors and publishers have made every effort to contact copyright holders of material used in this volume, they would be grateful to hear from any they were not able to contact.

Chapter 1

Unity in diversity

The world of the translator is inhabited by an extraordinary number of dichotomies, reflecting divisions which either exist or are supposed to exist between mutually exclusive opposites. Some of these are professional, corresponding to the traditional areas of activity of translators (the technical translator, the literary translator, the legal, the religious and so on). Others distinguish between different modes of translating: written, oral (such as simultaneous interpreting) and written-from-oral (such as screen subtitling), which again correspond to different professional orientations. A further set of dichotomies pertains to an age-old debate concerning the translator's priorities: 'literal' versus 'free', 'form' versus 'content', 'formal' versus 'dynamic equivalence', 'semantic' versus 'communicative translating' and – in more recent times – translator 'visibility' versus 'invisibility'.

This proliferation of terms and categories reflects the diversity of the translation world. Between the experience of the Bible translator, working in remote locations and with wholly unrelated languages, and that of the staff translator producing parallel copy of in-house documents in closely related languages, there is indeed a world of difference. Many of the concerns of the court interpreter are not shared, for example, by the translator of classical poetry. Indeed, their paths hardly ever cross. Yet there is a core of common concern which sometimes escapes unnoticed. It is striking that, beyond the widely diverging constraints which operate in different fields and modes of translating, so many of the intractable problems are shared. In this book, we propose to investigate areas of mutual interest and to uncover the striking uniformity which emerges when translating is looked upon as *an act of communication which attempts to relay, across cultural and linguistic boundaries, another act of communication (which may have been intended for different purposes and different readers/hearers)*. The common thread here is communication and, as the title of this book implies, our investigation is of communication strategies in the sense of the underlying principles behind the production and reception of texts – *all* texts, written and spoken, source and target, technical and non-technical, etc. The translator is, of course, both a receiver and a producer. We would like to regard him or her as a special category of communicator, one whose act of communication is conditioned by another, previous act and whose reception of that previous act is intensive. It is intensive because, unlike other text receivers, who may choose to pay more or less attention to their listening or reading, translators interact closely with their source text, whether for immediate response (as in the case of the simultaneous interpreter) or in a more reflective way (as in the translation of creative literature).

There are, as always, some apparent exceptions to the general rule. It may, for instance, be argued that poetry is essentially an act of self-expression and not one of communication. Therefore, an account of communication would be irrelevant to the work of the translator of poetry. But a poem which is to be translated has first to be read and the act of reading is, we submit, part of what we understand as communication. There may be all kinds of constraints which make the translation of poetry a special case, with its own concerns and problems, but the fact remains that there are a text producer and a text receiver, standing in some kind of relationship to each other. It is the nature of this relationship in general which interests us. The peculiarities of special cases, however constraining they may be, can only be truly appreciated once the underlying nature of the transaction is made clear.

The model of communication underlying all of our analyses will be the subject of Chapter 2. In this first chapter, we want to illustrate (from text samples in English, French and Spanish) some of the common concerns in all fields and modes of translating, to highlight what unites, rather than what divides them. In doing so, we hope to show the need for the (necessarily somewhat technical) description of text processing contained in the next chapter and how it will further our understanding of all kinds of acts of translating.

FIELDS OF TRANSLATING

Newmark (1981: 5–6) charts some of the false distinctions which have been made between literary and technical translation. At best these distinctions have been gross over-generalizations, such as the notion that the technical translator is concerned with content, the literary translator with form. But more often than not, they are simply misleading. Above all, they mask the essential similarities which may be perceived in texts of different fields, especially when communication is seen as more than a matter of exchanging words as tokens with fixed meanings. In discourse analysis, many works now subject literary and non-literary discourse to the same analysis and show similar linguistic processes at work. Fowler (e.g. 1986) illustrates many of the ways in which literary as well as non-literary texts create their effects. For the translator, one such shared concern may be the rhetorical structuring of a text and the use of logical connectors to enable readers to retrieve intended meanings. Text Sample 1.1 serves as a useful illustration of the point.

Sample 1.1

In the bar of the Hotel Cracovia, in fact, Oskar had already seen Gebauer hand over forged papers to a Jewish businessman for a flight to Hungary. Maybe Gebauer was taking a fee, though he seemed too morally sensitive to deal in papers, to sell a signature, a rubber stamp. But it was certain, in spite of his act in front of Toffel, that he was no abominator of the tribe. Nor were any of them. (. . .)

In this short fragment from Thomas Keneally's *Schindler's Ark* – described by the author as using the 'texture and devices of a novel to tell a true story' (Keneally 1982: 9) – coherence (the underlying continuity of sense of any stretch of language) can only be established by relating the sequence to its wider context, both linguistic and extra-linguistic. At this point in the narrative, Gebauer, a lieutenant in the German army, has been making pronouncements to his drinking companions, Schindler, Toffel and others, which would lead one to believe him to be wholly in favour of the SS policy towards the Jews in pre-war Germany. But Oskar Schindler, in fact, believes otherwise. In the fragment of interior monologue contained in Sample 1.1, he first entertains the notion that Gebauer's helpful gesture to a Jewish businessman may have been purely mercenary. Then he dismisses this notion and asserts his belief that Gebauer is 'no abominator of the tribe'. This rhetorical structure – putting one side of an argument and then dismissing it by stating more assertively the opposing point of view – is negotiated in Sample 1.1 through a series of connectors and modal adverbs: *in fact, maybe, though, but, nor.* If we now compare this fragment with its Spanish translation (Sample 1.2), we find a subtly different rhetorical structure: *la verdad era que, quizá, aunque, y, y tampoco* ('the truth was that', 'perhaps', 'although', 'and', 'and neither').

Sample 1.2

La verdad era que Oskar había visto a Gebauer mientras entregaba a un hombre de negocios judío, en el hotel Cracovia, documentos falsos para que pudiese huir a Hungría. Quizá Gebauer había recibido dinero a cambio, aunque parecía un hombre demasiado íntegro para vender papeles, firmas, sellos. Y estaba seguro, a pesar del papel que había representado ante Toffel, de que no odiaba a los judíos. Y tampoco los demás. (. . .)

[The truth was that Oskar had seen Gebauer while he was delivering to a Jewish businessman, in the Hotel Cracovia, false papers so that he might flee to Hungary. Perhaps Gebauer had received money in exchange, although he seemed too honest a man to sell papers, signatures, stamps. And it was certain, in spite of the role which he had played in front of Toffel, that he did not hate the Jews. And neither [did] the others.][1]

There are many interesting points in this translation, such as the stylistic 'flattening' of *abominator of the tribe* to *hate the Jews*, the kind of feature which can be described in the terms of **register membership** (see Chapter 2) and which we shall also describe as **discoursal** (that is, having to do with expression of attitude). But our main interest here is the structure of the argument concerning Gebauer. Sample 1.2 has 'And it was certain' whereas the source text reads *But it was certain.* Technically, what this translation does is to turn the belief that Gebauer did not hate the Jews into an addition to the caveat about his moral sensitivity: 'Perhaps . . . although he seemed . . . and it was certain . . .' This leaves room for doubt: perhaps he was pro-SS, perhaps not. The matter is left unresolved. The source text (1.1), on the other hand, strongly signals that Schindler does not believe Gebauer is pro-SS, even though he may have taken money in exchange for providing false papers. This is done by first suggesting a mercenary motive, which is immediately shown to be a weak hypothesis (though . . .), and then strongly asserting an opposing view. The difference between source and target text is subtle and depends upon interpretation of the function in this fragment of the connectors *But* (Sample 1.1) and *Υ* ('and' – Sample 1.2). Nevertheless, it provides some access into the signalling of intentions and attitude by writer to reader – here, in the field of literary translation.

Such processes are at work in technical translation too. Bédard (1986: 1) explodes the myth of technical translation being a matter of one-for-one exchange of technically precise vocabulary tokens and portrays it above all as *'un acte d'intelligence et de communication'*. Devoting a chapter to what he calls the demands of communication, he adduces an example which we reproduce here as Samples 1.3–5. Of these, 1.3 is the source text and 1.4 and 1.5 are variant translations.

Sample 1.3

The cost of operating an air conditioner is relatively low. However, there are many factors that contribute to cost of operation. Most important is proper capacity. Too small a capacity for the application would prove just as expensive as too large a capacity. Proper insulation and location of windows are other cost factors.

Sample 1.4

Le coût d'utilisation d'un climatiseur est assez modique, mais dépend bien sûr de divers facteurs, comme l'emplacement des fenêtres et le degré d'isolement. Il importe aussi de choisir une capacité appropriée à l'utilisation envisagée: un appareil trop petit se révélera aussi dispendieux à l'usage qu'un appareil trop puissant.
[The operating cost of an air conditioner is fairly modest but depends of course on several factors, such as the location of the windows and the degree of insulation. It is also important to choose a capacity appropriate to the expected use: too small a unit will prove as expensive in use as too powerful a unit.]

Sample 1.5

Le coût d'utilisation d'un climatiseur est normalement assez faible. Par contre, il peut s'élever dans certaines conditions: par

exemple si les fenêtres sont situées en plein soleil, si l'isolement
est mauvais ou si l'appareil choisi est trop faible ou trop puissant
pour les besoins.
[The operating cost of an air conditioner is usually fairly low.
Nevertheless, it may rise in certain conditions: for example if the
windows are situated in full sun, if the insulation is poor or if
the unit selected is too weak or too powerful for needs.]

The clarity of variant 1.5 is improved above all by the **explication**
of certain notions such as the location of windows – a decision
which will hinge on the translator's perception of the consumers of
the target text, an important factor in translating which we shall
refer to as **audience design**. But beyond this, there is a structural
similarity here to our literary examples (1.1 and 1.2). Here, source
and target texts all advance the notion that operating costs may be
fairly low and then counter this with a statement that costs can
be high in certain circumstances. But each translation conveys this
opposition in a different way. In Sample 1.4, the opposition is back-
grounded by (1) being placed in the same sentence and made
dependent on the same subject and (2) being accompanied by
the **modal** adverbial *bien sûr* ('of course'), which relays an **implicature** of the kind: 'but this is an obvious point, hardly worth
mentioning'. In Sample 1.5, the emphasis is quite different. The
use of *par contre* ('nevertheless' or 'on the other hand') in a second
sentence, juxtaposed to the first one, foregrounds an important
caveat, which might be glossed as 'but pay attention to high running
costs in certain conditions'. In no way can it be claimed that
the two variant translations are communicatively, pragmatically or
semiotically equivalent.

In our brief consideration of illustrations of counter-argumentation
structures in literary and technical texts, we have seen a variety of
degrees of emphasis and balance between opposing facts or points
of view which reflect differing attitudes on the part of text producers
towards what they have to say. The importance of structures such
as these in texts and translations will be discussed in Chapter 2 and
a categorization of the various sub-types of the structure will be
proposed in Chapter 8. The examples selected as 1.1–5 above
may, in themselves, seem slight in terms of the actual consequences
on users of the translations proposed. How much weight can be
attached, for example, to the alteration by a translator of an adversative to an additive marker of junction? But the point being pursued

here is not some plea for literalist adherence to the grammar of junction in the source text. Rather, we are interested in the signals that text producers send to text receivers about the way they view the world, in the way meaning is inferred beyond the words-on-the-page, so to say, and how the resources of language users for doing this kind of thing transcend any artificial boundaries between different fields of translating.

MODES OF TRANSLATING

In a similar way, it should not be assumed that because translating in the written and in the oral mode are known by different terms – translating and interpreting – they have little in common. Although the two activities are usually rigorously separated on translator/ interpreter training programmes, there is a strong case for creating a common core of fundamental issues to do with communication strategies. Many of the ways in which language users exploit the potentialities of the language system for particular purposes are common to both the written and the spoken modes. The case we shall explore here in order to illustrate the point is that of the **transitivity** system of languages and the way it relates to attribution of responsibility and/or blame.

In a study of bilingual interaction in American courtrooms, Berk-Seligson (1990) shows how various forms of passive or impersonal constructions can be exploited for the purpose of avoiding explicit blame. We reproduce here, as Sample 1.6, a particularly telling sequence. An attorney is examining a witness (a Mexican 'undocumented alien') in a case in which the defendant is accused of having smuggled the witness across the Mexico/US border in exchange for a fee. It is striking that, throughout this sequence, the attorney, by means of a series of passive constructions, avoids referring directly to the defendant, presumed to be the driver of the car.

Sample 1.6

Attorney: Do you remember, sir, being asked this question (. . .)?

Interpreter: ¿Se acuerda usted, señor, que le preguntaron esta pregunta (. . .)?
              [Do you remember, sir, that they asked you this question?]

Attorney:	Where were you going to be given a ride to, where was your destination?
Interpreter:	¿Cuál era el destino de ustedes, hacia dónde les iba a dar el ride?
	[What was your (plur.) destination, to where was he going to give you (plur.) the ride?]
Attorney:	Did you discuss with him where you were going to be taken?
Interpreter:	¿Discutió usted con él adónde lo iba a llevar?
	[Did you discuss with him where he was going to take you?]
Attorney:	When you were picked up by the car, did you, I take it that you got into the car, is that correct?
Interpreter:	Cuando los levantó el carro ... cuando lo levantó a usted el carro ... cuando a usted lo levantó el carro ... estoy asumiendo que usted se subió al carro, ¿es esto correcto?
	[When the car picked you (plur.) up ... when the car picked you (sing.) up ... when the car picked *you* (sing.) up ... I am assuming that you got into the car, is that correct?]

In translating the first question in this sequence, the interpreter avails herself of a Spanish-language device, the third-person plural impersonal with passive meaning: 'Do you remember, sir, that they asked you . . .?' This is one of a number of available ways in Spanish of expressing processes with passive effect. Although potentially ambiguous ('they' = specific persons or person(s) unspecified), it effectively relays here the agentless passive *being asked*. The modification is made necessary by the fact that, as Berk-Seligson notes, whereas use of the passive is extremely frequent in American English judicial settings, use of the true passive is relatively rare in spoken Spanish. However, in the following series of questions, instead of using one of the range of alternative Spanish devices for expressing passive effect and avoiding specifying an agent, the interpreter turns the attorney's passive into an active process, with either the defendant ('he') or the defendant's car in subject position. This attributes responsibility (for illegal acts) much more directly to the defendant than do the 'blame-avoidance' passives of the attorney. In interpreting the final question in 1.6, the interpreter, correcting herself twice, is very careful to relay the intended object pronoun in the intended grammatical case ('you', singular) and to emphasize it (*you* is in subject position in the source text), yet she ignores the English passive ('you were picked up by the car') and foregrounds the car as a responsible agent by making it the subject of the verb. Berk-Seligson's study adduces far greater evidence than what we have reproduced here and demonstrates convincingly that significant alterations do take place to the backgrounding or foregrounding of agent responsibility for blameworthy actions. In a judicial setting, such findings are clearly of great significance.

To see similar processes at work in a completely different mode of translating, let us now turn to the written mode and to the field of creative literature. Samples 1.7 and 1.8 are taken from Albert Camus's novel *L'Etranger* and a translation of it *The Outsider*.

Sample 1.7

Tout mon être s'est tendu et j'ai crispé ma main sur le revolver. La gâchette a cédé, j'ai touché le ventre poli de la crosse et c'est là, dans le bruit à la fois sec et assourdissant, que tout a commencé. (. . .) Alors j'ai tiré encore quatre fois sur un corps inerte où les balles s'enfonçaient sans qu'il y parût. Et c'était comme quatre coups brefs que je frappais sur la porte du malheur.
[My whole being tensed and I clenched my hand on the revolver. The trigger yielded, I touched the polished belly of the butt and it is there, in the noise both sharp and deafening, that everything began. (. . .) Then I fired four more times on an inert body into which the bullets sank without there being any trace. And it was like four brief knocks that I was striking on the door of misfortune.]

Sample 1.8

Every nerve in my body was a steel spring, and my grip closed on the revolver. The trigger gave, and the smooth underbelly of the butt jogged my palm. And so, with that crisp, whip-crack sound, it all began. (. . .) But I fired four shots more into the inert body, on which they left no visible trace. And each successive shot was another loud, fateful rap on the door of my undoing.

Here, we are once more in the presence of blameworthy events. In the following part of the novel, Camus's narrator, Meursault, will be tried and found guilty of murder on the basis of the events narrated here. And once again it is transitivity and agency which is in focus in these text fragments. Without delving into transitivity analysis,[2] it will be helpful here to note that processes of 'doing' are known as **material processes**, subdivided in turn into **action processes** (in which the actor is animate) and **event processes** (in which the actor is inanimate). Action processes may be further subdivided into **intention processes** (in which the actor performs the act voluntarily) and **supervention processes** (in which the process happens independently of volition). Of the eight material processes in the source text sample, four may be classified as event processes (*s'est tendu; a cédé; a commencé; s'enfonçaient*) and four as intention action processes (*j'ai crispé; j'ai touché; j'ai tiré; je frappais*). In this way a balance is achieved between Meursault's intentional actions and things or circumstances operating on him. An analysis of the wider co-text of the novel would show that this mix is characteristic of a narrative in which Meursault is both carried along by events and frankly admitting to being an active participant in them, with a high incidence of material intention processes beginning *j'ai*. . . . In our target text fragment, however, there is only one intention action process (*I fired*) while there are five event processes (*my grip closed;*[3] *the trigger gave; the underbelly jogged; it began; they left no trace*). The remaining two source text material processes have become, in the target text, what are known as **relational processes** (that is, processes of being: X 'is a' Y): 'every nerve was a steel spring'; 'each shot was another rap'. This sustained shift in transitivity patterns has the effect of presenting Meursault as more acted upon than acting – an effect which the translator may have wished to relay as reflecting what he saw as an overall characteristic of the source text.

Our concern here – and more generally throughout this book – is not to perform translation criticism nor to seek to impute particular motives to translators. Rather, we wish to bring out the importance of **context**ually determined communication strategies and the way they relate to the **structure** and **texture** of texts, be they oral, written, literary, technical or whatever. Thus, in Chapter 5, we shall examine **politeness** strategies in screen translating and in Chapter 7 the phenomenon of **reference switching** in the translation of sacred texts. Central to such analyses as these will be the sociolinguistic variables of **power** and **distance** – factors which are germane to the examples we have discussed here and which transcend particular fields and modes of translating. These phenomena and many of those we have described earlier in this chapter belong to the pragmatic and semiotic domains of context.[4] It will therefore be important to bear in mind throughout our analyses both the relation of utterances to the interpretation of their users' intentions (**pragmatics**) and the ways in which signs (from individual items to whole texts) interact within a socio-cultural environment (**semiotics**).

THE TRANSLATOR'S FOCUS

The third set of dichotomies identified at the beginning of the chapter had to do with translators' orientations: 'literal' vs. 'free', 'form' vs. 'content', and so on. The unsatisfactory nature of these distinctions and of the debates centred round them is amply documented. Various attempts have been made to replace them with other sets of terms, seen as being more closely related to what translators actually set out to achieve. Nida's (1964) 'formal equivalence' and 'dynamic equivalence' sought to distinguish between the aim to achieve equivalence of form between source and target texts and the aim to achieve equivalence of effect on the target language reader. Similarly, Newmark (1981: 39) distinguishes between 'semantic translation' (relaying as closely as the structures of the target language will allow the 'exact contextual meaning' of the source text) and 'communicative translation' (again, equivalence of effect). These polar opposites seem to have been interpreted as representing mutually exclusive alternatives and as an initial, free choice which a translator makes. Whatever the value of these distinctions, it is important to regard them as representing the opposite ends of a continuum, different translation strategies being more or less appropriate according to different translation situations. But it is the notion of *skopos* (or purpose of translating) which poses the greatest challenge to dichotomies of this kind.[5] Translators' choices are constrained above all by the 'brief' for the job which they have to perform, including the purpose and status of the translation, the likely readership and so on. To look at this in terms of examples discussed earlier, we can easily appreciate that the *skopos* of the American courtroom interpreter is remote from that of the translator of Albert Camus or Thomas Keneally, which again is wholly different from that of the technical report on air conditioning systems. Thus one key element of the *skopos* is the specification of the task to be performed, as stipulated by the initiator of the translation (employer, commissioner, publisher, etc.). Another key notion in our understanding of how text producers gear their output to receivers is **audience design** (A. Bell 1984). This notion will be developed in Chapter 5 and further in Chapter 9, where the variance between the audience design of the producer of the source text and that of the producer of the target text will be illustrated.

But, in addition to these fundamental differences of destination, the text itself will impose its own constraints. Where, for example, a news agency report quotes the controversial words of some foreign head of state, the translator's *skopos* shifts within the text from the sense and intended values of the source text to focusing on the words – often the form of the words. Where a source text departs from what is expected or ordinary and opts for unexpected or unusual expression, it is the linguistic, cultural and rhetorical significance of the departure which becomes the translator's focus. Consequently, a central issue for us will be what is known as **markedness** in texts. Conventionally, markedness is defined either as infrequency of occurrence (that is, less frequently occurring expressions are somehow more significant when they do occur) or as informativity (that is, the less predictable in context an item is, the more information it potentially relays).[6] A fuller account of this element of text is given in Chapter 2, where the notions of **static** and **dynamic** use of language will be introduced. Markedness is closely related to such pragmatic features as **presupposition** (what speakers/writers assume hearers/readers are likely to accept without challenge) and **implicature**s (as additional meanings which may be intended and/or perceived when communicative norms are flouted).[7] Now, judgements about presuppositions, implicatures and markedness in general can only be made in relation to the sociocultural context in which they occur. Thus the translator's inter-cultural judgement is inevitably brought into play in attempting to perceive and relay these extra layers of meaning. Indeed one might define the task of the translator as a communicator as being one of seeking to maintain **coherence** by striking the appropriate balance between what is **effective** (i.e. will achieve its communicative goal) and what is **efficient** (i.e. will prove least taxing on users' resources) in a particular environment,[8] for a particular purpose and for particular receivers.

Piecing together these word-level and text-level meanings to form an overall textual strategy is the unifying theme of this book and the guiding principle behind the analyses contained in each chapter.

In this sense some of the examples adduced here and in later chapters may, in themselves, seem slight. What, one might ask, is in the translation of an individual junctive such as 'and' or 'but' or of a concessive such as 'granted'? But our interest lies not in the translation of the words as individual items but in the clues these provide to an overall textual strategy and the way this may inform translators' decisions. In this chapter we have tried to show how such concerns are pertinent to all fields and modes of translating. The diversity – of texts and text forms, professional fields, purposes and ultimate destinations of translations – is manifest; the unity of what constitutes (source and target) text in context is less apparent. In order to pursue our investigation of these phenomena, we shall first present a model of the way texts work (Chapter 2) before applying it to a variety of translation situations (Chapters 3 to 9) and to issues in training (Chapters 10 to 12).

Chapter 2

Foundations for a model of analysing texts

To say that translators communicate may perhaps strike one as a fairly obvious claim to make. Yet, it is this very quest for the successful exchange of meanings that is at the heart of what we pursue as professional or trainee translators, teachers or critics of translation. Typically, one might say of translators that they are constantly exchanging something, not only by engaging in a dialogue with a source text producer and a likely target text receiver, but also by brokering a deal between the two parties to communicate across both linguistic and cultural boundaries. One way of getting to the core of what takes place and of unravelling this communicative game, is to chart the routes which the major players travel along and to see the entire exercise in terms of a set of parameters within which textual activities are carried out.

In any attempt to examine the communicative nature of the translating task, a number of assumptions will have to be made about texts, their users and the context in which they occur. Such assumptions will take the form of hypothetical statements which we as researchers make in the light of our current understanding of how communication works. It would of course be desirable to proceed by observation based solely on sound empirical evidence. But, texts being what they are – an imperfect record of communicative events – we sometimes find it necessary to settle for what may be described as heuristic procedures. Interaction makes its own rules, a process in which entire conceptual systems are involved, including those which have developed through our own experience with texts.

ASSUMPTIONS ABOUT TEXTS AND THEIR USERS

To illustrate what we mean by 'assumptions', let us consider what a particular text sample confronts us with as readers. In examining the intricacies of this process, we shall eclectically use elements from a number of fairly standard models of text processing.[1] The stretch of text in Sample 2.1 is part of an article on the subject of heritage, published in the UNESCO *Courier*. For ease of reference, the sample is presented here sentence by sentence.

Sample 2.1

1 The greatest and most tragic clash of cultures in pre-Columbian civilization was recorded by some of those who took part in the conquest of Mexico.

2 Hernán Cortés himself sent five remarkable letters (*Cartas de Relación*) back to Spain between 1519 and 1526;

3 and the soldier-chronicler Bernal Díaz del Castillo (c. 1492–1580), who served under Cortés, fifty years after the event wrote his *Historia verdadera de la conquista de la Nueva España* ('True History of the Conquest of New Spain').

4 The vanquished peoples also left written records.

5 A manuscript dated 1528, now in the Bibliothèque Nationale in Paris, recounts in Nahuatl, the language of the Aztecs, the traumatic fate of the Indians.

Seen within the context of the entire article, Sample 2.1 appears to meet a number of standards which, when fulfilled, uphold textuality and ensure that a stretch of language is successful as a communicative event. To start with, the sample is **cohesive** in the sense that the various components of the surface text (the actual words we see) are mutually connected within a sequence of some kind. In terms of both lexis and grammar, that is, the surface components depend upon each other in establishing and maintaining text continuity. Consider, for example, the additive function of *also* in sentence 4:

4 *The vanquished peoples also left written records.*

In this context, this item serves to add a further participant (*the vanquished peoples*) to two previously mentioned participants (*Cortés* and *Díaz del Castillo*). But it is a recognized fact that it is just as easy to find sequences of elements which, although displaying all these lexico-grammatical dependencies, still fail the textuality test. The dependencies might be insufficient to reflect a recognizable pattern of concepts and relations which we can relate to recognizable portions of reality or what we shall refer to as a **text world**. The underlying concepts and relations must also appear to the reader to be mutually relevant and accessible in establishing and maintaining sense constancy or **coherence**.[2] Let us look at the relationship between sentences 4 and 5 in Sample 2.1:

4   *The vanquished peoples also left written records.*
5   *A manuscript dated 1528, now in the Bibliothèque Nationale in Paris, recounts in Nahuatl, the language of the Aztecs, the traumatic fate of the Indians.*

Here, sentence 5 'substantiates' what is said in the preceding sentence, with the cohesive links between *records* and *manuscript* and between *peoples* and *Aztecs* helping to establish coherence. It also serves as an elaboration, providing another 'aspect' of the scene originally set in sentence 1:

1   *The greatest and most tragic clash of cultures in pre-Columbian civilization was recorded by some of those who took part in the conquest of Mexico.*

The two text-centred notions of cohesion and coherence incorporate elements of what we shall refer to as the **texture** and **structure** of texts. These are areas of text organization involving both the way texts are put together and the way the emerging patterns link up with some model of reality. To approach these aspects of textuality from a procedural point of view, we can now put forward the following assumption:

Assumption 1

Text users (writers, readers, translators, etc.) engage in a form of negotiation which moves in a text-to-context direction, as a point of departure for the way a text is composed in accordance with certain communicative requirements.

At this elementary stage of text processing, we suggest, contextual requirements related, say, to the structure of texts will normally be extremely unclear or fuzzy. As texts unfold, however, a fuller picture gradually emerges, fleshing out the bare details of the scheme within which they might be envisaged. For example, in dealing with Sample 2.1, a 'scene-set-then-expanded' format gradually comes into view, as in Figure 2.1. At the same time as this format is emerging, readers try to match elements of meaning yielded by this **bottom-up** processing activity with their expectations of what either a detached or a committed review of events might look like. Expectations may be defied or fulfilled, but the final arbiter is always the analysis of text in context. In the light of this, we may now formulate our second assumption:

Assumption 2

Simultaneously with bottom-up analysis, text users take contextual factors into consideration and assess them in terms of the way they impinge 'top-down' upon actual texts as these unfold in real time.

What are the contextual requirements which a sequence of cohesive elements must fulfil to be recognized as ultimately coherent? To examine this interaction between text and context, we must consider the standard of **intertextuality**. This builds on the fundamental notion that the various surface elements of a text, together with their underlying conceptual meaning potential, are in effect 'signs' which play a role in the signification process. This **semiotic** process

1 THE GREATEST CLASH OF CULTURES IN PRE-COLUMBIAN CIVILIZATION WAS **RECORDED.**

2 CORTES SENT FIVE LETTERS BACK TO SPAIN.

3 DIAZ DEL CASTILLO WROTE 'TRUE HISTORY'.

4 THE VANQUISHED PEOPLES ALSO LEFT WRITTEN RECORDS.

5 A MANUSCRIPT DATED 1528 RECOUNTS THE TRAUMATIC FATE OF THE INDIANS.

Figure 2.1 Scene set and expanded

includes all those factors which enable text users to identify a given text element or sequence of elements in terms of their knowledge of one or more previously encountered texts or text elements.

The dependency on a prior text is usually indicated by linguistic and/or non-linguistic means at any level of text organization: phonology, morphology, syntax or the entire compositional plan of the text. The source of the intertextual reference could, to start with, be any one of a myriad of what we shall call **socio-cultural objects** (e.g. 'Job' as in the phrase 'the patience of Job'). Such entities are conventionally recognized as being salient in the life of a given linguistic community, often reflecting commonly held assumptions. Consider, for example, the following lexical elements from Sample 2.1:

> *pre-Columbian civilization* (in which the arrival of a European is seen as the main historical milestone, as opposed to 'pre-Montezuma', for example);

> *the Indians* (which is consistent with a Euro-centric, Columbian nomenclature, as opposed to, say, 'ancient Mexicans' or 'Aztecs').

But intertextuality may and often does involve aspects which are more challenging than the socio-cultural. The reference could indeed be to entire sets of rhetorical conventions governing **text**s, **genre**s and **discourse**s. Texts involve the language user in focusing on a given rhetorical purpose (arguing, narrating, etc.). Genres reflect the way in which linguistic expression conventionally caters for a particular social occasion (the letter to the editor, the news report, etc.). Finally, discourses embody attitudinal expression, with language becoming by convention the mouthpiece of societal institutions (sexism, feminism, bureaucratism, etc.). These categories are part of what we shall term the **socio-textual practices** of communities of text users.[3] As we have already hinted, by the way Sample 2.1 develops (Figure 2.1) we recognize it as an instance of predominantly detached **exposition** and not, say, committed **argumentation**.

Seeing intertextuality at work in this way now enables us to formulate our third assumption:

Assumption 3

Values yielded by top-down analysis tend to cross-fertilize with features identified in bottom-up analysis. Together, these regulate the way texts come to do what they are intended to do. As part of this process, intertextuality is a semiotic parameter exploited by text users, which draws on the socio-cultural significance a given occurrence might carry, as well as on recognizable socio-textual practices (texts, discourses and genres).

Now, text users have intentions and, in order to indicate whether a text is of this or that type, or whether a given text element invokes this or that socio-cultural concept, a text producer will engage with another contextual criterion, known as **intentionality**. Taken out of context, a particular sequence of sounds, words or sentences is often neutral as to its intertextual potential. Intended meaning materializes only when **pragmatic** considerations are brought to bear on what the text producer does with words and what it is hoped the text receiver accepts. For example, an intertextual reference to 'Canute' is in itself static and may at best yield values such as 'he was the king who, in his arrogance, claimed he could order the tide not to come in'. However, the way the reference is made on a particular occasion by a pro-Conservative British newspaper, the *Daily Mail*, in a non-neutral piece of reporting headlined 'Canute Kinnock', the term takes on added values such as 'the newly-elected Labour Party leader is unfit to govern'. Does it not then become a matter of who utters what and for what purpose?

Intentionality can be seen in both highly abstract and relatively concrete terms. At a fairly high level of abstraction, intentionality involves the text producer's attitude that the text in hand should constitute a cohesive and coherent whole and that it should inter-textually link up with a set of socio-textual conventions recognizable by a given community of text users. For example, the producer of Sample 2.1 has made sure that sufficient cues are provided not only to show that the text hangs together but that it also serves a particular text-type focus (i.e. detached exposition):

X himself sent . . .; and Y wrote . . . Z also left.

These cohesion and coherence relations are part of overall intentionality. At a more concrete level of analysis, on the other hand, intentionality comprises a set of goals (e.g. to assert, to substantiate, etc.). These may be achieved locally by relaying intended meanings or globally by contributing to the mutual dependence of the various intentions within an overall plan of the entire text. In fact, it is the overall plan, seen within the socio-textual practices of a given community of text users, that is the primary driving force in the act of signification. The text producer consistently seeks not only to indicate the relevant socio-cultural values which the text is intended to represent (*pre-Columbian, Indians*), but also, and perhaps more significantly, to define the socio-textual focus of the text as a whole (detached exposition).

Casting this in procedural terms, we can now formulate our fourth assumption, thus:

Assumption 4

Text producers' intentions, beliefs, presuppositions and inferences are brought to bear on the analysis and perception of a given unit of meaning. Meaning is here understood to cover areas of both socio-cultural and socio-textual practice.

In pursuing intended goals, translators (as a special category of text receivers and producers) seek to relay to a target reader what has already been communicated by a text producer and presented with varying degrees of explicitness in the text. The question we ought to address at this juncture is whether a given sequence of cohesive and coherent linguistic elements, intended to display a particular intertextual potential, is actually appropriate to a given situation of occurrence. This property of texts is known as **situationality**.

As a standard of textuality, situationality is taken to mean the way text users interact with register variables such as **field**, **mode** and **tenor**. Items such as *civilization, record, conquest, vanquished,* establish historical writing as the predominant subject matter; there is a general air of formality and the mode is one that is typical of a text written to be read rather reflectively. Defining the register membership of the text in this way provides us with the basis for our fifth assumption about what goes on in the production and reception of texts:

Assumption 5

Register membership is defined in terms of a number of parameters which constrain the communicative transaction. These include field (or subject matter), tenor (or level of formality), and mode (or the distinction between spoken and written). It is by recognition of such factors that registers are defined.

The various standards of textuality and the domains of context to which they relate may now be presented schematically as in Figure 2.2. The static nature of diagrams like this, however, can obscure the true complexity of interaction. For example, in opting for *pre-Columbian*, the producer of Sample 2.1 has made a deliberate choice to avoid alternatives such as 'pre-Montezuma'; either option would have equally effectively served the subject matter of historical writing. But the two alternatives would not have served the same social institutions or social processes involved. As we suggested earlier, *pre-Columbian* makes the arrival of a European the main historical milestone, whereas focusing on the indigenous man could among other things highlight commitment to a pro-Mexican cause.

Furthermore, the various choices which superficially relay a formal tenor, in reality reflect a more **power**-oriented stance, which may in practice be considered characteristic of 'expert' historical

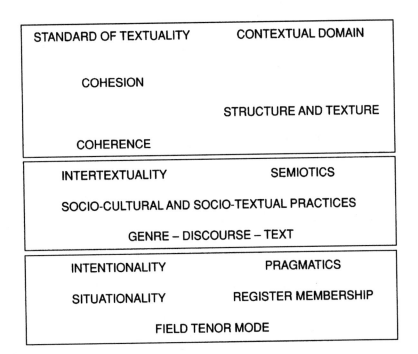

Figure 2.2 Standards and domains of textuality

writing. Different choices in mood or modality, for example, could have relayed an attitude of greater **solidarity**: is it simply 'X sent ... and Y wrote ...' or could it be 'about this, X and Y would/might be expected to write'? By incorporating into our analysis these additional layers of meaning which accrue from the options actually selected, we gain more insight into the issue of tenor and our view of formality. Here, what is at stake is the issue of **social distance**: it is the social roles enacted in establishing a particular relationship between producer and receiver and between both of these and their subject matter that motivate the various choices and indicate the appropriate degree of formality.

Finally, the variable of mode also takes us beyond the elementary distinction between spoken and written. Distance is once again involved here; but this time, it is intended in the 'physical' and not the 'social' sense. Mode thus includes the degree of **physical proximity** between producer and receiver, as well as between users and subject matter. In this respect, the producer of Sample 2.1 strikes us as being physically distant. The distance could have been reduced had the intention of the producer been to talk less 'like a book' and more intimately as colleague to colleague.

REGISTER AS A SOCIAL SEMIOTIC

This view of register membership is both richer and more far-reaching than earlier distinctions.[4] Here, intentionality is inevitably involved in the text producer's desire to be part of particular social institutions and processes, to be power- or solidarity-oriented, or to adopt a particular distance with regard to the addressee and the object of description. Furthermore, such communicative goals are purposeful in that they ultimately link up with the way we partition and view reality (the semiotics of culture). Cumulatively, all of the values yielded by the various domains of context referred to above contribute to and are shaped by the culture of a community. The trend of historical writing to which the producer of Sample 2.1 subscribes, for example, may be seen as a cultural manifestation in its own right, with its own ideology, aims and assumptions. Such a trend brings together those who have access to the socio-textual practices which distinguish them from other 'fraternities'. The professional expert as a member of such an institution tends predominantly to use particular genres (e.g. the review of events), particular texts (e.g. the narrative) and particular discourses (e.g. the authoritative) as vehicles through which to promote the ideas and ideals of the institution in question.

This more comprehensive view of field, mode and tenor, together with a more active notion of intentionality, takes us directly into language as a social-semiotic. There is, however, a further dimension to register which relates the genesis of communication to the actual words finally chosen in the composition of the text. First, within the category 'field', language users generate **ideational** meanings which are ultimately realized in the actual choices made within linguistic systems such as those of **transitivity** (the way we view reality and represent it in the arrangement of the clause in terms of participants, processes and circumstances).

To illustrate transitivity in texts, let us look at the thematic choices made in the four sentences of Sample 2.1. The passive in sentence 1 has the effect of making more salient the notion of the clash of cultures and in the process deflecting attention from the true agency of some of those who took part in the conquest. A static view is relayed which may be glossed as 'there is nothing new here; those who wrote about it are listed below with the main ones first'.

Second, the category 'tenor' relates to choices made within the **interpersonal** function of language, and finds expression in the **mood** and **modality** in actual texts. Mood covers the three basic sentence forms: the declarative, the interrogative and the imperative. Modality reflects the attitude towards the status of what is expressed. In Sample 2.1, the declarative 'statement' form which predominates, together with the associated modality of conviction, organize texture in support of a given structure format and text type focus. In this way, mood and modality are linked to the social institutions and processes involved (field), this time via the notion of social distance.

Finally, mode (which we characterized above in terms of the physical distance between producer and receiver, and between producer and object of description) also motivates various procedures undertaken within the so-called **textual** function of language. In Sample 2.1, the thematic chain *Hernán Cortes > Díaz del Castillo > the vanquished peoples*, introduced in the three sentences following the initial passive sentence (texture) supports the format of setting a scene and providing details (structure). An expository focus (**text type**) is intended and maintained (pragmatics) in the interests of serving a given ideological stance (semiotics).[5]

Taking all these things together, we can now represent in diagrammatic form (Figure 2.3) the way in which the individual categories

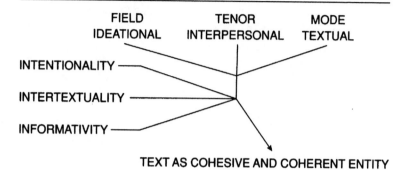

Figure 2.3 The interaction of text with context

interact with each other to produce new meanings and relay new values which contribute to the cohesion and coherence of the text. To fulfil the various standards of textuality, then, a given sequence of sentences must be one that:

1 is relevant to a situation of occurrence (situationality);
2 has components of surface realization which are intended to be mutually connected (intentionality and cohesion);
3 has underlying concepts and relations which are mutually accessible and relevant (intentionality and coherence);
4 shows dependence on recognizable prior texts and text elements (intertextuality).

MOTIVATEDNESS IN THE USE OF LANGUAGE

It is important to understand that underlying the whole model presented above is the notion of **motivatedness**. It is this notion which provides the essential link between textural occurrences and the context in which they are embedded. Bearing in mind the global view of field, tenor and mode outlined above, we can identify register features as performing a variety of individual tasks that add up to particular ideational, interpersonal and textual orientations. Take, for instance, **nominalization** (the conversion of an agent-verb sequence into a single noun as in 'someone criticized' vs. 'there has been criticism'). This is a device which may be used locally in texts to serve a variety of global ideational aims such as the expression of 'alienation', a theme which dominates George Orwell's *1984*. In an insightful study of the uses of passivity in this novel, Kies (1992) provides us with a catalogue of devices used to suppress agency. Three characteristic sentences from the novel are reproduced here as Sample 2.2.

Sample 2.2[6]

1 There was a long nagging *argument* that went round and round, with *shouts, whines, tears, remonstrances, bargaining.*
2 He tried to squeeze out some childhood memory . . . he *could* not remember.
3 *His thin dark face had become* animated, *his eyes had lost* their mocking expression.

(italics added)

Sentence 1 illustrates the use of nominalization referred to above. If 'alienation' or 'powerlessness' is a global theme, it may also be relayed by exploiting the interpersonal resource of modality, as in sentence 2. Finally, the depersonalization of themes together with the use of the past perfect tense may be exploited as textural resources in the service of an overall procedure which is globally intended to cater for a given theme such as 'alienation', as in sentence 3.

In discussing intentionality, we emphasized the need to recognize a global and a local level. As we pointed out, intentions may globally relate to the text producer's attitude that a given set of textual occurrences is a cohesive and coherent whole instrumental in fulfilling specific goals within specific plans (e.g. to present people as passively subjected to historical events as opposed to actively involved in shaping them, to project an authoritative image, to sound objective and analytical). Text producers would seek to attain these goals through a set of micro-intentions (e.g. the use of the passive to present people as acted upon rather than acting, the use of a particular modality to minimize involvement and increase distance, etc.). It is through the mutual relevance and accessibility of the various micro-intentions that the condition of overall purpose is satisfied.

A similar scheme may be envisaged for intertextuality. At a global level, a set of socio-textual and socio-cultural practices is identified, with intertextuality seen as the mechanism which regulates the way we do things with texts, genres and discourses (e.g. the review of events undertaken authoritatively in a narrative form). At a more local level, on the other hand, individual elements of socio-textual and socio-cultural practice are employed. Here, a variety of micro-signs (concepts, values, etc.) will typify the ways a given community uses particular texts, genres and discourses or represents the socio-cultural. For example, the use of straightforward, intertextually inactive words such as 'ironing' can acquire significant socio-cultural values when uttered in a particular context. For example, looking at a slim, glamorous and enviably beautiful model in a television commercial, an older woman was heard to say: 'when does she do her ironing, I wonder?' This utterance involves the use of terms from a cultural code with which the speaker identifies in putting her feelings into words.

STYLISTIC INFORMATIVITY

In addition to the various characteristics identified above, texts fulfil a further criterion, namely **informativity**. This notion concerns the extent to which a communicative occurrence might be expected or unexpected, known or unknown, certain or uncertain and so on. Here too, the notion of 'communicative occurrence' and the idea of 'knownness' may be seen at a global and a local level. On the one hand, an occurrence, expected or unexpected, may be viewed in concrete terms as yielding varying degrees of 'interestingness'. For instance, the informativity of terms such as 'sectioned' or 'specialed' is extremely slight when occurring in a medical report. However, higher degrees of informativity are detected when such medical jargon intrudes into the speech of, say, an ordinary person complaining about the standards of health care provision, as in Sample 2.3.

Sample 2.3

She is *sectioned* in the hospital; she became one of those called *specialed* which means you have a nurse following you every-where you go.

Informativity can also be seen in a more abstract sense. Here, the various occurrences would provide evidence for a particular text type, genre or discourse, whether expected or unexpected. In other words, entire stretches of language may come to fulfil or defy our expecta-tions, and thereby display varying degrees of informativity. What is

involved here is a variety of signs that in varying degrees of explicitness relay semiotic values. For example, the informativity of Sample
2.1 (on Mexican heritage) is relatively low, assuming a readership that
subscribes to a fairly conventional way of writing history. The text,
discourse and genre seem to fulfil expectations and do not in the least
take the audience of receivers by surprise. On the other hand, higher
degrees of informativity would no doubt be encountered if a patently
legalistic genre were used in an informal, conversational setting. This
fulfilment or defiance of expectations is at the centre of communicative or stylistic creativity. It has to be noted, however, that too much
informativity would be as communicatively problematical as too
little. To prevent this from happening, communicative systems are
self-regulating in this respect, and, in their search for equilibrium, text
users tend to identify appropriate points on the scale between two
extremes, the least and the most expected.

COMMUNICATIVE STABILITY VS. TURBULENCE

The notion of the continuum seems to be an ideal way of accounting
for the intricacy of communication, not only in the area of informativity but with respect to the other standards of textuality. In
dealing with any of these standards, it would appear that we can
identify a scale of values ('more of this or less of that' and not 'either
this or that'). At one extreme, there will be those local- and global-
level textual occurrences which display maximal cohesion and
consequently maximal coherence, where intertextuality is least
intricate, intentionality least opaque, situationality least cumbersome
and informativity sparingly used. At the other extreme, there will
be local- and global-level textual occurrences where cohesion is not
straightforward and where coherence is problematical to retrieve.
In such cases, values yielded by other factors such as intentionality
and intertextuality become slightly less transparent. This continuum
may be schematically represented as in Figure 2.4. Looking at this
continuum from the vantage point of users' expectations, we can
now identify the left-hand side as an area of textual activity characterized by maximal stability, in which expectations are invariably
fulfilled, the interaction of signs highly uniform and norms of
language use strictly adhered to. The right-hand side represents an
area of textual activity where stability is minimal and where expectations are often defied, the interaction of signs is turbulent and

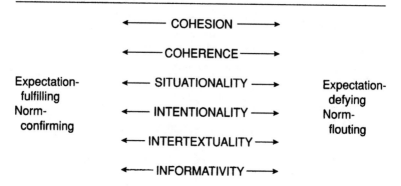

Figure 2.4 The static/dynamic continuum

norms are systematically departed from. We shall refer to instances of language use characterized on the left in Figure 2.4 as **static**, while those on the right may be termed **dynamic**. These will be key notions in our analysis of the translation process and the role of the translator as communicator.

Let us now show these processes at work in some actual examples of language use. Francis and Kramer-Dahl (1992) make a useful comparison between the uses of language illustrated in Samples 2.4 and 2.5.

Sample 2.4

Presentation at an unusual angle, without kinesthetic clues
Familiar faces
Photographs of 16 famous people, politicians, heads of state, actors, etc., recognition of whom was expected for her [the patient's] educational level, were presented individually. She recognized only President Kennedy. .... From a live line-up of 2 very familiar persons and 6 strangers, *she could not pick out her* sister.

(italics added)

Sample 2.5

For he [the patient] approached these faces – even of those near and dear – as if they were abstract puzzles or tests. He did not relate to them, he did not behold. No face was familiar to him, seen as a 'thou', being just identified as a set of features, an 'it'.

Samples 2.4 and 2.5 are drawn from comparable sections of two neuropsychological case histories, one published in a professional journal (2.4), the other appearing in what has been described by the author himself as a 'clinical tale'. The striking point of comparison between the two instances is that the same experience which is succinctly represented by the single sentence *she could not pick out* in 2.4, is encoded by no less than four 'mental' process clauses in 2.5. In raising these issues here, our aim is merely to illustrate what we take to be static or dynamic uses of language. If context tells us that what we are reading is a report of a medical case history, then Sample 2.4 fulfils expectations and the communication would be maximally stable (i.e. static). However, given the same expectations on the part of the reader, a not unlikely proposition, Sample 2.5, would conversely be disconcerting in the way it defies expectations, albeit in an interesting fashion.

Before relating our model of textuality to the activity of translating, it is perhaps helpful to underline a number of basic points. First, it must be stressed that there is nothing pejorative about the use of the term static to describe certain textual occurrences, nor is there anything particularly privileged about occurrences being described as dynamic. Being static or dynamic is a normal condition of natural language use; and opting for one or the other is a matter of choice informed by factors such as register membership, the purpose for which utterances are used, as well as wider socio-textual and socio-cultural considerations. As suggested above, to be viable, communication constantly finds its most suitable location on a scale between complete defiance of expectations and complete fulfilment of expectations. This is in line with an all-important characteristic of communicative behaviour, namely that too much stability is as undesirable as too much dynamism, and that language users have a way of striking a balance, thus avoiding either extreme. In the words of Beaugrande and Dressler,

> Complete knownness – or, in cybernetic terms, total stability – is evidently uninteresting to the human cognitive disposition. Communication therefore acts as the *constant removal and restoration of stability through disturbing and restoring the continuity of occurrences.*
> (1981: 36)

The next point regarding the model of text processing presented above relates to our use of terms such as 'minimal' or 'inaccessible' or stability being 'removed'. Here, we do not in any sense imply that a given stretch of linguistic material has degenerated into a 'non-text'. When stability is said to be minimal, this is simply a reference to cases where the process of retrieving coherence and matching textual material with a text world becomes more challenging. In these cases, intensive processing effort has to be expended, and reading for intention becomes less straightforward (i.e. becomes interesting). By the same token, removal of stability is seen as an attempt to minimize boredom, to shock, to be creative.

Another point relevant to the discussion of our approach to the processing of texts concerns the motivations which often lie behind the way utterances take on static or dynamic values. The varying degrees of stability or dynamism are the outcome of purposeful linguistic behaviour. We relay or perceive a certain degree of, say, dynamism when it is appropriate and not gratuitous. One or two examples should make these points clearer. Returning to Samples 2.4 and 2.5, we can now see that the dynamic use of language brings the medical case history to life and restores human beings to the centre of action. More significantly, perhaps, text producers use dynamism as a vehicle for promoting certain ideals and for the fulfilment of important rhetorical purposes. Through the kind of writing we have seen in Sample 2.5, for example, Oliver Sacks has sought to question the ideology encoded in the 'standard' texts on neuropsychology and to warn 'of what happens to science which eschews the judgmental, the particular, the personal, and becomes entirely abstract and computational' (1985: 19).

THE STATIC AND THE DYNAMIC IN TRANSLATION

The model proposed above has a number of implications for the work of the translator, acting as both receiver and producer of texts. Where a source text is situated towards the stable end of the scale, a fairly literal approach may and often will be appropriate. That is, least intervention on the part of the translator is called for – unless the brief for the job includes different requirements. On the other hand, where the source text displays considerable degrees of dynamism, the translator is faced with more interesting challenges and literal translation may no longer be an option. Sample 2.6 as a source text is a clear illustration of the dynamic use of language and the translation procedures required to handle it.

Sample 2.6

It was the best of times, it was the worst of times, it was the age of wisdom, it was the age of foolishness, it was the epoch of belief, it was the epoch of incredulity, it was the season of light, it was the season of darkness, it was the spring of hope, it was the winter of despair, we had everything before us, we had nothing before us, we were all going to heaven, we were all going direct the other way ...

Here, the formal parallelism together with the conceptual juxtaposition of opposites constitute interesting departures from norms and hence call for greater processing effort. A motivation can be perceived on the part of the text producer, namely, to convey irony. These manifestations can easily be overlooked in translation, as Gutt (1991) demonstrates. For example, a Russian version (Sample 2.7) has the effect of restabilizing what is dynamic and thus neutralizing unexpectedness.

Sample 2.7

It was the best and worst of times, it was the age of wisdom and foolishness, the epoch of unbelief and incredulity, the time of enlightenment and ignorance, the spring of hope and the winter of despair.

Let us take another example where the problems which the translator confronts regarding source text dynamism may this time be seen more in terms of cross-cultural difficulties. Sample 2.8 is a formal translation of a passage from an Arabic novel.[7]

Sample 2.8

[I was 24 years old. I was enamoured with gambling. The matter started with small, easy things, like so many things in life, such that one never dreams that one's whole life would change. At first we would *play for* walnuts. Then we began to *play for*

poultry. And then came the day when I *played for* the three calves
I had. And finally I *played for* the trees.]

(italics added)

The Arabic text purposefully establishes lexical cohesion via recurrence of the lexical item *play for*. The motivation behind this
exaggerated reiteration may be explained in terms of the prominence which the concept of gambling assumes in the context of the
passage and indeed the whole novel. The sin is magnified and the
gradual lapse into frittering away all that one holds dear, including
self-respect, is foregrounded. The procedure involved in this
fragment of text may be seen in the light of a basic rhetorical maxim:
'opt for lexical variation unless there is a good reason for doing
otherwise'.

This maxim is probably a universal rhetorical convention.
However, the distinctive socio-textual practices of different communities promote different thresholds of tolerance for features such as
recurrence and degree of lexical variation. That is, while recurrence
is an option available to users of both Arabic and English, the latter
generally see it as a heavily marked form which, to be sustainable,
must have some special motivation. Now, it may be argued that this
holds for Arabic too. However, cross-cultural variation is often
detected in this area, and what speakers of Arabic see by way of
motivation may differ in both kind and degree from that which
speakers of English appreciate as such. Thus, in the published
English translation (Sample 2.9), the rhetorical thrust of the Arabic
text went by and large unheeded:

Sample 2.9

I was 24 years old and fond of gambling. Like so many things
in this world, the whole thing started in a very small way. In such
cases you never dream that your whole life is going to change
as a result. At first we used to *gamble* with walnuts; then we
began to *play for* poultry; and then came the day when I *gambled*
with the three calves I had. Finally I *threw* the trees *in*.

A mere glance at the translation in terms of the cohesive devices
used would immediately reveal some striking discrepancies. Some
of these are probably inevitable and may be justified in terms
of the aversion of English idiom to certain source text patterns of

cohesion. For example, the addition of *in such cases* abstracts the content of the preceding discourse and links it up with the succeeding part of the text. The Arabic source text did not require this anaphoric link whereas the English text seems to call for the logical connection. Such devices are in fact available in Arabic and we may assume that their exclusion here is motivated. Indeed, reactions of English-language readers, when informally canvassed, suggest that the superimposition of this logical veneer on the translation has detracted from the 'literariness' of the text and rendered it rather 'cold'.

Of immediate relevance to our purposes here, however, is lexical cohesion and whether this is established through variation or reiteration. In the English translation, the particular reiterative chain which dominates the source text has not been observed and variation is opted for instead. Such a format has the effect of compromising the rhetorical purpose of the original, distracting the reader's attention from the gradual build-up through recurrence of the loss-of-self-respect theme. Again, an informal survey of English-language readers suggested that recurrence throughout in the translation would have been readily acceptable.

It is never possible to be certain about the motivations underlying particular translation choices. In the case of Sample 2.9, an uncharitable view might lead one to assume that the link between reiteration in the source text and the theme of loss of self-respect was not perceived at all. On the other hand, one could adopt a less extreme position and suggest that the translator probably felt that the socio-cultural issue in question and the text world depicted (the depravity associated with the loss of self-respect) are not sufficiently significant to be singled out in this way. In other words, the translator may have seen the recurrence for what it is but decided that the target reader would not be able to see the rhetorical motivation behind its use, or would see it but reject the linkage as too nebulous.

To end this brief exercise in translation criticism on a more positive note, let us take another example where socio-cultural dynamism in the source text has been skilfully handled by the translator. Sample 2.10 is a formal translation of a passage from an Arabic novel by the Egyptian Nobel Prize winner Naguib Mahfouz.

Sample 2.10

[She *woke up* at midnight. She always *woke up* then without having to rely on an alarm clock. A wish that had taken root in her *woke* her *up* with great accuracy. For a few moments she was not sure she had been *woken up* . . .

Habit *woke* her *up* at this hour. It was an old habit she had developed when young and it had stayed with her as she matured. She had learnt it along with the other rules of married life. She *woke up* at midnight to await her husband's return from his evening's entertainment. Then she would serve him until he went asleep.]

(italics added)

Here, lexical cohesion is once again established via recurrence of the lexical item *woke up*. The motivation behind the excessive re-iteration in this sample may be explained in terms of the social comment which the passage is intended to relay: an ironical portrayal of the 'never-endingness' characteristic of the plight of the average Arab housewife in her domestic situation.

In the published English translation (Sample 2.11), an interesting solution to the form-function problem is opted for. The translators were no doubt aware that the incessant recurrence in the Arabic text might seem inappropriate in English idiom and should therefore somehow be neutralized. But they appear nevertheless to have been loath to part with the function which this device is meant to serve in the original. The solution opted for was thus to preserve the recurrence as well as the motivation behind it through using various forms of the same root word *wake*. In other words, a compromise was struck between source text rhetorical meaning and target text rhetorical conventions.

Sample 2.11

She *woke* at midnight. She always *woke up* then without having to rely on an alarm clock. A wish that had taken root in her *awoke* her with great accuracy. For a few moments she was not sure she was *awake* . . .

Habit *woke* her at this hour. It was an old habit she had developed when young and it had stayed with her as she matured. She had learnt it along with the other rules of married life. She *woke up* at midnight to await her husband's return from his evening's entertainment. Then she would serve him until he went asleep.

Behind all this, one cannot help feeling that a general trend in translation seems regrettably to point in the direction of cultural hegemony and the prestige of certain languages at the expense of other, less privileged ones. The pull of a powerful target language such as English generally motivates the interventions made by translators, as Venuti (1995) suggests. Ideology may come into this and Sample 2.1 is a case in point. So far, we have chosen not to focus on the fact that the text is actually a translation of a Spanish source text. Assuming that there is nothing untoward, the target text reader would have no reason to suspect that the textual profile of the Spanish text is any different from what we are presented with in translation. This is how we normally approach any translation, taking it for granted that it is an accurate record of the original.

Closer scrutiny of translations, however, can reveal interesting discrepancies, and Sample 2.1 is no exception. In terms of register membership for example, the translated sample subscribes to a conventional mode of historical writing which grants text producers authority and a considerable measure of power and calls for fairly uniform textualization procedures. The Spanish source text, on the other hand, subscribes to a different, less conventional mode of writing history: less authority is exercised, there is more reader involvement and a more emotive form of expression. The aim is to present a set of events from a more human and more committed perspective. Such issues of ideology in translating will occupy us in Chapter 9, where the two texts are discussed in greater detail. Suffice it here to say that some interesting divergences are readily apparent when source and target texts are compared and different world views or ideologies emerge. Also implicated are intentionality, sociocultural and socio-textual practices and the realization of these in the actual texture and structure of texts.

Chapter 3

Interpreting: a text linguistic approach

The principal aim of this chapter is to explore possible applications of text linguistics to the training of interpreters. Focusing on those aspects of our discourse processing model which relate to the oral mode of translating, we shall see how distinctions such as the static vs. the dynamic (Chapter 2) are of concern to the interpreter as well as the translator. Rather than emphasizing differences due to field of translating, mode of translating or translator focus, we will in this chapter explore areas of common interest in the processing of texts. The central theme however is interpreting. In particular, the three strands of textuality – texture, structure and context – will be shown to correlate in a number of interesting ways and to varying degrees of relevance, with the three basic forms of interpreting – **liaison, consecutive** and **simultaneous**.

HOW TEXTS HANG TOGETHER

The three basic domains of textuality identified in Chapter 2 are texture, structure and context. The term 'texture' covers the various devices used in establishing continuity of sense and thus making a sequence of sentences operational (i.e. both cohesive and coherent). We can illustrate the operational nature of texts with the help of a number of examples seen from the perspective of oral translating. Our first Sample (3.1) is taken from the edited text of President Bush's declaration on 25 February 1991 concerning strategy in the Gulf War.

Sample 3.1

(. . .) (1) The coalition will, therefore, continue to prosecute the war with undiminished intensity. (2) As we announced last night, we will not attack unarmed soldiers in retreat. (3) We have no choice but to consider retreating combat units as a threat, and respond accordingly. (4) Anything else would risk additional coalition casualties. (. . .)

Adopting a bottom-up approach to the processing of this text, the receiver will first respond to the various clues that lend the text its quality of being a cohesive and coherent whole. One such clue is connectivity, a factor that is crucial in, for example, perceiving the contrast signalled implicitly in sentence 3 above:

We have no choice but to consider retreating combat units as a threat.

This may be glossed as 'however, we have no choice but . . .', a reading that is possible only when we set sentence 3 against the background provided by sentence 2 and examine the various cohesive relationships that hold the text together. It is interesting to note, particularly from a translation perspective, that this kind of implicit connectivity is discouraged if not totally disallowed in a number of languages (e.g. Arabic) and the relationship involved may thus have to be made explicit. However, even if we were to restrict the discussion to those languages in which implicit connectivity is not unusual, the texture of 'contrast' would still have to be properly appreciated. Only through such an appreciation would we be able to see, for example, the important distinction introduced in an inconspicuous way between *unarmed soldiers in retreat* and *retreating combat units*, which can easily be overlooked as it is presented here.

THE COMPOSITIONAL PLAN

Another source from which texts derive their cohesion and acquire the necessary coherence is structure. This assists us in our attempt to perceive specific compositional plans in what otherwise would only be a disconnected sequence of sentences. Structure and texture thus work together, with the former providing the outline, and the latter fleshing out the details. For example, the text fragment in Sample 3.1 constitutes a conclusion, signalled by *therefore* and comes at the end of a long stretch of utterance in which Saddam Hussein's 'non-compliance' with the will of the international community is assessed. It also takes on a counter-argumentative text structure of its own, via the implicit contrast noted above.

Sample 3.2

Saddam's most recent speech is an outrage. He is not withdrawing. His defeated forces are retreating. He is trying to claim
victory in the midst of a rout. And he is not voluntarily giving
up Kuwait. He is trying to save the remnants of power and control
in the Middle East by every means possible. And here too,
Saddam Hussein will fail.

   Saddam is not interested in peace, but only to regroup and
to fight another day. And he does not renounce Iraq's claim to
Kuwait . . .

   He still does not accept UN Security Council resolutions, or the
coalition terms of February 22 . . .

   The coalition will, therefore, continue to prosecute the war
with undiminished intensity. As we announced last night, we
will not attack unarmed soldiers in retreat. We have no choice
but to consider retreating combat units as a threat, and respond
accordingly. Anything else would risk additional coalition
casualties . . .

Diagrammatically, this text-within-text structure format may be
represented as in Figure 3.1.

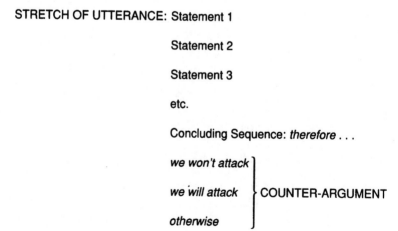

Figure 3.1 Text within text

CONTEXTUAL FACTORS

Rhetorical purpose in texts

In dealing with structure and texture, we rely on higher-order contextual factors which determine the way in which a given sequence of sentences serves a specific rhetorical purpose such as arguing or narrating (i.e. becomes what we have called 'text'). The longer sequence presented as Sample 3.2 serves a mixture of rhetorical purposes and may therefore be described as 'hybrid': while seemingly operating within the communicative brief of **monitoring** a situation (exposition being the rhetorical purpose served), the text producer is in fact involved in **managing** the situation, steering the text receiver towards the acceptance of his own goals (the overall rhetorical purpose being 'to argue a case').

Attitudinal meanings in discourse

In Sample 3.2, the speaker adopts an attitude which attenuates what is in fact a dire warning, couching an expression of military hegemony in more acceptable defence jargon. Discoursal meanings such as these influence the way texts are put together (duality of text function, opaqueness of compositional plans and subtleties of the words chosen). The suppressed *however* in Sample 3.1 is an instance of a deliberately **marked** use of language, defying normal expectations and thereby exhibiting a certain degree of discourse dynamism. Implicitness of this kind cannot be dismissed simply as unfortunate phraseology. Rather, it is an ideological ploy, highly motivated in contexts of language use such as this. Texture, structure and text type focus are all involved and together reflect deeper underlying meanings that are essentially discoursal (i.e. serve as the mouthpiece of institutions).

Genre as a fashion of speaking

All of the factors mentioned so far – rhetorical purposes, attitudinal meanings, structure and texture – are deployed to meet the requirements of particular social occasions (e.g. the diplomat's ultimatum). Genres are conventionalized forms of language use appropriate to given domains of social activity and to the purposes of participants in them. As the text sample considered so far shows, genres have by common consensus attracted particular forms of linguistic expression and have thus acquired a formulaic status. There are strict do's and don'ts regarding who the participants are, what to say and how to say it within certain formats generally sanctioned by the community of text users.

The interaction of text with text

Through the principle of intertextuality, text users recognize the various texts, discourses and genres, and their linguistic expression, as signs. At the global level, argumentation-disguised-as-exposition would be recognized as a particular text form, the masking of real intentions as a particular discourse function and the diplomat's ultimatum as a particular genre. Alternatively, whether the issue under discussion is one of 'retreat' or 'withdrawal' or indeed 'regrouping' would, at a more local level – that of individual lexico-grammatical choice – depend very much on one's semiotic perspective.

Intended actions

For Peirce (1931–58), 'a sign . . . is something which stands to somebody for something in some respect or capacity' (1931: 135). Here, intention is a key concept, regulating another set of conventions, this time pragmatic in nature, to do with our ability to 'do things with words'. Within pragmatics, the minimal unit of analysis is the **speech act** which, like the sign, may be identified at a local level of interaction, or can indeed be global, spanning entire texts, discourses or genres, as we have demonstrated in Chapter 2. In Sample 3.2, the sentence:

He is not withdrawing.

could be anything from a speech act 'representative' of a given state of affairs, to a 'complaint', a 'cry for help' or an 'expression of defiance'. But, uttered by George Bush about Saddam Hussein in 1991, the utterance is bound to take on an intentionality that drastically narrows down its potential meanings. This will become even clearer when the utterance is situated within the text act sequence with which Bush's statement begins:

Saddam's most recent speech is an outrage. He is not withdrawing. His defeated forces are retreating.

INTERPRETING AND THE STANDARDS OF TEXTUALITY

Having studied aspects of the texture, structure and context of Sample 3.2, let us now look at it from the perspective of the interpreter. George Bush's declaration is ideal material from which the manifold demands made on the interpreter may be illustrated. It is the kind of statement that is often required to be simultaneously interpreted if made at an international forum, for example, or consecutively relayed if delivered, say, at a press conference. One could easily imagine similar rhetorical purposes being involved in a question-and-answer briefing session, relayed by a liaison interpreter.

The three principal modes of interpreting (the simultaneous, the consecutive and the liaison) inevitably place different demands on the interpreter. It is true that all well-formed texts, oral and written, possess all of the following characteristics:

1　They are cohesive in texture.
2　They are coherent and exhibit a particular structure.
3　They serve a clear rhetorical purpose as texts.
4　They relay specific attitudinal meanings as discourse.
5　They are in keeping with the requirements of certain conventional formats as genres.
6　They serve a set of mutually relevant communicative intentions pragmatically.
7　They stand out as members of distinct registers.

It is also true that, whatever the mode of interpreting, input or output will have to display all of the above characteristics. However, the three modes of interpreting mentioned above seem to focus on different areas of text production and reception. The various domains of textuality – context, structure and texture – are not equally prominent. To reflect this varying degree of prominence we now put forward a set of hypotheses.

A SET OF HYPOTHESES

1　Bearing in mind the nature of the demands made on the interpreter by the situational constraints normally associated with each of the three basic modes, it may be assumed that the simultaneous interpreter has to settle for a partial view of both context and text structure and has therefore to rely more heavily on the emerging texture in order to make and maintain sense. This is because, in this mode of interpreting, reception and production of text take place at more or less the same time.

2   The consecutive interpreter, whose output comes after the source text has been delivered, tends to focus on information relevant to text structure as this outweighs that yielded by context or texture in what is noted down and used as a basis for delivery.

3   Finally, the liaison interpreter has access only to a partial view of texture and structure, both of which would be unfolding piece-meal in the two-way exchange. In this case, context would seem to be the main resource which the interpreter draws on in the task of maintaining the continuity of the exchange.

In terms of the demands on the interpreter, then, particular strands of textuality remain partly inaccessible, leaving the interpreter to make fuller use of those which are more readily available. Some might argue that 'inaccessibility' is perhaps too strong a word for what must potentially be present, even if it is incomplete. While not wishing to make too much of the issue of accessibility, we can from the interpreter's point of view take the following as a fair representation of what actually happens:

(a) In the case of simultaneous interpreting, context and structure are revealed only piecemeal and can thus be accessed more effec-tively via texture,[1] i.e. the words as they are spoken.

(b) In the case of consecutive interpreting, texture and context are retained only in a most short-lived manner and can thus be stored more effectively via structure.

(c) In the case of liaison interpreting, texture and structure are manifested only partially and can thus be negotiated more effectively via context.

In short, it is our contention that only the most 'local' and hence insuf-ficient information is made available regarding context and structure in simultaneous interpreting, texture and context in consecutive inter-preting and texture and structure in the case of liaison interpreting. Schematically, this may be represented as in Figure 3.2. At some stage in the interpreter's processing, no doubt, the shaded areas in each case become less inaccessible and expectations are formed. However, these remain to be confirmed and may have to be discarded if forthcoming textual evidence runs counter to initial expectations. For example, let

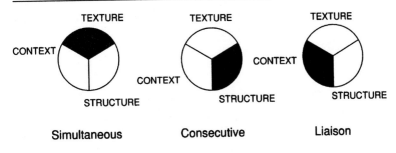

Figure 3.2 Accessibility of context, structure and texture

us imagine a simultaneous interpreter working with Sample 3.2. Textural clues would be the main guiding principle and inter-sentential relationships something to be monitored closely. In negotiating the initial segment:

> *Saddam's most recent speech is an outrage.*

the interpreter is bound to expect in what follows a substantiation of this claim. Thus, a hypothesis is developed capturing this insight. Indeed, the next sentence is:

> *He is not withdrawing.*

But how does sentence 2 relate to sentence 1? Is the 'outrage' the fact that he is not 'withdrawing', in which case a likely option to follow would be: 'but we are not going to stand idly by'? Or is it an ironic, even sarcastic, statement ridiculing Saddam's use of the word 'withdrawing', in which case we might expect Saddam's actual words to be juxtaposed to what, in the view of the speaker, he should have said instead? This may be represented graphically as in Figure 3.3.

OPTION 1

SPEECH = OUTRAGE   BECAUSE   HE IS NOT WITHDRAWING

OPTION 2

SPEECH = OUTRAGE   BECAUSE   USING THE WORD 'WITHDRAW'
IS OUTRAGEOUS

Figure 3.3 Two readings of 'withdrawing'

Note that, whereas in option 2 the focus is on the interpretation of a word (texture), option 1 takes the entire structural element and fits it into a conceptual scheme of some kind (context). In fact, it is the second option which is acted upon in sentence 3:

His defeated forces are retreating.

Relying on texture, the interpreter would perceive the juxtaposition of the item *withdrawing* to its counterpart *retreating*. This will set up the expectations of parallelism: *claim victory* vs. *in the midst of a rout* and *voluntarily giving up Kuwait* vs. *trying to save the remnants of power*. It is primarily in perceiving this textural contrast that the interpreter may be able to predict how the speech is to develop.

Let us now re-express our initial set of hypotheses in the light of these observations:

1 Input for simultaneous interpreting is characterized by context and structure being less readily usable than texture.
2 Input for consecutive interpreting is characterized by context and texture being less readily usable than structure.
3 Input for liaison interpreting is characterized by texture and structure being less readily usable than context.

A corollary to this set of basic hypotheses is that, whatever the form of the deficit or the compensation strategy, it is our contention that texture may be treated as a privileged category. Texture is necessarily available at all times, providing the interpreter with a point of departure. It is the mainstay of the simultaneous interpreter's activity; it is there to help the consecutive interpreter retrieve the sought-after structure; and it is there to help the liaison interpreter reconstruct the required context for the one or two utterances dealt with at any given time. This is the basic position which we will now try to elaborate, using examples of authentic interpreting data.

THE PROMINENCE OF TEXTURE IN SIMULTANEOUS INTERPRETING

In simultaneous interpreting, the input is received piecemeal, and the interpreter's task is basically to react and interact with utterance 1, then utterance 2 and so on, allowing for the inevitable overlap between the various elements of the sequence. (For a brief overview of the factors involved, including short-term memory, see Chapter 4.) Of course, experienced interpreters use all kinds of anticipation strategies which enable them to formulate in advance plausible hypotheses regarding both context and structure. But, even when prior expectations are sufficiently focused, the processing is still tentative and the various hypotheses must be confirmed or disproved by the forthcoming textual evidence. Thus the rich variety of texture signals have to be relied upon as the most tangible point of reference.

To illustrate how texture comes to the fore, guiding the interpreter's efforts in negotiating meanings, let us consider an example drawn from a real interpreting situation. Sample 3.3 is a formal translation of an extract from the original text of a speech delivered in Arabic at the United Nations by King Hussein of Jordan. Sample 3.4 is a verbatim transcript of the simultaneous interpretation into English of the extract.

Sample 3.3

King Hussein (formal translation from Arabic):
[It is a great honour for me to take part in celebrating the fortieth anniversary of the establishment of the United Nations as the greatest international organization which set its goal in the very first words of the Preamble to its Charter: 'to save succeeding generations from the scourge of war and to push social progress ahead and to raise the standard of life in an atmosphere of freedom that is larger'. (. . .)

In the past 40 years, the world has, in the nature of things, witnessed a number of developments and changes which were distinguished from those of previous times by their speed and tremendous diversity. With every social or scientific advance emerged a new reality, carrying within it remarkable ironies. The great aspirations stemming from development soon collided with the negative aspects and the apprehensions arising from that development.

During the past 40 years, the world knew the nuclear era with its destructive bombs and its power-generating plants. Mankind enjoyed the fruits of massive progress in science and technology to live in constant terror of lethal weaponry made possible by this progress. And distance between states and nations shrank as a result of the communications revolution. And international terrorism in turn prospered. The degree of consciousness among peoples of the world regarding their common concerns rose to be met by the division of the world into a north largely affluent and pioneering and a south largely impoverished and recipient.]²

Sample 3.4

King Hussein (interpretation from Arabic):
It is a great honour for me to take part in celebrating the fortieth anniversary of the United Nations. Established as the paramount international organization, its goals were set in the very first words of the Preamble to its Charter, namely: 'to save succeeding generations from the scourge of war and to promote social progress and better standards of life in larger freedom'. (. . .)

In the past 40 years, the world has inevitably undergone a number of developments and changes characterized by unprecedented speed and diversity. Every social or scientific advance has brought with it a new reality, fraught with striking ironies. Great aspirations inspired by a particular development soon collided with apprehensions and negative effects arising from the same development.

During the same period, the world was thrust into the nuclear era with both its destructive devices and its power-generating plants. Mankind enjoyed the fruits of massive progress in science and technology only to live in constant terror of lethal weaponry made possible by the same progress. Similarly, the communications revolution has brought states and nations dramatically closer, but has also enabled international terrorism to prosper. The nations of the world have become more conscious of their common concerns, but at the same time have been forced to face the reality of a world divided into a largely affluent and pioneering North and a largely impoverished and recipient South.

Readers may assess for themselves the aspect of texture which relates to lexical choice in this highly competent interpreting performance. Consider for example the English *inevitably* for what is literally in Arabic 'in the nature of things', *unprecedented* for 'distinguished from those of previous times', *fraught with* for 'carrying within it', and so on. These are important manifestations of texture and show how collocation is crucial in establishing lexical cohesion.

Of more immediate interest for our purposes is how the interpreter relies on what the text offers by way of textural clues, that is, devices serving anaphoric (backward) and cataphoric (forward) reference, substitution, ellipsis, conjunction and indeed lexical cohesion, and how these devices are then used as clues to the way the text is developed. To illustrate this, a few examples may be drawn from Sample 3.3 above:

Example 1

Arabic:
[... celebrating the fortieth anniversary of the establishment of the United Nations as the greatest international organization which set its goal in the very first words of the Preamble ...]

English:
... celebrating the fortieth anniversary of the United Nations. Established as the paramount international organization, its goals were set in the very first words of the Preamble ...

Having disposed of the formulaic expression of 'honour', the interpreter identifies the concept of 'establishment' as somehow superfluous in sentence 1. This item is not discarded, however, but used as the starting point of sentence 2 which cataphorically relates 'establishment' to 'goals', thus propelling the text forward. The cataphora is also an ideal way of breaking up a long awkward sentence. All this is done without altering the sequence of source text elements. This close monitoring of texture has the advantage of generally upholding idiomaticity in English and of avoiding the increased pressure which would have been entailed by reordering the parts.

Example 2

Arabic:
[... enjoyed the fruits of massive progress in science and technology to live in constant terror ...]

English:
... enjoyed the fruits of massive progress in science and technology only to live in constant terror ...

Obviously the Arabic 'to live' is not a straightforward infinitive of purpose. The restriction (*only to*) is a cohesive device equivalent to an adversative ('but', 'however'). This emphasizes the contrast between 'progress' and 'terror' and anticipates what is to follow (a series of similar contrasts).

Example 3

Arabic:
[And distance between states and nations shrank as a result of the communications revolution. And international terrorism in turn prospered.]

English:
Similarly, the communications revolution has brought states and nations dramatically closer, but has also enabled international terrorism to prosper.

Faced with two 'and' connectors (one genuinely additive, the other in fact an adversative) the interpreter has responded to the contrast perceived earlier between 'progress' and 'terror' by maintaining it here as intended.

Example 4

Arabic:
[The degree of consciousness among peoples of the world regarding their common concerns rose to be met by the division of the world into a north largely affluent and pioneering and a south largely impoverished and recipient.]

English:
The nations of the world have become more conscious of their common concerns, but at the same time have been forced to face the reality of a world divided into a largely affluent and pioneering North and a largely impoverished and recipient South.

Drawing on textural clues, the interpreter has now successfully established the contrastive pattern and used this as a basic anticipation strategy. In this way, the initially inaccessible structure and context gradually materialize but only through the piecing together of a variety of textural devices.

THE PROMINENCE OF STRUCTURE IN CONSECUTIVE INTERPRETING

The input processed by the consecutive interpreter is a text that can be said to be complete and autonomous. Consecutive interpreting thus affords the interpreter the advantage of not having constantly to wait for or anticipate the next fragment of input. Conversely, whereas in simultaneous mode, the interpreter has at least something to embark upon, the consecutive interpreter has to wait before he or she can deliver. There is, in other words, an added pressure and an extra load on memory, which have the result that information relating to texture and, perhaps to a lesser extent, context become rather too detailed to be retainable. In note-taking, it is not words in themselves that are recorded but rather arrangements of ideas in relation to each other. In this way, consecutive interpreters seem to use manifestations of texture and of context not as ends in themselves but as the means to gain access to structure.

In consecutive interpreting, then, effective reception and storage of information will involve focusing on the way a text is put together in response to context, and to the way texture is utilized to implement this. Effective consecutive output thus exhibits a clear outline of the way a text is structured. This compositional plan of the text will be the overall arrangement within which only relevant details of texture and context are to be found. Certain kinds of contextual and textural information are liable to be jettisoned if they do not fit within the compositional plan in a way which contributes to making a sequence of sentences operational.

To illustrate this reliance on indications of structure, we reproduce as Sample 3.5 a short sequence from a speech used as a consecutive interpreting test. Successful negotiation of this difficult passage would depend upon recognition of the counter-argumentative structure it contains and note-taking which clearly reflected this, in particular, the identification of 'codification' with 'legislation' and the contrast of these to 'institutions'.

Sample 3.5

Dans ce contexte, la première des réponses, c'est la transparence. Et la transparence ne résulte pas seulement de dispositions législatives. Bien sûr, la codification est très importante. Mais il n'y a pas que la codification. Je voudrais profiter de ce débat pour dire que je crois qu'il y a aussi une lisibilité des institutions elles-mêmes . . .

[In this context, the first response is transparency. And transparency does not result just from legislative measures. Of course, codification is very important. But there is not just codification. I would like to use the opportunity of this debate to say that I believe that there is also a [problem of] legibility of the institutions themselves . . .]

Candidates in the test were clearly divided between those who had relied over-much on the texture of 'I would like to use the opportunity . . .' and thus allowed themselves to be diverted from the structural arrangement (making an entirely new point out of 'also . . .') and those who had picked up the counter-argumentative signal *bien sûr* ('of course') and used it to structure their output. This clue to structure is all the more important in that the source text is elliptical, saying 'there is also legibility . . .' but meaning 'there is also a problem of legibility (i.e. transparency)'. Only through perception of the structure of the text can this meaning be retrieved.

THE PROMINENCE OF CONTEXT IN LIAISON INTERPRETING

Liaison interpreting input bears an interesting resemblance to that of simultaneous: in both cases the interpreter receives a first instalment of a longer text and more or less immediately embarks upon delivery. But the resemblance ends here: while the second instalment of simultaneous input is never long in coming, providing the interpreter with more textural information to be processed, the liaison interpreter has to treat the first portion as a self-contained unit. Although the situation improves as the interaction develops, the fact that liaison interpreters are left to work out how the exchange has reached a given point and, perhaps more importantly, where it is likely to go next has serious implications for the way they go about their business. Textural clues would at best be incomplete, restricted to what may be described as 'local' cohesion (i.e. covering a sequence of not more than two or three sentences, if not less). Similarly, indications of structure will hardly reveal a coherent and complete design. Yet, it is the task of liaison interpreters to make sense of whatever texture they are provided with, and it is also their task to negotiate with an interlocutor a text design of some kind. That is, on the basis of the separate instalments of input, linked with each other only at the highest level of text organization (i.e. that of the entire interaction), each chunk of output is expected to be coherent in its own right contextually.

To cope with this incompleteness of texture (continuity of sense) and structure, liaison interpreters seem to put to best effect whatever clues are encountered in these domains. For this limitation to be properly overcome, interpreters resort to a more readily accessible strand of textuality and one that ultimately determines how the text is developed. This, we suggest, is context (register membership, pragmatics and semiotics). But why should contextual input be so prominent in comparison with other strands of textuality?

To answer this question, let us consider the situation of the liaison interpreter. Whether the session involves questions and answers or negotiation of some sort, there will be unpredictability at the outset as to how the dialogue will develop and what the long-term significance of current lexical choice or local cohesion will be. Of course, the interpreter has some awareness of the issues involved, of the participants concerned and usually of the topic tackled. But these are not necessarily reliable clues to the way the two-way interaction will develop and conclude. Consequently, contextual clues tend to assume greater importance as long-term guides.

Furthermore, even at the most local level of linguistic expression, context seems to be a much richer category than texture or structure. There are important indications as to register membership, intentionality and intertextuality, with the latter encompassing a variety of relevant genres and discourses. But, perhaps more significantly, it is the intertextual potential of text type that is the prime determinant in the production and reception of texts. Here, a focus emerges that, on the one hand, brings together contextual information from a number of different contextual sources and, on the other, almost causally determines the way both structure and texture appear in texts.

Let us illustrate this with an example from a real-life situation. Although involving a communication breakdown, it is hoped that the following example will demonstrate not only what can go wrong but also what should ideally happen, underlining in the process the role of context in liaison interpreting. For whereas context is, we are suggesting, the key domain in liaison interpreting, it may, by the same token, become the main source of problems (cf. a similar example in Chapter 10).

Sample 3.6

> Interviewer: What were the contents of the letter you handed to King Fahd?
>
> Tunisian Government minister: This matter concerns the Saudis.
> (as relayed by interpreter)

In Sample 3.6, the interviewer asks a very pointed question. The minister is reported to have replied rather curtly in Arabic, in terms which the interpreter has relayed verbatim into English. The wrong impression has been conveyed, however, and the intended sense should have been relayed as:

> This is a matter solely for the Saudis' consideration!

The error may be attributed to lack of awareness of contextual specifications which surround utterances and dictate the way they should be interpreted. Relevant contextual factors include:

1 the register membership of the text (journalese, diplomacy, etc. as fields; formality of tenor, etc.);
2 the pragmatic force of the utterance (what is intended and not explicitly stated – here, unwillingness to give a direct answer to a question);
3 the culture-specific genre requirement that journalists do not overstep the mark; the discourse of rebuttal; and the text-type focus on managing a situation.

In addition to these factors, much contextual information lies outside the text, in the area of prior expectations – about the line of questioning pursued and even beyond this about the whole speech event which ultimately culminates in the form of words used (i.e. in the utterance proper). True, the word *concern* carries a considerable amount of textural information; but in the absence of contextual indications from both within and outside the currently unfolding interaction, this particular word could mean anything and could thus function in a variety of speech acts, one of which is the 'representative statement' erroneously opted for. The utterance was obviously intended to function as:

(a) a diplomat's way out of journalists' awkward questions;
(b) an intended 'telling-off': do not pursue this line of questioning, or else!;

(c) a socio-cultural sign carrying a specific attitudinal meaning (resenting nosiness), a certain genre specification (the familiar parrying of nosy journalists' questions) and a particular rhetorical purpose (steering the text receiver in a direction favourable to the text producer's goals).

The English journalist who asked the question would no doubt have appreciated the kind of meanings yielded by the register membership of the utterance ((a) above), its pragmatic meaning (b) and its semiotic significance (c). However, lured by the kind of 'inviting' answer which he received through the interpreter, the journalist pursued the initial line of questioning, only to be rebuked a second time.

PEDAGOGIC IMPLICATIONS

In the preceding sections, we have argued for the need to view texts in terms of a model of textuality within which we recognize three basic strands of textual activity: the contextual specification of texts, their structure and their texture. But these aspects of textuality cannot be equally prominent in all situations of text use. In interpreting, for example, as the nature of the task varies, text utilization strategies seem to vary and different ones are resorted to. Take for instance the case of consecutive interpreting. Here, given ideal conditions of performance, interpreters cannot hope to avail themselves of what a text offers by way of cohesion, theme-rheme progression and so on. In these circumstances, text structure must be paramount in a skill that involves rendering in a reduced form a text delivered at natural speed, often in a style that is less than fully coherent.

Incidentally, this kind of casual style of delivery raises an important issue that has been used by critics of applied text linguistics. In the context of interpreter training, the argument would no doubt be that, if very few speakers structure their texts as the discourse analyst would have them do, what is the point of telling the consecutive interpreter about text structure? Or, if very few politicians stick to the point or speak in context, what is the point of telling the liaison interpreter about the role of context in the development of texts? Or, if very few international delegates produce texts that are at all times both cohesive and coherent, what is the point of telling the simultaneous interpreter to heed texture in his or her attempts to listen and deliver intelligibly?

To this, we can only say that such impressions of what goes on after dinners, in interviews or in international conferences are all true regarding what happens in real life most of the time. But it is this very fact that makes it that much more worthwhile to tell interpreters about this or that strand of textuality and about how it relates both to text and to a given interpreting task. The fact that texture could be lacking, for example, can only support the argument that learning to operate with an idealized **norm** is a sure way of spotting and dealing with **deviation**s. Being trained to respond to the various manifestations of texture, structure or context is thus a crucial part of guaranteeing that the interpreter is on the alert.

Interpreter-training institutions the world over tend to combine training in different forms of interpreting. The philosophy behind such an approach seems to be that interpreters must be prepared to handle whatever is thrown at them. However, as we have just seen, the various standards of textuality are not implicated to the same extent in all forms of interpreting. Thus, through some form of needs analysis, in the light of trainee interests or staff competence or simply as a convenient pedagogic device, we ought to be able to narrow the set of options and identify certain useful trends. A well-thought-out programme should reveal that in a given situation, this interpreting skill is more in demand than others. In cases like these, it is essential that specialized training modules be developed to focus our efforts on the discourse mechanics of a particular skill.

The simultaneous module

In the light of this, we suggest that the simultaneous module should include intensive training in the appreciation and re-production of those devices that lend texts their quality of being viable units of communication (for examples of cohesion devices and how these are always employed in the service of coherence, see Chapter 4). Within texture, there is also the factor of **staging** or **theme-rheme** organization, including thematic progression and the way this links up with text type focus. To illustrate this, let us consider Sample 3.7, a formal translation of a speech delivered in Arabic at the UN by the representative of Egypt:

Sample 3.7

[Egypt has in its statement today delivered before this august council a great honour which it cherishes, and a great responsibility which it appreciates in the way it should be appreciated. For Egypt, taking pride in the honour of acting as Chairman of the African Group for this month, appreciates at the same time the responsibility of expressing honestly and sincerely the African position with regard to . . .]

Sample 3.8 is the verbatim transcript of the simultaneous interpretation into English of the above extract:

Sample 3.8

'It is a great and cherished honour, as well as a grave responsibility, for Egypt to speak today in the Council. . . . While taking pride in the honour of acting as Chairman of the African Group for this month, Egypt is also aware of the responsibility of expressing honestly and sincerely the African position with regard to . . .'

One of the basic assumptions of **functional sentence perspective** (**FSP**) is that the point of departure in a sentence (theme) tends to reflect given information which is less taxing on short-term memory. On the other hand, what is said about the theme (rheme) tends to carry new information which is consequently more taxing on short-term memory. In dealing with Sample 3.6, the interpreter placed the last received part of a chunk of input first without losing the rhematic status of 'most important information'. He achieved this through the use of a cleft sentence structure ('it is . . . that'). Thus, through a proper appreciation and a skilful manipulation of texture, the most burdensome task has been accomplished first, reducing the pressure on processing the rest of the utterance. Note also that this strategy enabled the interpreter to edit out and compensate for what would have only been cumbersome phraseology in English:

Arabic:
[a great honour which it cherishes, and a great responsibility which it appreciates in the way it should be appreciated.]

English:
a great and cherished honour, as well as a grave responsibility.

In this area of texture, diction, metaphors, irony and so on, together with the underlying contextual principles that regulate such modes of expression, are also bound to feature prominently. Providing the interpreter with the necessary tools to deal with such clues is therefore vital for the student of texture in the context of simultaneous interpreting.

The consecutive module

The consecutive module would obviously focus on the notion of text structure. But this will not be seen in isolation. Rather, it is the way structure is closely bound up with both texture and context that must form an important part of learning to negotiate text designs properly. Consider this example:

Sample 3.9

Formal translation from the Arabic of a Saudi minister's reply:
[Travelling between the countries of the Cooperation Council is the easiest thing to do, and the Gulf citizen does not need a visa. *Then*, the passport is the only proof of identity and is thus indispensable to retain]

In dealing with this series of utterances, the interpreter uncritically retained the sequential/additive form and function of *then*. This particular text, however, is structured along different lines: a claim is cited then countered, an adversarial relationship that would in English be better served by the use of something like 'but then'. Thus, while one particular strand of textuality is to the fore in a given interpreting situation (contextual focus in the present example from liaison interpreting), it is misleading to suggest that this could be focused on in isolation from, say, texture and structure.

The liaison module

Finally, the liaison module would introduce trainees systematically to the various facets of context. There will be special training in interacting with the intertextual potential of signs (texts, discourses, genres and other smaller-scale socio-cultural objects). The latter category may be illustrated from the ITN interview with president Saddam Hussein during the Gulf War. In dealing with the following utterance:

Sample 3.10

(Saddam Hussein, in Arabic)
We are *victimized* (*mustadeafuun*)

the interpreter first opted for 'we are hopeless', then, seeing that this was glaringly inadequate, revised it to 'we are helpless', and finally to 'we are hopeless and helpless'. These semantic values are all present in the original word, but the meaning of a given, say, lexical item is not always merely the sum total of its semantic features mechanistically put together. There is something else which was missing in the way the interpreter tried to cope. This is the intertextual potential of the item in question as a 'sign' and how an equivalent sign has to be created for the target listener. The Arabic *mustadeafuun* is intertextually linked to 'the victimized on earth', a motto which Immam Khumeini had used for his Party of God in Iran and elsewhere. He had borrowed this from an even more profound source – a Qur'anic verse which hinges on the notion of victimization. It is the retrieval of this intertextual set of meanings which interacts with semantic values such as 'hopeless' and 'helpless' that might have been what is needed for relaying the intended effect.

Pragmatics, speech acts uttered both individually and in sequence, politeness and so on would supplement this semiotic dimension and provide the interpreter trainee with insight into intentionality and the way we do things with words. There is also the role which register variation plays in the negotiation of context as the mainstay of liaison interpreting. Field, mode and tenor, and the way these vary, are important factors in promoting awareness of the kind of social institutions and social processes being served by a given text.

THE STATIC AND DYNAMIC DISTINCTION REVISITED

It is perhaps instructive at this stage to link the issue of the pedagogic implications of the text linguistic model outlined above for interpreting with the distinction we developed earlier between the 'static' and the 'dynamic'. It will be recalled that by static we mean a type of textual activity that is maximally stable and one where expectations are invariably fulfilled. The dynamics of textuality, on the other hand, subsumes cases where such a stability is all but removed as a result of expectations being invariably defied.

Given this spectrum of variation, students of interpreting may first be introduced to what we have described as static in the way texts are developed. At this stage, interpreting materials would be of well-known registers (journalistic, political, etc.), specially selected to illustrate the most 'unmarked' forms of how journalists or politicians genuinely operate. Strategies for getting round the jargon will have to be developed, but, as what is being handled is very much 'unmarked' use of language, processing difficulties are bound to be minimal and the tasks involved fairly manageable. As we have pointed out, the static nature of interaction in this domain of register variation is partly due to intentionality being fairly transparent: when journalists or politicians stay within their brief in using language and simply speak as journalists or politicians, there will be maximal predictability of the way things are said and meant. Predictable will also be text type in these domains of conventional practice. There would be few surprises in the way news reporters 'monitor' or politicians 'manage' a given situation. Also predictable would be the operative nature of the politician's discourse and the detached attitude ideally adopted by the journalist. Finally, genres would be fairly stable and manipulation of convention fairly infrequent.

Inevitably, the above account will have raised one or two eyebrows: where and when are we ever going to come across such an undiluted form of, say, politics or journalism? Perhaps never. However, as we pointed out above, a theoretical case may be made, and theoretical norms could conceivably be established, supported by authentic data, extremely rare as this might be. This is justifiable for the kind of initial-stage training we have in mind, and as a prelude to further stages in the training process.

Once the introduction to the rudimentary stylistics of the communicative act is covered (and this is not expected to be a long-drawn-out affair), we should be able gradually to expose our trainees to 'real' communication. Here, journalists would have 'an axe to grind' in evaluating as well as monitoring a situation, politicians would suddenly 'go coy' while borrowing from the detached discourse of, say, a 'historian' what would ultimately be used to further their own interests, and so on. In liaison, consecutive and simultaneous, this **hijacking** of someone else's discourse becomes a real problem that the interpreter must be trained to cope with.[3] Consider, for example, the following text sample:

Sample 3.11

A 'domestic' they call it; they [the police] don't give a stuff.

Two layers of meaning may be distinguished in what the woman had to say. First, there is the genuine discourse of the text producer: an ordinary housewife resenting what she perceived as a dismissive, indifferent attitude on the part of the police. The second layer of what we may here call the **absent discourse** is not that of the woman, but of someone else. That is, the term 'domestic' is not part of the 'cultural code' with which the woman may identify, but of some other culprit institution, in this case the police. The way this latter level of meaning is hijacked has contributed to the overall meaning and rhetorical effect of the utterance as a whole.

THE WAY FORWARD

In this chapter, the process of interpreting has been viewed from the vantage point of a discourse processing model within which we distinguish three basic domains of textuality: context, structure and texture. These are seen to correlate in subtle and meaningful ways with the three basic types of interpreting: liaison, consecutive and simultaneous. The basis of the relationship is the need on the part of the interpreter to focus on the particular strand of textuality that is made prominent by the requirements of one skill and not of another. In liaison interpreting, it has been suggested that, given a necessarily least readily accessible structure and texture, the interpreter needs to acquire facility in reacting to and interacting with the various vectors of context. The simultaneous interpreter, on the other hand, would seem to handle less readily available context and structure by heavily relying on texture, maintaining text connectivity through interacting with the various aspects of cohesion, theme-rheme progression, etc. Finally, less readily available context and texture in the kind of short-term storage of input that is characteristic of consecutive interpreting entails the category of structure being utilized to best effect.

In conclusion, it may be appropriate to enter one or two notes of caution to restrain the scope of what our proposals could be taken to suggest. First, the atomism that might strike one in the neatness of the various trichotomies (less readily available X and Y, with Z predominating) should be viewed as a methodological convenience and not an accurate reflection of the real situation. As far as interpreter performance and the training required are concerned, the reality is far more involved than could be accounted for by the kind of idealized theory outlined. As far as text processing is concerned, on the other hand, the reality is even fuzzier. The variables of context, structure and texture intermesh in subtle and intricate ways, and the interdependence of the various interpreting skills is normally too complex to be discussed in definitive terms.

But theorizing has a role to play in the maze of the various processes involved. Certainly, most of the statements we have made in the course of the above discussion are hypothetical at this stage and are in need of further corroborative evidence. Nevertheless, research into the nature of the interpreting process, which in certain quarters is already underway,[4] must start somewhere, and it is in this spirit that we have advanced what in our judgement are plausible hypotheses in need of further investigation.

Chapter 4

Texture in simultaneous interpreting

In focusing our attention now on one of the prominent modes of conference interpreting, namely simultaneous interpreting, our aim is to show how the particular constraints associated with this mode of translating affect performance and to subject to some degree of scrutiny our hypothesis concerning the prominence of texture (relative to structure and context) in simultaneous interpreting. The interpreter, like the translator, is both a receiver and a producer of text but, in the case of the former, the near simultaneity of the reception and production processes and the fact that there is no opportunity for working on successive drafts of text output create differences which are important both in terms of performance and in the use of performance as research data. In order to appreciate the particular constraints under which the simultaneous interpreter works, let us briefly review the salient features of this mode of translating.

RELEVANT FEATURES OF SIMULTANEOUS INTERPRETING

Divided attention

Speaking at the same time as the source text producer, interpreters have to run several processing activities concurrently. In addition to processing current input, they have to translate the immediately preceding input, encode their own output and monitor it (the interpreter's headset incorporates feedback from microphone to earpiece of his/her own voice so that output can be monitored). Time available for evaluative or reflective listening is thus curtailed. Shlesinger (1995) notes that this constraint entails a trade-off among the separate components of the task. For example, if syntactic processing becomes especially burdensome at a particular juncture, then time available for, say, lexical searching will be reduced (see Gile 1995: 172–3).

Ear-voice span

The necessary time-lag between reception of source text and production of target text has been called the ear-voice span (EVS – see, for example, Gerver (1976), Goldman-Eisler (1980)) and is said to vary from two to ten seconds approximately, depending for example on individual style, on syntactic complexity of input and on language combination. Variations in EVS can, of course, be taken as a rough measure of the size of the stretch of source text currently being processed. In general terms, the shorter the EVS, the closer will the translation adhere to the form of the source text. The correspondence is however not absolute. But whereas EVS is at least measurable, the length of text being processed at any given time during written translation is not observable in the same way. Thus, some insight into the translator's mode of operation is available in simultaneous interpreting. Most importantly, EVS imposes strain on short-term memory and, if it is allowed to become too long, breakdown can occur.

Audience design

In a seminal article, Bell (1984) drew attention to the ways in which text producers adapt their output to what he called **audience design**, that is, the perceived receiver group. It is important to realize that the interpreter, as a receiver of the source text, is not the intended addressee.[1] But speakers accommodate to their addressees in a variety of ways. As Shlesinger (1995) points out, speakers at a specialist conference gear their output to an expected level of specialized knowledge on the part of their audience, knowledge which the interpreter would often not share. Speakers also rely on feedback from their addressees, judging the extent to which even a very passive audience is following, becoming involved, losing interest, etc. In most cases, feedback from the interpreters in their booths will not be available (or even of interest) to the speaker. Thus the interpreter cannot be said to be a ratified participant in the speech event but, rather, an overhearer (cf. Bell (1984) and below, p. 83). Further, speeches for simultaneous translation tend to be of a particular kind. In many cases (although not in committee work), the mode of the source text will be written-to-be-read-aloud and the propositional content will be non-trivial with sustained and planned development of a single topic. Pace of delivery will of course be affected by whether the source text is spontaneous speech or written text (and may even be influenced by the fact that the text is to be simultaneously translated). But it will not be affected by the pressures of face-to-face interaction. Indeed, the simultaneous interpreter is in a totally different situation from that of the participant in a speech exchange who negotiates meaning with an interlocutor. The interpreter is rather what we may call an 'accountable listener', in the sense that the product of their listening is held up for scrutiny in a way which the ordinary listener is not subject to. And the interpreter's response will not be one of interaction with an interlocutor but rather of sympathetic impersonation of a source text speaker – with a similar group of addressees in mind to that of the speaker.

Continuous response

A further concomitant of the situation is that, given the requirement of divided attention and immediacy of response, the simultaneous interpreter concentrates on processing only current input. In other words there is likely to be less matching of current input with previous text than is the case in other forms of processing such as listening to a monologue or, especially, reading. Whereas co-textual clues do form an important part of the interpreter's understanding of text, preference is probably granted to the immediate pre-text over earlier text segments. Studies have shown that recall of verbal material is less after simultaneous interpreting than after other forms of processing, probably due to phonological interference between input and output (Darò and Fabbro 1994).

Our hypothesis is, then, that the simultaneous interpreter relies on textural signals. Context is muted because the interpreter is not a ratified participant in the speech event and because the constraints of immediacy of response and the focus on short units deny the interpreter the opportunity for adequate top-down processing. The same constraints – only a very small segment of text in active storage, the narrower processing channel – affect appreciation of structure. Structure is then something which may be inferred from textural clues such as those to be listed below but it is not available to the receiver in its entirety in the same way as it is to the consecutive interpreter or the receiver of written texts.

To illustrate these processes at work, we shall look at some evidence forthcoming from the work of trainee interpreters. There is no claim here that the evidence to be presented constitutes a scientific validation of our hypothesis since it cannot be claimed that our sample is in any sense representative of French-to-English interpreting in general or that the output of one group of trainees is representative of the work of professionals. One advantage, however, of observing trainees is that many output versions are produced of the same source text input, showing trends among an interpreter group which is relatively homogeneous in terms of previous training and exposure both to simultaneous interpreting and to the source language.[2] Further, evidence of self-correction (repair), hesitation, false starts and so on may be less readily available from the polished performance of seasoned professional interpreters than it is from the work of trainees. Yet such evidence is valuable for the insight which it gives into the communication difficulties involved in the process itself. Thus, the examples to be quoted are in no sense intended as some kind of error analysis. What interests us in this instance is not the accuracy of the interpreter's output so much as what it suggests about what is actually going on during the process of interpreting.

Our first data sample involves the responses of a group of thirty–two trainee interpreters to certain features of a speech sequence which had originally been delivered to the European Parliament by J. Delors, in his capacity as President of the Commission, on the topic of the next stage of European integration.[3] Sample 4.1 reproduces this speech sequence.

Sample 4.1

Bien entendu, un tel effort de clarification et de codification ne saurait prétendre, vous en êtes d'ailleurs convaincus, à résoudre tous les problèmes qu'auront à traiter les Etats membres lors de leur rendez-vous institutionnel de 1996. Je n'en citerai que quelques-uns.

Premièrement, la vision générale de l'organisation de la grande Europe, la finalité étant d'étendre – la finalité est notre devoir historique – à tous les pays de ce continent les valeurs de paix, de liberté et de reconnaissance mutuelle qui constituent l'âme et

le ciment de la construction européenne. J'ajoute que les élar-
gissements successifs ne sauraient nous dispenser de cette
réflexion à la fois géopolitique et institutionnelle.

Deuxièmement, la vision et l'héritage des pères de l'Europe
restent-ils valables alors qu'un débat s'est engagé à ce sujet? Il
me sera possible, en temps opportun, de démontrer qu'au-delà
des contingences de l'après-guerre, ces personnalités avaient vu
juste, loin et large. [. . .]

Troisièmement, s'il s'avérait inévitable de prendre acte des
positions opposées des Etats européens quant à la finalité de la
construction européenne, quel cadre conviendrait-il d'adopter
pour permettre à certains pays de partager une part notable de
leur souveraineté pour l'exercer ensemble? Et ce, sans pour
autant ne pas participer à la création de la grande Europe? Le
projet de Constitution propose, je l'ai dit, un mécanisme institutionnel. Sera-t-il suffisant? Sera-t-il opérationnel? C'est un beau
sujet de débat en préliminaire à la conférence intergouverne-
mentale de 1996.

Et enfin, quatrième problème, le 'comment procéder' reste au
coeur de toute ingénierie de la construction européenne. Une fois
acquise entre les pays la nouvelle frontière qu'ils veulent
atteindre, il reste à définir la stratégie et le cheminement, question posée depuis les premiers pas de 1948–1950. [. . .]

At the beginning of this speech sequence, the speaker (to use our
terminology, the text producer) embarks upon a new structural
section which is clearly signalled in the following manner:

> *Bien entendu, un tel effort de clarification et de codification ne saurait prétendre*
> *. . . à résoudre tous les problèmes . . . . Je n'en citerai que quelques-uns.*
> [Of course, such an effort of clarification and codification could
> not claim to solve all of the problems . . . . I shall cite just some
> of these.][4]

This utterance commits the text producer in various ways. Its effect
is to set up a number of expectations in the mind of the receiver
(in our case, the interpreter), who is bound to use these as guidelines
for what is to follow. The expectation-creating signals here are (1)
the use of *bien entendu* ('of course'), which habitually signals a counter-
argumentative structure; (2) the announcement of a thesis cited
('unresolved problems') to be opposed at some later stage; (3) these
two signals also imply that the text cannot reach its conclusion

before a more optimistic ('despite the problems') counter-argument appears; (4) the use of *quelques-uns*: the thesis cited will adopt an enumerative structure ('problem one, problem two', etc.). So, a list of problems will be expected. The immediately following item of input confirms this expectation. *Premièrement* not only signals the exposition of a 'problem to be overcome' but also that more will follow.

Enumerations of this kind may, in French as in other languages, adopt various structural formats (a list of noun phrases, a list of full clauses, a list of infinitive constructions) but an intertextually established convention is that parallelism of structure will be employed to reinforce the cohesion of the enumeration (e.g. while we are still hearing noun phrases, we are still within the list). Consequently, the interpreter, on hearing *premièrement*, cannot tell whether a noun phrase (NP) or a full sentence is to follow. The next items, *la vision générale*, give no syntactic clue as to whether this is a theme to which a rheme will be appended or just a topic announced as a rubric without comment. In other words, the interpreter may expect either:

(a) *Premièrement, la vision générale de l'organisation de la grande Europe. Deuxièmement, . . .*

or:

(b) *Premièrement, la vision générale de l'organisation de la grande Europe reste à définir . . .* (or some such rheme)

The interpreter's only clue as to the syntactic format to be followed is to be found in another textural device,[5] namely the pattern of intonation of the source text producer (rising on *Europe* if a rheme is to follow) which may be more or less distinct in practice. The first question to be asked of our data is then: what strategy do the interpreters adopt in processing the segment immediately following *Premièrement?* EVS has a role to play in this choice of strategy; if the span is a long one (different interpreters have different styles in this respect) then the interpreter may hope to delay committing him/herself until the source text syntactic format becomes clear; if the span is short, then an immediate output-processing decision must be made: either to opt for a NP rubric or for a theme-rheme utterance.

In practice, 24 out of the test group of 32 opted for the 'rubric' NP. Of these, 11 signalled by intonation an end-pattern after their translation of the items *la grande Europe*. In this way they clearly signalled that the first problem on the list had now been stated and that what immediately followed was comment on this. For this sub-group, the expectation which may be inferred is that the whole list of 'problems' is to follow an NP-rubric-plus-comment format. Another sub-group (13), however, opted for the NP-rubric but maintained level intonation, indicating that the rubric did not finish at *la grande Europe* but was to continue. This is entirely consistent with the source text, which continues with *la finalité étant d'étendre* ... ('the aim being to extend ...'). But in most such cases the syntactic link of *étant* was missing from the target language output, thus affecting the coherence of the whole sequence. The longer the sequence proceeds without falling intonation, the greater is the receiver's expectation of a finite verbal clause rather than a rubric, as may be appreciated from the following output sample:

> Firstly the general vision for Europe~ and European integration~ the aims of this~ ... and ensuring that all the countries of the continent have freedom, peace and recognition~ which is vital for European integration#
> [Key:[6] ~ = level or rising intonation; # = sentence-end pattern of intonation; ... = pause or hesitation]

Another strategy, well attested in observation of interpreters' performance, is to supply a verb in order to turn the rubric NP into a statement. Thus:

> Firstly there is the overall vision of an enlarged Europe#

Eight of the group opted for this solution, although not always appropriately:

> First of all the general vision of Europe as a whole# ... is important~
> And the vision for a great Europe is becoming a reality#

What may be observed at this point is that most of the group reproduced the NP-rubric syntactic pattern but a significant number avoided committing themselves to it, either by avoiding the sentence-end intonation pattern or by supplying a verb. In this way, the interpreters keep their options open for whatever is to follow. Let us now return to the source text, to see how it evolves beyond this point and what are the textural signals to which the interpreter has to respond.

The signal *Premièrement* commits the source text producer, as we have seen, to produce another signal to be realized as *Deuxièmement* or *Ensuite* or some such. In fact, the signal duly appears after another

38 seconds of input text. Given the intertextual expectation of parallelism, interpreter expectations – assuming that textural information remains in active or semi-active storage for that long – will now be that a NP rubric, however long or structurally complex, is to follow rather than a theme-rheme utterance of the syntactic format of (b) above. These expectations are however not borne out and what the interpreter has to deal with is not just a finite-clause utterance but an entirely unexpected complex interrogative as well. To appreciate what is involved here, one must imagine the interpreter processing the input *Deuxièmement, la vision et l'héritage des pères de l'Europe* ... ('Secondly the vision and the legacy of the founding fathers of Europe'), which, thus far, appears syntactically parallel to the earlier *Premièrement, la vision générale de l'organisation de la grande Europe*.... That is, the syntactic signal of the question form, the inversion of subject and verb, is delayed until five seconds after the beginning of the sentence. Evidence of a different intonation pattern is similarly delayed. Our next examination of the data is then to ascertain how the trainee interpreters coped with this unexpected/counter-expected texture. Is there evidence of the use of parallelism by the interpreter to expect a listing without a finite clause? Included in this must be the evidence of output intonation patterns, which are often subject to modification and repair as output proceeds.

It is striking that no fewer than 14 of the group reproduced the question as a statement that the vision and legacy were indeed still valid. From a contextual point of view, it would probably be apparent to readers of this sequence as a written text (that is, with more processing time and capacity available) that, if the vision and legacy remain valid, then this is less likely to be a 'problem' than if they do not remain valid. But the simultaneous interpreter is generally denied the luxury of such contextual inferencing and runs the risk of being misled by a close adherence to textural patterns of the source text. Most of the group (17), nevertheless, were able to respond to the signal of the interrogative. Of these, five seem to have been influenced by the parallelism expected following the NP-rubric format of 'problem one', in that they reproduce 'problem two' as an NP rubric and then signal the interrogative in a second sentence, either lexically:

Secondly the vision and the legacy of the founding fathers of Europe# We must ask ourselves whether these principles still hold true to-day~

or by inversion:

> Secondly the vision and the legacy of the founding fathers of Europe# Will it remain valid during such a debate?#

The remaining 12 output sequences are a close calque of the texture of the input text. Thus, at one and the same time, they reproduce an NP-rubric format but without sentence-end intonation and continue with an inversion of verb and subject pronoun uncharacteristic of the target language, e.g:

> Second~ the vision and the legacy of the fathers of Europe~ is it . . . is it valid (. . .)

> Second~ the vision and the heritage . . . or the legacy rather of the founding fathers of Europe~ will it still be valid when a new debate is taken up~

Beyond the calque, inappropriate as it is in English, what is perceptible is the general reluctance of the interpreters to curtail their options by closing their sentence. There is a striking tendency to hedge one's bets as long as possible, in order to be in a position to handle whatever syntactic pattern is to follow.

Further textural pitfalls await the interpreter of the speech sequence in sample 4.1. Mention of the third item in the list is followed by what in English linguistics is known as a *wh*-question, again delayed well beyond the beginning of the utterance by a subordinate conditional clause:

> *Troisièmement, s'il s'avérait inévitable de prendre acte des positions opposées des Etats européens quant à la finalité de la construction européenne, quel cadre conviendrait-il d'adopter . . .*
> [Thirdly, if it proved inevitable to acknowledge the opposing positions of the European states concerning the end-result of European integration, what framework should be adopted . . .?]

Here at least the initial conditional *si* ('if') signals that the utterance will not be complete until a full sentence format is achieved. A phrase-by-phrase calque of the source text format will, in this instance, serve the interpreter well and, indeed, 14 of our group of 32 follow this procedure. What is surprising, however, is that no fewer than 13 of the group miss the *si* cue and turn this clause ('if it were inevitable') either into a statement ('it is inevitable') or a question ('is it inevitable?'). Why should this happen in so many cases? A clue to what may have happened during processing is to be found in the following version:

> Thirdly~ whether it would be necessary to take opposing views . . . if this were necessary with regard to the final object of European construction# What framework would we need to adopt (. . .)

If an expectation is set up in which each ordinal number is immediately followed by a rubric which states a 'problem', then the input sequence *si* . . . may easily be wrongly processed as representing 'problem no. 3', that is 'the problem is whether it is inevitable . . .'. The intonation pattern of the version quoted above suggests that the source text has been processed in this manner. Given the already noted tendency to turn rubrics into verbal clauses, 'problem no. 3' may alternatively be reformulated as 'Thirdly it is inevitable . . .', a pattern followed by 10 of the group. There is, then, some evidence – which is far from being conclusive – of expectations based on previous textural patterns being used to process incoming text.

The next item in the enumeration of *problèmes*, which is immediately signalled as the closing item (*Et enfin, quatrième problème* . . . 'And finally, fourth problem') adopts a syntactic format not hitherto encountered in the list, a statement of the format X = Y, incorporating a finite verb form:

> *Et enfin, quatrième problème, le 'comment procéder' reste au coeur de toute ingénierie de la construction européenne.*
> [And finally, the fourth problem, the 'how-to-proceed' remains at the heart of all planning of European integration.]

The relevant question here might be: is there evidence that the earlier format of the enumeration sequence influences interpreter choice of output format? Given a climate of unpredictability, do interpreters commit themselves or do they hedge their bets? An immediate output of 'the fourth problem is how to proceed' allows the option of either ending the utterance at this point or continuing it (if it should turn out that the source text input is not yet complete) by: '. . . and this is . . .' or some similar device. An additional complication here is that the subject NP in the source text, *le comment procéder* ('the how-to-proceed'), is not easily calqued by an NP of the same form in English; the gloss provided above as a guide to source text format is, of course, inappropriate as natural TL text. (An appropriate NP translation might be 'the logistics of . . .'.) The interpreter is thus forced, in some measure at least, to depart from the syntactic format of the source text. Which options are in fact selected by the interpreters in our test group?

The format suggested above, namely, supplying a verb and thus making a sentence of the form 'the fourth problem is how to proceed', was selected by 23 of our group of 32 interpreters, showing a clear preference for keeping options open as far as possible. Of these, 15 ended their sentence-intonation pattern at this point and began a new sentence to deal with the following input (. . . *reste au coeur* . . .) while 8 continued without falling intonation, using either 'and . . .', a relative clause or some other device:

> And the fourth problem is how should we progress~ . . . and this is something which lies at the heart of (. . .)
> And finally the fourth problem is the . . . procedure~ which is the main problem of setting up the Union#

A sub-group of six echoed the NP-rubric format of 'problem one' and then embarked upon a new statement to incorporate the rheme element of the source text, thus:

> And finally~ the fourth problem~ how to achieve this# This is at the heart of European construction#
>
> And lastly~ the fourth problem~ how to proceed# This remains at the heart of all the institutions of the European Union#

Of this sub-group, five had also used the NP-rubric pattern following *Premièrement* and two additionally following *Deuxièmement*. There is consequently some – strictly limited – evidence of the interpreter's working memory intervening to ensure TT parallelism (and consequently cohesion) where this particular cohesive device does not occur in the source text.

In the data we have looked at so far, it is clear that the relative unpredictability of source text texture does create problems for this group of trainee interpreters, who will tend to adhere to source text textural patterns where possible and may create their own expectations based on source text patterns still present in short-term memory. But in a situation in which there is textural instability, the interpreters tend to hedge their syntactic bets by adopting formats which will allow them maximum flexibility in dealing with whatever is to follow. Overall, the numbers of successful negotiations of unpredictable patterns may point to the active use of source text intonation patterns, as a more reliable textural clue than syntactic patterns, which may evolve in unpredictable ways.

In our final instance, it is a marked use of verbal tense which creates a sudden dynamism in the source text, posing a problem for the interpreter. The source text here (extracts are reproduced below as Sample 4.2) is an official statement to the European Parliament by a Commission spokesman on the situation of the Leyland-DAF vehicle manufacturer. Our data consist of 31 trainee simultaneous interpreter versions.

Sample 4.2

Monsieur le Président, le 2 février 1993, Daf et sa filiale britannique, Leyland-Daf, qui comptent parmi les premiers constructeurs de poids-lourds, ont annoncé leur effondrement financier et ont demandé la protection de leurs créanciers aux Pays-Bas, en Belgique et en Grande Bretagne. Ces sociétés ont été placées sous administration judiciaire, le consortium bancaire de Daf, le gouvernement néerlandais et les autorités de la région flamande n'étant pas parvenus à un compromis sur un plan de restructuration et sur son financement. [. . .]

Depuis lors, les administrateurs judiciaires – dans le cas de Leyland-Daf, *the receivers* – dirigent les sociétés et ont réussi, sur la base de financements à court terme, à relancer la production qui s'était arrêtée après l'effondrement financier de Daf.

Le lundi 8 février, la presse a publié un plan de restructuration qui aurait été préparé par les administrateurs judiciaires de Daf aux Pays-Bas, sur la base d'études effectuées par deux sociétés de conseil, l'une spécialisée en gestion et l'autre en comptabilité. Sur base de ces études, un plan de restructuration a été élaboré, qui prévoit la création d'une nouvelle société anonyme qui absorberait la totalité des activités de Daf aux Pays-Bas et en Belgique dans le secteur de la construction des camions et des poids-lourds, ainsi que, peut-être, des opérations d'assemblage de Leyland-Daf à Leyland au Lancashire. Ce plan entraînerait également d'importantes suppressions d'emplois, estimées à plus de 5000 postes, ainsi que la fermeture de certains sites au Royaume-Uni. Les communiqués de presse indiquent qu'un financement de l'ordre de 1,5 milliard de florins serait nécessaire au cours de la période 1993–1995. A la suite d'une demande adressée par la Commission, les autorités néerlandaises ont précisé, le 10 février, que les parties concernées ne s'étaient pas encore complètement entendues sur le plan de restructuration, dont certains éléments doivent être examinés ultérieurement. Dans ces conditions, toute déclaration sur ce dossier présente pour le moment un caractère provisoire.

Déjà avant l'effondrement de Daf, la DG IV avait examiné deux cas d'aides non notifiées concernant un financement à court terme que les gouvernements néerlandais et flamand avaient accordé. Ces deux gouvernements ont annoncé qu'ils apporteraient encore leur soutien, à condition que toutes les parties arrivent à un accord sur un plan de restructuration complet. Etant donné que cela entraînerait certainement d'importantes aides d'Etat, la DG IV suit l'affaire avec attention. [. . .]

From the outset of the source text speech, a narrative sequence is signalled:

> . . . *le 2 février 1993, Daf et sa filiale britannique, Leyland-Daf . . . ont annoncé leur effondrement financier . . .*
> [on 2 February 1993, Daf and its British subsidiary, Leyland-Daf, announced their financial collapse . . .]

This narrative text focus is reinforced in the following co-text by a series of narrative events in sequence:

> . . . *ont demandé la protection de leurs créanciers* [asked for their creditors to be protected]
> . . . *ces sociétés ont été placées* . . . [these companies were placed]
> *Le lundi 8 février la presse a publié* . . . [On Monday 8 February, the press published . . .]

It is to be expected on the basis of these indications that receivers will activate a narrative frame, in which events will continue to be related until some conclusion is reached. An element of instability disturbs this routine sequence of events, however, when a conditional of allegation (. . . *un plan de restructuration qui aurait été préparé par les administrateurs judiciaires* – 'a rescue plan which [lit.] would have been drawn up by the receivers') interrupts the series of narrative verb tenses. In using this 'conditional of allegation or rumour' in French, a text producer can avoid stating an event as fact and shed responsibility for the truth of what is being reported. In this instance, since the text producer is relying on newspaper reports alone for his information, it is only natural that he would wish to exercise caution in attributing authorship of the rescue plan to a particular person or body; however probable that it was indeed the *adminstrateurs judiciaires* who drew up the plan, he simply cannot be sure. There are, of course, conventional ways of achieving the same illocutionary force in languages such as English, for example by the use of modal adverbs such as 'apparently'. But in terms of the linear development of the source text received by the interpreter as input, what is significant here is the sudden departure from factual reporting of events to expression of modality. This becomes increasingly important as the text unfolds in that it becomes apparent that a mild discourse of reproach is being injected into what otherwise would be a detached report of a factual matter. The Commission is, in fact, discreetly making it clear that it feels it should have been consulted about the rescue plan from the outset instead of having to rely on press reports. Later utterances such as:

> *A la suite d'une demande adressée par la Commission, les autorités néerlandaises ont précisé, le 10 février, que . . .*
> [Following a request from the Commission, the Dutch government explained on 10 February that . . .]

show that the Commission was anxious to reaffirm its authority and a reference to two previous cases which had not been notified to it (*deux cas d'aides non notifiées*) reinforces the reprimand. But at the juncture of the source text where the first conditional of allegation occurs, the interpreter (unless briefed in advance on this point) cannot know what is to follow and can only respond to the textural detail of the modalized verb form, the only evidence currently available. Now, one of the questions which were raised in Chapter 3 was: how do interpreters react when stability is removed? Given reliance on the texture of the input text, does the expectation of an unfolding narrative lead the interpreters to 're-stabilize' the instability, to 'hear' the conditional of allegation as an actual event in the sequence being related?

There is some evidence of this occurring, in that 10 out of a group of 29 trainee interpreters processed this item as a simple narrative event (e.g. 'a rescue package which was prepared by the receivers . . .'). But what is altogether more striking is the range of other options resorted to by the group. These include:

> 'had been prepared by . . .' (sub-group of 10); here, the compound element of the source text item is registered and reproduced but, again, within an entirely narrative and non-modal framework;

'was to be prepared by . . .' (sub-group of two)
'was to have been prepared by' (sub-group of one); in these cases, an element of conjecture or hypothetical reporting is introduced in response to the source text signal but the pragmatic effect is wholly different to that intended;

'would have been prepared by . . .' (sub-group of two)
'should have been prepared by . . .' (sub-group of two); in these versions, modality is relayed. The first of them is a calque of the source text form but the modal values of both of these English verb forms is different to that relayed by the source text form.

'was probably prepared by . . .' (sub-group of one)
'a plan which . . . it is said that this has been produced by . . .' (sub-group of one)

These versions do relay values similar to those implied in the source text and show an automatic interpreter response to a correctly perceived signal.

It is important to stress at this point that what interests us here is not some kind of evaluation of interpreter performance. It may well be the case that this group of trainees was less sensitive to the value relayed by the conditional of allegation than a professional interpreter would be. More importantly, however, it is probably fair to say that relaying the particular item we have been studying is not crucial to an appropriate interpretation of this speech. The aims of the simultaneous interpreter are not those of the written translator and, whereas it will always be important to relay the discoursal values of a source text speaker, these will become apparent at other junctures and do not rely on a single textural detail such as that considered here. In this sense, the translation of an individual verb form is scarcely significant. But this chapter is about observing interpreter behaviour in response to given stimuli in order to shed some light on relevant aspects of the interpreting process. It is in this sense that the reactions of our trainee interpreter group, reproduced above, are interesting. In the majority of cases, the interpreter response shows instant reaction to the dynamic element which suddenly intrudes in the texture of the source text. The signal is recognized and responded to but the full discoursal value of what is merely an item of texture cannot yet be realized by the interpreter who is, at this stage in the unfolding of the source text, deprived of the necessary contextual and structural clues to its appreciation. Further research is needed – for example, a verbal protocol questionnaire to interpreters immediately after the event might afford insight into the extent to which the interpreters are relying on texture and the kind of mental model of text development they have built.

Nevertheless, there are certain features which have emerged from this observation of trainee interpreter performance. They may be summarized as follows:

- There is a tendency to follow source text textural patterns where possible.
- Even isolated textural signals tend to evoke some response in target text output.
- The inadequacy of many responses may be traceable to lack of an adequate overview of context and structure.
- Some use is made of previous textural patterns still in active storage.
- In situations of relative unpredictability, there is a tendency to opt for syntactic structures which do not reduce future options.
- Source text intonation patterns may be the element of cohesion on which interpreters rely most strongly.

All of these trends would need to be tested in a far more systematic way than has been possible here. But what we hope to have elaborated in Chapters 3 and 4 is an overall discourse/text processing framework within which research into this and other forms of oral translating may take place.

In Chapter 3 we surmised that the context and structure 'deficit' of the simultaneous interpreter has implications for syllabus design in interpreter training programmes. At the end of this brief glance at the interpreter in action, we can at least appreciate that it would be fairly pointless to rely, in training sessions, on a *post hoc* appreciation of the full context of this sequence (the Commission intends to use this opportunity of a report to the Parliament to issue a veiled reproach) or of the full structure (a detached report is followed by a statement of the Commission's role and then of the Commission's attitude). Rather, it might be fruitful to consider key textural signals of discoursal or textual trends-to-come, not necessarily as items to be responded to immediately but as important indicators of what may be expected as the text unfolds. Certainly, the conditional of allegation is one such feature, in that it is so often used not in isolation but in support of a whole discoursal attitude. Being able to anticipate changes of direction or the introduction of a new stance or attitude is what will most assist the interpreter in the booth.

Chapter 5

Politeness in screen translating

We now turn to an entirely different mode of translating, that of film subtitling, in order to show discourse processes of a similar kind at work. In this chapter, the emphasis will be on the pragmatic dimension of context and we shall see how the constraints of particular communicative tasks affect variously the textural devices employed both in original screen writing and in the writing of subtitles. It will immediately be realized that we are here confronted with mixed modes. Unlike the dubber, who translates speech into speech, the subtitler has to represent in the written mode what is spoken on the soundtrack of the film.

It would be superfluous here to enter into a detailed description of the task of the subtitler (for a full account of what is involved, see for example Vöge (1977), Titford (1982)). For our purposes, it will suffice to summarize the main constraints on subtitling, which create particular kinds of difficulties for the translator. They are, broadly speaking, of four kinds:

1 The shift in mode from speech to writing. This has the result that certain features of speech (non-standard dialect, emphatic devices such as intonation, code-switching and style-shifting, turn-taking) will not automatically be represented in the written form of the target text.

2 Factors which govern the medium or channel in which meaning is to be conveyed. These are physical constraints of available space (generally up to 33, or in some cases 40 keyboard spaces per line; no more than two lines on screen)[1] and the pace of the sound-track dialogue (titles may remain on screen for a minimum of two and a maximum of seven seconds).

3 The reduction of the source text as a consequence of (2) above. Because of this the translator has to reassess coherence strategies in order to maximize the retrievability of intended meaning from a more concise target language version. In face-to-face communication, the normal redundancy of speech gives hearers more than one chance of picking up intended meaning; in subtitling, the redundancy is inevitably reduced and chances of retrieving lost meaning are therefore fewer. Moreover, unlike other forms of written communication, this mode does not allow the reader to back-track for the purpose of retrieving meaning.

4 The requirement of matching the visual image. As Chaume (forthcoming) points out, the acoustic and visual images are inseparable in film and, in translating, coherence is required between the subtitled text and the moving image itself. Thus, matching the subtitle to what is actually visible on screen may at times create an additional constraint.

Some of the studies which have been carried out have concentrated on the effect of these constraints on the form of the translation. Goris (1993) and Lambert (1990) note the levelling effect of the mode-shift and, in particular, the way in which features of speech which are in any way non-standard tend to be eliminated. Lambert speaks of '*un style zéro*' and Goris, comparing user variation in subtitling and dubbing, observes that, in the latter, social dialect is under-represented in terms of prosodic features of speech but quite well represented lexically; in subtitling, on the other hand, neither prosodic features nor variant lexis appear to be represented.

POLITENESS

In an earlier study (Mason 1989), we observed that one area of meaning which appeared consistently to be sacrificed in subtitling was that of interpersonal pragmatics and, in particular, **politeness** features. In what follows, we hope to illustrate how politeness is almost inevitably underrepresented in this mode of translating and to suggest what the effects of this might be. Additionally, we shall point to further research which might be carried out in this particular area of translation studies.

We use the term politeness in the sense intended by Brown and Levinson (1987), on which much of this chapter is based. It is important to establish immediately that the term is not used here in its conventional sense of displaying courtesy but rather it is intended to cover all aspects of language usage which serve to establish, maintain or modify interpersonal relationships between text producer and text receiver.

Brown and Levinson's theory rests on the assumption that all competent language users have the capacity of reasoning and have what is known as '**face**'. Face is defined as:

> the public self-image that everyone lays claim to, consisting of two related aspects:
>
> (a) negative **face**: the basic claim to freedom of action and freedom from imposition;
> (b) positive **face**: positive self-image and the desire that this self-image be appreciated and approved of.
>
> (Brown and Levinson 1987: 61)

Now, because language users are aware of each other's face, it will in general be in their mutual interest to maintain each other's face. So, speakers will usually want to maintain addressees' face because they want addressees to maintain their face. Above all, speakers want to maintain their own face. They are however aware that some linguistic actions they may wish to perform (such as asking for a favour) intrinsically threaten face. These are referred to as '**face-threatening acts**' (**FTA**s). Normally, a speaker will want to minimize the face-threat to the hearer of an FTA (unless their desire to carry out an FTA with maximum efficiency – defined as 'bald on-record' – outweighs their concern to preserve their hearer's or their own face). So, the more an act threatens the speaker's or the hearer's face, the more the speaker will want to select a strategy that minimizes the risk.

Strategies available to speakers for this purpose are (in order of increasing face-threat):

1 *Don't carry out the FTA at all.*
2 *Do carry out the FTA, but off-the-record,* i.e. allowing for a certain ambiguity of intention.
3 *Do the FTA on-record with redressive action (negative politeness).* This will involve reassuring hearers that they are being respected by expressions of deference and formality, by hedging, maintaining distance, etc.

4 *Do the FTA on-record with redressive action (positive politeness).* This will involve paying attention to hearers' positive face by, e.g., expressing agreement, sympathy or approval.

5 *Do the FTA on-record, without redressive action, baldly.*

To illustrate this, let us imagine that A wants B to lend her money, in itself an FTA. Strategy 5 above would involve A making a direct request of the type: 'lend me twenty pounds' – a threat to B because it seems to lack respect; and a threat to A because it is not good for her self-image. For both of these reasons, A is more likely to opt for a less face-threatening strategy. Strategy 4 might involve an utterance along the lines of: 'We're old friends and I know I can rely on you. Please lend me . . .' The threat, although still direct, is slightly mitigated by the attention paid to B's self-image. Strategy 3 would involve expressions of the kind: 'I hate to ask you this but could you possibly . . .?' Again, this is still a direct request for money, although the way it is put makes it slightly easier for B to refuse without losing face and without causing A to lose face. On the other hand, strategy 2 (e.g. 'I'm desperately short of money. I wonder where I could get twenty pounds from.') allows A to protest, if challenged by B, 'Oh, but I wouldn't dream of asking *you*!'

Crucially, it should be added that the seriousness of an FTA is a cultural variable; it cannot be assumed that the same act would carry the same threat in different socio-cultural settings. Moreover, the weight of an FTA is subject to the variables of the social **distance** and relative **power** of speakers and addressees. A direct request for a favour is less face-threatening between friends than between people who are relative strangers to each other or whose relationship is hierarchical (employee to employer, for example). Thus, in languages which have distinct pronouns of address to encode addresser/addressee relationship (French *tu* and *vous*, for example), a switch from the use of one form to the other form may in itself constitute a potential FTA – to the addressee because the sudden reduction of the social distance between him or her and the speaker may be unwelcome; and to the speaker because he or she runs the risk of being rebuffed by non-reciprocal use by addressees. In addition, if a speaker who is in a hierarchically superior position to a hearer initiates the change, then threat to face may stem from the hearer's impression that this is an attempt to exercise power, i.e. encode the non-reciprocal relationship. Consequently, pronouns of address are often the site for complex negotiation of face.

Brown and Levinson present evidence from three unrelated social and linguistic cultures to show that, whereas the linguistic realization of politeness varies considerably, there is a remarkable uniformity of underlying strategy, which might suggest that politeness is a universal feature of natural language communication. From a translation point of view, what this might suggest is that the dynamics of politeness can be relayed trans-culturally but will require a degree of linguistic modification at the level of texture.[2] Relaying the significance of the shift from *vous* to *tu* mentioned above, for example, is a familiar problem for screen translators as well as translators of novels.

At the same time, as suggested above, the particular constraints under which the film subtitler works make it impossible for all of the meaning values perceived in the source language soundtrack to be relayed. Indeed, it would be fair to say that this is not even an aim of the subtitler, who seeks to provide a target language guide to what is going on in the source text. Meaning is then to be retrieved by cinema audiences by a process of matching this target text guide with visual perception of the action on screen, including paralinguistic features, body language, etc. Consequently, any phrase-by-phrase comparison of source text and target text for the purposes of translation criticism would be an idle exercise and our analysis below should not be construed as having any such intention. What is an altogether more legitimate subject of investigation, however, is to ascertain whether there is any consistent pattern in the kinds of values/signals/items which are perforce omitted in translated dialogue. Such research would require the analysis of a wide variety of acts of subtitling of various kinds and in widely differing languages. Here, we can do no more than provide some initial evidence which would point in the direction such research might take.

AUDIENCE DESIGN

Before proceeding to the analysis of our data, it is important to consider the nature of film dialogue. As with all works of fiction, the dialogue is 'authentic' only in a special sense. Characters on screen address each other as if they were real persons while, in reality, a script-writer is, like a novelist, constructing discourse for the sake of the effect it will have on its receivers, in this case the cinema audience. Consequently, in the case of film dialogue, some refinement is needed to our key notions of text producer and text receiver. Thus, potentially

Text producer 1 = scriptwriter (film director, etc.)
Text producer 2 = character A on screen
Text receiver 1 = character B on screen
Text receiver 2 = cinema audience
(Text receiver 3 = other potential receivers)

A. Bell (1984) provides a taxonomy of categories of text receiver and shows how speech style is affected above all by what he calls '**audience design**', that is, the extent to which speakers accommodate to their addressees. He argues convincingly that style is essentially a matter of speakers' response to their audience, who include four potential categories. **Addressee**s are known to the speaker, ratified participants in the speech event and directly addressed; **auditor**s are both known to the speaker and ratified participants but they are not being directly addressed; **overhearer**s are known by the speaker to be present but are neither directly addressed nor ratified participants; finally, **eavesdropper**s are those of whose presence the speaker is unaware. Bell's hypothesis is that the text producer's style is affected most of all by addressees, to a lesser extent by auditors and less again by overhearers. (Eavesdroppers, being unknown, cannot, by definition, influence a speaker's style.) Adapting this classification now to film dialogue, we may say that characters on screen treat each other as addressees within a fictional world in which the cinema audience is like an eavesdropper. What we know, however, is that in reality the screenwriter intends the dialogue for a set of known, ratified but not directly addressed receivers – i.e. the cinema audience, who then according to the above classification may be considered to be auditors. (Other categories of potential receivers, such as film festival juries, boards of censors, etc. may then be considered as overhearers.)

In the case of mass communication, furthermore, Bell argues that audience design is not so much a response to the audience (since the communicator cannot know exactly who is being addressed) but rather an initiative of the communicator, who forms a mental image of the kind of (socio-cultural) group he or she knows to be the likely receivers. He also suggests that this kind of communication inverts the normal hierarchy of audience roles, since 'mass auditors are likely to be more important to a communicator than the immediate addressees' (A. Bell 1984: 177). Thus, it could be said according to·this hypothesis that the style of a film script is more subject to influence by the auditors than by the immediate addressees within the fictional dialogue. For example, in the data to be discussed below, a fictional character appearing on screen for the first time at a dinner-table conversation, begins:

> *Ce que je trouve navrant – et c'est ce que j'essaie de dire dans mon dernier livre – c'est que . . .*
> [What I find upsetting – and this is what I attempt to say in my latest book – is that . . .]

It seems plausible that what is primarily involved here is a scriptwriter's signal to mass auditors that the character who is being introduced is pompous or pretentious; secondarily, the fictional character is seeking to establish his intellectual authority with his interlocutors. In other words, the pretentious style is both addressee-designed and auditor-designed but, in terms of cinema as communication, the orientation towards the mass auditors is perhaps the overriding consideration.

The relevance of these audience-design distinctions to our consideration of the subtitler's task may now become apparent. As a translator, the subtitler is seeking to preserve the coherence of communication between addressees on screen at the same time as relaying a coherent discourse from screenwriter to mass auditors. Given the severe constraints of the task as detailed above, hard choices have to be made. Elements of meaning will, inevitably and knowingly, be sacrificed. On the basis of our observation, we wish to suggest that, typically, subtitlers make it their overriding priority to establish coherence for their receivers, i.e. the mass auditors, by ensuring easy readability and connectivity; their second priority would then be the addressee-design of the fictional characters on screen (particularly in terms of the inter-personal pragmatics involved). Specifically, there is systematic loss in subtitling of indicators of interlocutors accommodating to each others' 'face-wants'. In the remainder of this chapter, we shall illustrate such processes at work.

THE DATA

The examples of screen translating reproduced below are taken from the English-subtitled version of the French film *Un coeur en hiver*

(Claude Sautet, 1992). This film was chosen for the following reasons. First, being a recent, widely-distributed, full-length feature film, the quality of subtitling is high. Second, a theme of the film is the establishment, maintenance and modification of personal relationships and the ways in which these are or are not made explicit in language. Thus, our central concern, which we described above as interpersonal pragmatics, is always to the fore in this film. Third, the film contains many sequences of verbal sparring, in which characters on screen seek to get the better of each other, impose their will or improve their image among others present (cf. the notions of face and threat to face, outlined above). This confronts us with an abundance of the politeness phenomena referred to earlier.

In the film, Stéphane, a violin-maker, is attracted to Camille, a musician, who is involved in a close relationship with Stéphane's colleague, Maxime. Camille is attracted to Stéphane but the latter's reticence and unwillingness to commit himself is a growing problem between them.

The sequences from which our examples are taken are (Sample 5.1) a rehearsal by Camille and two (male) fellow-musicians of a Ravel sonata, witnessed by Stéphane, who has improved the sound of Camille's violin. In the sequence, the dialogue is between Camille and Stéphane. Camille speaks first; (Sample 5.2) a dinner-table conversation between guests, including Stéphane, Camille and Maxime, and their hosts.

Positive and negative politeness

Sample 5.1

– Ça vous convient?[3]	Like it?
[Does that suit you?]	
– Oui, m . . .	Yes, but . . .
[Yes, b . . .]	
– Dites.	Go on.
[Say it]	
– Vous n'avez pas joué un peu vite?	You took it a bit fast.
[Didn't you play rather fast?]	
– Si. Vous voulez l'entendre à sa	Yes. You want to hear
vitesse.	it at the right tempo?
[Yes. You wish to hear it at its	
normal pace.]	

– Oui, si ça ne . . . [yes, if it's not . . .] (Music)	If you wouldn't mind.
– Alors? [well?]	Well?
– C'est très beau [It's very beautiful.] (Pause)	It was beautiful.
– Vous partez déjà? [You're leaving already?]	Leaving already?
– Oui. [Yes.]	
– Vous avez d'autres rendez-vous? [You have other appointments?]	Other business?
– Non mais j . . . je dois vous laisser travailler. Au revoir. [No but I . . . I must let you work. Goodbye.]	No, I must let you work. Goodbye.
– Au revoir. [Goodbye.]	Goodbye.
(Other musicians) – Salut! – Salut! [Cheerio!]	

In Sample 5.1, what is really going on is apparent not so much from the propositional meaning of what is said but from what is implicated in what is said. Camille is seeking to provoke Stéphane and get behind his defences. Her utterances constitute direct threats to his face. Stéphane, on the contrary, is self-effacing and defensive; his whole strategy is to avoid going on-record and his embarrassment is apparent not only in his speech but also in his facial expression. Camille's directness is also apparent in her gaze. To an extent, then, these paralinguistic features will convey the interpersonal meanings to the cinema audience without the need for them to be explicitly encoded in subtitles. But let us look more closely at what is going on here. Camille's initial question asks bluntly whether her rendering 'suits' Stéphane (rather than simply whether he likes it). What is implicated in such an utterance is that Stéphane is the kind of person who requires things to suit him. This threatens his face in two ways. First, to accept the question as it stands implies acceptance of the implicature that he would wish it to 'suit' him – which, in turn, commits him to something which is face-threatening to his interlocutor. Second, it commits him (a non-musician) to going on-record in expressing an opinion of a concert-violinist's work. In reply, Stéphane's strategy is consequently one of minimization of face-loss; he wishes to express a point of view (the music was played too fast) but he cannot afford either to agree or disagree with the question as put and so opts for a 'yes, but' which is, even then, not fully stated but just alluded to (*Oui, m* . . .). Not content to allow Stéphane to be so evasive, Camille insists, with a bald, on-record imperative: 'say it!' Now Stéphane can no longer avoid expressing an opinion. But his main concern is still to protect his own face. Again, he takes redressive action by putting his view in the form of a question, thus allowing himself the let-out 'I didn't say it was too fast' and implicating 'this is only my view: you're the expert'. Not to be outdone, Camille replies as if Stéphane's view had been intended as an instruction. Her rejoinder *Vous voulez l'entendre à sa vitesse* ('You wish to hear it at its own tempo') is uttered with the intonation of a statement of confirmation, not with that of a question. Stéphane, again recognising the face-threat involved in saying either 'yes' or 'no', is once more equivocal and hesitant: 'Yes, if it's not . . .' It is as if he dare not finish his utterances for fear of going on-record.[4]

In the remainder of the exchange, three things are evident. First, Camille's direct (bald, on-record) strategy continues, with short questions which function either as instructions (*Alors?* = 'State an opinion') or as reproaches (*Vous partez déjà?* and *Vous avez d'autres rendezvous?* may implicate 'You're not really interested in me or my music'). Second, Stéphane's evasiveness is further served by his ambiguous reply *C'est très beau*, which can be understood either as 'Your rendering was beautiful' or as 'The music (but not necessarily your rendering of it) is beautiful.' Again, he avoids committing himself any more than necessary. Finally, the artificial distance between Stéphane and Camille is thrown into sharp relief when their formal leave-taking (– *Au revoir*, – *au revoir*) is echoed in much less formal terms (*Salut!*) by the two other musicians, whose relations with Stéphane are apparently casual and unproblematic.

Thus far in our analysis, the textural encoding of politeness has included lexical choice, sentence form (imperative, interrogative), unfinished utterance, intonation, ambiguity of reference. These then are the linguistic features which constitute the best evidence of the management of the situation, the interpersonal dynamics and the progress of the conflictual verbal relationship. We now turn to the sequence of subtitles to consider the extent to which the implicatures are still retrievable from the target text. Unsurprisingly – and almost inevitably – a different picture emerges.

The preference for brevity and ease of readability accounts for such translations of Camille's questions as 'Like it?', 'Leaving already?', 'Other business?' Yet this concise style, omitting the subject pronoun, is conventionally associated in English with familiarity and solidarity (in terms of politeness theory, it is a way of minimizing face-threat by 'claiming common ground') – the opposite of the strategy adopted by Camille, who, in the source text, does nothing to reduce threat to face. This different, altogether more conciliatory Camille also emerges in lexical selection (asking someone about 'likes' is far less face-threatening than asking about what suits him; 'Go on' is a conventional way of encouraging a speaker to say more, whereas 'Say it!' is a direct challenge). Finally, the mode-shift from speech to writing requires choices to be made in punctuation. Camille's question delivered as a statement (*Vous voulez l'entendre à sa vitesse*) has become 'You want to hear it at the right tempo?' – again suggesting a more conciliatory stance.

Turning now to Stéphane, we find that several of the politeness features observed above have disappeared. His off-record strategy of tentativeness, vagueness and ambiguity is not recoverable from the subtitles. *Oui m . . .* has become 'Yes, but . . .'; *Oui si ça ne . . .* has become 'If you wouldn't mind' and the hesitation in *Non mais j . . . je dois vous laisser travailler* is, in translation, the more assertive 'No, I must let you work.' The verdict 'It was beautiful' no longer allows the inference that the comment *C'est très beau* refers to Ravel rather than Camille. Likewise, the redressive action which mitigates the threat to face in *Vous n'avez pas joué un peu vite?* (see above) is no longer perceptible in the pronouncement 'You took it a bit fast.' In other words, the translated Stéphane is pursuing a different strategy. Finally, the opposition *Au revoir / salut!*, so important in the encoding of social relations that it must be supposed to be primarily a signal from the scriptwriter to the auditors, is not relayed; the audience relying on the translation is unaware of the stark contrast between Stéphane's and Camille's leave-taking and that of the two other musicians.

From the point of view of the verbal exchange in Sample 5.1 as a whole, it could be argued that enough is apparent from facial expression and gesture for all of these interpersonal dynamics to be retrieved without the need for them to be made explicit in the target text. There is no doubt some substance to such a claim and our analysis cannot do full justice to the visual image which the subtitles are intended to accompany. Nevertheless, if indicators of politeness in the target text are at variance with those suggested by the moving image, then a discordance is created which may need more processing time to resolve than the cinema audience has available to it. The problem is not so much that explicit markers of politeness are just absent from the translation; rather, that subtitling may create a substantially different interpersonal dynamics from that intended.

In Sample 5.1, the general brevity and spacing of the (source text) exchanges mean that the subtitler's task is not as constrained as it usually is when the density of source text dialogue requires to be significantly abridged in translation. Indeed, more space was theoretically available for the representation of Camille's and Stéphane's politeness features than was actually used, although subtitlers invariably opt for the briefest translation compatible with establishing coherence. We shall return to this point at the conclusion of this chapter. Now, let us proceed to Sample 5.2, where the dialogue is rapid and the translator's leeway consequently far less.

Sample 5.2

(Speakers are identified as follows: L = Louis, the host; X = an unnamed guest, who is a writer; C = Camille; M = Maxime, her partner; S = Stéphane)

X:	Mais non Camille, c'est pire. Toutes ces foules sans aucun repère qui piétinent dans les musées. [But no, Camille, it's worse. All those drifting crowds trampling in the museums.]	No, Camille, it's worse! Herds of people drifting around art galleries ...
C:	Mais si dans ces musées au milieu de cette foule qui ne voit rien il n'y a qu'une seule personne qui rencontre une oeuvre qui la touche, qui va peut-être changer sa vie,	But if, among that drifting herd ... ... one person sees a painting that moves him and may change his life –

c'est déjà beaucoup, non?
[But if in those museums
amid that crowd which
sees nothing there is just
one person who finds a
work of art which moves
him/her, which may change
his/her life, that's already
a lot, isn't it?]

isn't that good?

X: Mais ça s'est toujours
passé comme ça.
[But it has always
happened like that.]

That's nothing new.

C: Je ne crois pas.
[I don't think so.]

I think it is.

S: Au fond vous êtes à peu
près d'accord. Vous
aussi vous parlez de la
sensibilité de l'individu
en face d'une masse qui
serai aveugle.
[Basically you more or less
agree. You too speak of
the sensitivity of the
individual confronted with
a blind crowd.]

Basically, you agree.

You also talk about one
sensitive person in a dull
herd.

C: Je n'ai pas dit ça.
[I didn't say that.]

I didn't say that.

M: Non, ce que tu as dit je
crois, c'est qu'à chances
égales, il y aurait comme
une sélection des gens qui
seraient destinés à . . .
[No, what you said, I think,
was that, all things being
equal, there might be some
kind of selection of those
who might be destined
to . . .]

You said that, in any group,
a select few are more
likely to . . .

C: Mais pas du tout.
[But not at all.]

I did not!

M:	Tu as dit que certains voient des choses que d'autres ne voient pas. [You said that some see things that others do not.]	You said some people see what others don't.
S:	Oui, c'est ce que vous avez dit. [Yes, that's what you said.]	That's what you said.
C:	Oui mais . . . non. Enfin, moi, je n'exclus personne. [Yes but . . . no. Well, I exclude no-one.]	Yes . . . no! I exclude nobody.
X:	Mais moi non plus. [But neither do I.]	Neither do I.
S:	Bien sûr. [Of course.]	Of course.
L:	Et toi, tu n'as pas d'avis sur la question? [And you, have you no opinion on the question?]	And you? Have you no opinion?
S:	Non. [No.]	
C:	Aucun. [None.]	None?
L:	Il est au-dessus du débat. [He is above the discussion.]	He's above it all.
S:	Non, j'entends des arguments contradictoires et tous valables. [No, I hear arguments which are contradictory and all valid.]	No, I hear conflicting arguments, all valid.
C:	Tout s'annule, c'est ça. On ne peut plus parler de rien. [Everything cancels everything else out, that's it. One can no longer talk about anything.]	They cancel each other out, so we may as well shut up?
S:	C'est une tentation, en effet. Je n'ai pas votre bonne volonté. [It's a temptation, indeed. I do not have your good intentions.]	It's a tempting thought. I lack your good intentions.

L:	Bien, nous respectons ton silence.	All right.
	[Good, we respect your silence.]	We'll respect your silence.
C:	Evidemment si on parle, on s'expose à dire des conneries. Si on se tait, on ne risque rien, on est tranquille, on peut même paraître intelligent.	Of course
		If we speak, we run the risk of being wrong.
	[Of course if one speaks, one exposes oneself to talking rubbish. If one keeps quiet, one risks nothing, one is unconcerned, one may even appear intelligent.]	It's easier to keep quiet and appear intelligent.
S:	Peut-être simplement qu'on a peur.	Maybe it's just fear.
	[Perhaps simply one is afraid.]	

In Sample 5.2, threats to face come thick and fast. At a dinner table discussion initiated by someone who holds controversial opinions and is unafraid to go on-record with them at some length (X has expounded his views in the immediately preceding sequence), it becomes increasingly difficult to challenge these views without exposing oneself to attack. Camille, however, attempts this, only to find herself flatly contradicted and then reinterpreted by others. Noticing that Stéphane is not similarly prepared to put himself on the line, she goes on to the attack. The subtitler's difficulties may be appreciated even from the script of the source text reproduced here. To this must be added, of course, the pace of the conversation on the sound-track, the need to represent each voice separately and identify it with a particular character on screen. If politeness features were difficult to relay in Sample 5.1, they will be all the more difficult to accommodate in Sample 5.2.

Rather than attempt a complete analysis of the interaction in this sequence, we propose to focus on selected features in order to add to what has already been said. They are (1) Camille's disagreement with the writer 'X'; (2) Maxime's attempted reconciliation; and (3) Camille's challenge to Stéphane.

1 Disagreement

The counter-argumentative structure employed by Camille ('I agree
... but') at the beginning of Sample 5.2 is a conventional form of
positive politeness, claiming common ground before committing the
face-threatening act of disagreeing. (On the use of this text format
and politeness in written texts, see Chapter 8.) This is so conventional that, especially in spoken French, the first half of the structure
is commonly omitted and utterances begin *Mais . . ..* What is noticeable here, however, is the power differential referred to earlier.
As a recognized writer, X has status within the situation and his
opinions are valued. Camille, on the other hand, is relatively powerless in this situation (her recognized expertise lying elsewhere). Thus,
she must pay full attention to her interlocutor's face (using the full
counter-argumentative structure and putting her view as a question
– *C'est déjà beaucoup, non?*) whereas he need make only the minimal
ritual gesture (*Mais non, Camille, c'est pire* and *Mais ça c'est toujours passé
come ça*). In translation, X is even more direct, without a hint of
positive politeness ('No, Camille, it's worse' and 'That's nothing
new'). In this sense, the translation, although it modifies the interpersonal relations, does so in the intended direction: the power
differential between Camille and X is heightened.

2 Attempted reconciliation

Stéphane, feels the need to reconcile the two opposing viewpoints.
Yet it will be extremely face-threatening to suggest to two people
who have gone on-record as having diametrically opposed views
that they are, in fact, in agreement with each other. Consequently,
Stéphane adopts the negative politeness strategy of hedging:

> **Au fond**, *vous êtes* **à peu près** *d'accord* (emphasis added to show
> hedges)

as redressive action to his interlocutors' want to be unimpinged
upon. By inserting these hedges, Stéphane also protects his own face
by implicating 'I didn't say that you agree in all respects.' Camille,
relatively powerless in her confrontation with X, is on the other
hand far more confident of her position now: she can afford to be
direct: *Je n'ai pas dit ça* ('I didn't say that'). This is, of course, a direct
threat to face. Maxime seeks to retrieve the situation by hedging
still more. First, he agrees: *Non* (= no, you didn't) and then goes on

record in restating Stéphane's view but with redressive action: *ce que tu as dit*, *je crois* (= I may be wrong) *c'est qu'à chances égales* (= 'only in some circumstances') *il y aurait* (= hypothetical) *comme* (= 'not exactly') *une sélection des gens qui seraient* (= hypothetical) *destinés à* . . .. Once again, we can see how it is in the textural detail that evidence of the maintenance and development of relations between characters is revealed. And once again, the subtitles reflect an entirely different politeness strategy: 'You said that, in any group, a select few are more likely to . . .' Here, the translated Maxime appears altogether more defiant.

3 Challenge

Among the interesting features of Camille's subsequent attack on Stéphane are use of intonation, irony and use of pronouns. It is worth noting that, when Stéphane admits to Louis that he has no opinion, Camille, as in the sequence in Sample 5.1, challenges him with what might seem to be a question ('None at all?') but is uttered with the intonation of a statement, creating an implicature along the lines of 'You simply have no view.' This is, of course, an altogether more face-threatening act than the 'None?' of the subtitle. It provides an opportunity for Louis to accuse Stéphane of remaining aloof. The latter employs positive politeness in suggesting that the contradictory views he has heard are equally valid. To counter this, Camille employs irony (an off-record strategy listed by Brown and Levinson 1987: 214):

> *Tout s'annule, c'est ça. On ne peut plus parler de rien.*

The expression *c'est ça* ('that's it') is a strong signal of the ironic intention, indicating that the opinion being stated is not sincerely held and that the words used are intended to mimic or parody another person's words. In this way, Camille can strongly implicate that Stéphane's position is absurd ('no-one can talk about anything'). Interestingly, there is another instance of this use of irony (in a sequence of the conversation not reproduced in Sample 5.2) when X, feeling that he has been accused of being 'traditional', exclaims:

> *La tradition, c'est ça, je suis réac!* [tradition! that's it, I'm reactionary]

This utterance is to be compared to the discussion at the end of Chapter 3 of the 'hijacked' discourse. By hijacking the discourse of the political left (*réac* is a ritual term of abuse used to describe anyone with conservative views) and attaching it ironically to his opponent in argument, X can implicate 'Your view is no more than the knee-jerk response of the extremist.' This use of irony as an off-record strategy by X and by Camille is scarcely retrievable from the subtitled versions ('Tradition? So I'm a reactionary?' and 'They cancel each other out, so we may as well shut up?').

Our final point concerns the use of personal pronouns. The way in which speakers exploit personal reference for purposes of positive and negative politeness is analysed in Stewart (1992) and (1995). In addition to their core values, some pronouns can be used to refer to other individuals or groups. For example, 'you' can refer to people in general ('generic reference', as in 'On a clear day, you/one can see the coast of France'). There is no space here for a complete analysis of pronominal use in *Un coeur en hiver*, including, for example, the mutual use of *tu* by most of the friends in the film, contrasting with the studied *vous* of Camille and Stéphane to each other – a feature which, as noted earlier, the subtitler cannot easily relay. But let us take one significant instance – the use of the French impersonal pronoun *on* ('one') by Camille. It is Stewart's (1995) insight that speakers exploit the ambiguity of reference of *on* for purposes of face-protection and redressive. action. Camille's final attack on Stéphane is a case in point:

> *Evidemment si on parle, on s'expose à dire des conneries. Si on se tait, on ne risque rien, on es tranquille, on peut même paraître intelligent.*
> [Of course, if one speaks one exposes oneself to talking rubbish. If one keeps quiet, one risks nothing, one is unconcerned, one may even appear intelligent.]

The implicature is clear: Camille is referring to her own earlier willingness to go on record as disagreeing with the writer and to Stéphane's silence in the discussion. By using *on*, which can be used for self, other and generic reference, she avoids explicit self-reference and thus protects her own face from the threat of admitting that she might have been 'talking rubbish'. Conversely, by using the same pronoun to refer to Stéphane's silence, she can carry out the face-threatening act of accusing him but with the negative politeness strategy (strategy 3) of indirectness; that is, 'if one keeps quiet, one can appear intelligent' has the potential meaning 'if people keep quiet, they can appear intelligent'. No-one would misunderstand who her real target is but, with her redressive action, Camille avoids a bald, on-record FTA which might provoke a confrontation (they are in company and, at this stage in the film, Camille has been acquainted with Stéphane only for a short time). That Stéphane himself does not mistake the target of the accusation is apparent from his defensive response: *Peut-être simplement qu'on a peur* ['Perhaps simply one is afraid'], which serves to protect his own face. How is all this to be relayed in translation? The pronoun 'we' in 'If we speak . . .' partly fulfils the same function as *on* but, if repeated several times, would sound unnatural in English. The translator is therefore forced into the use of impersonal expressions (Camille: 'it's easier to keep quiet' and Stéphane: 'it's just fear'). The politeness strategies – and consequently the interpersonal dynamics – of the exchange are only partly relayed.

There are many more points that could be made and readers may find other significant details in samples 5.1 and 5.2. Subtitlers may also object that it is quite unjust to subject to such scrutiny of detail a translation which is in any case intended to be partial and is normally 'consumed' in real time. The objection would be valid if the objective had been to criticize subtitlers or subtitling. But, as has been made clear, given that some elements of meaning must be sacrificed, our interest lies in the kinds of meaning which tend to be omitted and in the effects such omission may have. We hope to have shown that, in sequences such as those analysed, it is difficult for the target language auditors to retrieve interpersonal meaning in its entirety. In some cases, they may even derive misleading impressions of characters' directness or indirectness. In order to test the generalizability of these limited findings to other films and other languages, far more empirical research would be needed. In particular, one could test source language and target language auditor impressions of characters' attitudes. Beyond this, our data provide some insight into the problems involved (in any mode of translating) in relaying interpersonal meaning generally and politeness in particular. Politeness will be referred to again in Chapters 7 and 8, from a cross-cultural perspective and applied to written text. Indeed, there is overlap between what has been shown here and all that is said elsewhere in the book on the topic of pragmatic meaning in translation. In our discussion of subtitling, we have gone beyond the limits of this particular mode of translating and observed discourse at work.

Chapter 6

Register membership in literary translating

The common thread which, we suggested in Chapter 1, unites all types of translating, including literary and non-literary translating, is by now familiar to the reader. Differences in the prominence of particular features, procedures and translator focus in different translation tasks cannot and should not be overlooked. But, from the perspective of a view of textuality which holds that the structure and texture of texts is subject to higher-order contextual requirements, the differences have to be seen in the light of the register-based, pragmatic and semiotic features which determine the communicative potential of all utterances.

The field to be investigated in this chapter is literary translating and aspects of literary expression. At the same time, we shall concentrate on one particular domain of context, namely **register** membership, through the analysis of an instance of register variation. In discussing literary language in terms of use- and user-related categories of register variation, issues of common concern to literary and non-literary translating will emerge and contribute to our broad view of a unified text strategy. From this perspective, our discussion will encompass both semiotics and pragmatics, which will be seen to work in harness with register in shaping the actual structure and texture of texts.

THE TRANSLATION OF IDIOLECT AND TENOR

The translation problem tackled in this chapter relates generally to the techniques adopted in handling literary discourse. In this domain of translating, however, a common concern of both literary and non-literary translators will emerge. It has to do with user-related aspects of the message such as idiolect and use-related categories such as **tenor**. By idiolect we understand the individual's distinctive and motivated way of using language at a given level of formality or tenor. To demonstrate the validity of this approach to a common problem in translation (i.e. informal, idiolectal use of language), we take a literary text (Shaw's *Pygmalion*) and focus on the way translators have dealt with the Flower Girl's idiolectal use of tagged statements such as *I'm a good girl, I am*, and the general informality characteristic of the tenor of a dialect such as Cockney English.

What we hope to show in this exercise, then, is that features of idiolect or tenor are not the exclusive preserve of one variety rather than another (e.g. spoken, non-literary language), but have wider currency across domains of language use as varied as literature and factual reporting. More specifically, we intend to show that, preoccupied with surface manifestations, some translators of *Pygmalion* have not been entirely successful in tackling subtle aspects of discoursal meaning. In the case of Arabic – a language from which we wish initially to illustrate success or failure in establishing translation adequacy – the straightforward and rather static approach to the entire play has been to opt for a high and a low variety of the language to relay formal and informal tenor respectively, dealing rather casually with idiolectal meaning as not being particularly noteworthy. With some exceptions, this procedure is not untypical of the way translation problems of this kind are tackled in other languages.

In this discussion, we shall also address some wider issues. Contextual categories such as tenor, although universal in the sense that every language in the world is bound to possess some sort of scale of formality, are in fact language-specific when it comes to (a) the way the formal-informal distinction is operationally perceived (i.e. where to draw the line between formal and informal), and (b) the way formality or informality is linguistically realized (i.e. the options selected in the actual production of texts). Categories such as tenor thus become a problem in translation between languages in which the formal-informal distinction does not operate in the same way.

IDIOLECTAL USE: THE TRANSLATOR'S OPTIONS

Let us now consider Shaw's *Pygmalion* as a source text and reflect on the kind of translation procedures which might be adopted in Arabic to handle formality. At the disposal of the translator, there would be many language varieties and a fundamental choice to be made between the classical and one of the vernaculars (Moroccan, Egyptian, etc.). Broadly speaking, the following options are possible. Translators may opt for the classical variety throughout (hypothetical version 1), one of the vernaculars throughout (version 2) or one of the vernaculars for less formal speech and the classical for more formal speech (version 3).

Leaving aside the thorny issue of whether the translation is intended to be read or to be performed, version 1 would most certainly be well received, as classical Arabic is felt by many to be the only variety compatible with the written mode in fields such as creative literature. But this solution is surely far from satisfactory as it cannot possibly reflect source text variation in tenor and idiolectal use. Version 2 no doubt goes some way towards preserving this variation, but also remains lacking in consistency as far as general translation strategy is concerned: how informal should a source text utterance be to be marked as such within the vernacular, and which vernacular is to be chosen? Version 3 shares some of the problems of inconsistency suffered by version 2 but would also attract much louder criticism not only from the classical Arabic language establishment who would decry this abuse, but also from those whose vernacular happens to be used for informal speech.

In fact, the Arabic version of *Pygmalion* which we have consulted adopts a solution of the type of version 3 above: a combination of classical and vernacular to render the formal and informal parts of the text. But, as we shall demonstrate in the following critique, none of the three types of approach seems adequately to address the real issues. The problem is that a scale of categories (of formality in this case) which works for English is naively imposed on languages in which it may not necessarily be applicable. In the context of Arabic, to borrow the scale of formality from English and use it uncritically would inevitably entail the erroneous assumption that categories such as classical/vernacular always correlate with standard/non-standard English, on the one hand, and with formal/informal speech, on the other. What is suspect in this kind of approach to language variation is not only the unconstrained positing of correlations, but also, and perhaps more significantly, the perpetuation of the notion that varieties such as RP and cockney or classical and vernacular Arabic are mere catalogues of static features, to be called up mechanistically with little or no regard for what is actually going on in communication.

TOWARDS A MORE WORKABLE SOLUTION

As will become clearer in the course of the following discussion, simple solutions to complex problems such as dialectal fluctuation in Shaw's *Pygmalion* invariably run the risk of glossing over a basic text linguistic principle governing language variation in general. This is the requirement that, whatever options are selected to uphold the register membership of a text, they should always be adequately motivated. Register is a configuration of features which reflect the ways in which a given language user puts his or her language to use in a purposeful manner. This intentionality acquires its communicative thrust when intertextuality comes into play and utterances become signs (socio-textual/rhetorical or socio-cultural/semantic) – cf. Chapter 2, where these notions are explained.

We are all familiar with the way advertisers, for example, take meticulous care in their choice of what kind of speaker or professional activity is appropriate to given settings for selling certain products. It would indeed be bizarre if a speaker of southern British English were used to sell the traditional qualities of Yorkshire bitter or if a strongly-marked regional accent were used to sell pharmaceutical products. Advertising copy-writers make sure that this does not happen. What is involved here is precisely an advertiser's attempt at being, perhaps intuitively, in tune with the way texts develop in natural settings. A given register thus takes us beyond the geographical provenance of, say, the beer drinker or the consumer of pharmaceutical products to questions of identity (i.e. self-image). Register consequently carries all kinds of intended meanings and thus functions as the repository of signs, whose range of semantic as well as rhetorical values is intuitively recognized by all textually competent speakers of a language.

To illustrate this notion of 'motivation' from a well-known literary text, let us consider the following example from Eugene Ionesco's play, *The Lesson*. The play is about the interaction between a professor and his 18-year-old pupil. The interactive dynamic hinges on the way the professor and the pupil behave towards each other at the start of their encounter and how they end up behaving. The nervousness and diffidence of the professor is contrasted with the dynamism and liveliness of the girl in the beginning. Gradually attitudes are reversed and a powerful climax ensues.

Simpson (1989) analyses this reversal from the perspective of politeness theory (cf. Chapter 5) and traces the professor's movement (as shall we with that of *Pygmalion*'s Flower Girl) from utterances such as 'You are . . . er . . . I suppose you really are . . . er . . . the new pupil?' to 'Be quiet. Sit where you are. Don't interrupt.' Hesitancy or confidence are aspects of behaviour which find expression in actual patterns of language use. These tend to be both recurrent and functional and must therefore be heeded as such by readers or translators. The need to be aware of variation and of the underlying motivations becomes even more urgent in domains such as literary analysis or literary translation, where some of the most elliptic or opaque forms of utterance (and hence the easiest to overlook) come to occupy a crucial position in the literary work, serving as important clues in the portrayal of a certain scene or persona.

THE STATIC AND THE DYNAMIC IN REGISTER SPECIFICATION

Registers, then, have a pragmatic and a semiotic meaning potential. We can see this potential in terms of the marked vs. unmarked use of language referred to in Chapters 1 and 2. As we have shown in the analysis of a number of texts so far, a register feature, like any other instance of language use, may be seen as unmarked when expectations are upheld and when the text world is unproblematic and retrieved without difficulty (i.e. maximally stable): lawyers speak like lawyers, scientists like scientists, and so on. Markedness, on the other hand, arises when expectations are defied, and when lawyers' language, for example, is borrowed and used to best effect by, say, an anguished housewife, resentful of the deplorably indifferent attitude of the police (see Sample 3.11 in Chapter 3) or indeed by a politician, relaying a particularly detached, cold-blooded attitude towards some humanitarian issue (see Sample 11.3 in Chapter 11). In these highly dynamic uses of language, communicative stability has been gradually removed, intentions are blurred and intertextuality is less than straightforward.

Let us return to *Pygmalion*. In dealing with this play, translators would be confronted with similar dynamic uses of language. Firstly, they would have to account for a number of register features intended to relay special effects and which go beyond established, unmarked characteristics. To be fully appreciated, such features must first be seen against the background of some unmarked 'norm' and then within the wider perspective of pragmatic action and semiotic interaction. In both these domains, intended actions and conventional signs can and often do display remarkably high levels of dynamism. To explain these adequately, we have to detect the rhetorical purposes which they serve (in the text), the attitudinal meanings they express (in discourse) and the social activity they perform (in genre).

Register, then, is not always a neutral category. The more creative the text is, the more dynamic language use must be. In order to illustrate this, we shall, in the following discussion of literary translation, merge values yielded by tenor with idiolectal use of language. With the use and user of language implicated in this way, we shall seek to show that the preservation of these aspects of the construction of meaning is not only crucial but is also a concern for both the language user and the literary critic.

IDIOLECTAL MEANING

Within register, the 'user' dimension includes variation due to geographical, temporal, social and idiolectal factors. Of particular interest to the translation assessment exercise conducted in this study is idiolectal/tenor variation. Idiolectal meaning enjoys a special status within the dialectal spectrum. An idiolect subsumes features from all of the other aspects of variation and, before developing as an idiolect, has its origin in straightforward dialectal use of language envisaged along geographical, historical, or social lines. For example, the Flower Girl's idiolectal use of the peculiar form of tagging (*I'm a good girl, I am*) is undoubtedly shared by many speakers and bears traces of Cockney English, a London dialect spoken by a particular class of people at a particular stage in time.

In this way, idiolect incorporates those features which make up the individuality of a speaker or writer. Now, this varies in scope from what may be described as a person's idiosyncratic way of speaking (a favourite expression, a quaint pronunciation of particular words, the over-use of certain syntactic structures and so on) to more collectively shared sets of features that single out entire groups of users and set them apart from the rest in certain respects (e.g. the tagging feature to be discussed here or frequent use of the 'posh' pronoun 'one'). Another equally attractive feature of idiolects is that, contrary to common belief, they are not peripheral. They are in fact systematic, their use is often linked to the purpose of utterances and they are frequently found to carry wider socio-cultural significance. It is the task of the translator to identify and preserve the purposefulness behind the use of these seemingly individualistic mannerisms.

In classifying idiolects, it is particularly useful to make a distinction, on the one hand, between the transient and the durable (along what we shall call the 'recurrence' continuum) and, on the other hand, between functional and non-functional (the 'functionality' continuum). The two axes overlap in the sense that, if idiolectal occurrences happen to be short-lived, they will also tend to be afunctional (a category which would include instances of the person- or group-oriented idiosyncracies discussed above). But it is recurrent and functional idiolectal features which are by far the more interesting as carriers of both pragmatic and semiotic meanings. In actual texts, these tend to recur systematically and, in so doing, consistently relay a variety of rhetorical values which have to be properly appreciated for the overall effect to be preserved.

For example, like the professor's um's and ah's referred to above, the far-from-logical over-use of the connector *on the other hand* by the miser in the musical *The Fiddler on the Roof* is an instance of a functional feature of idiolect. This recurs systematically and, every time it is uttered, it serves more or less the same rhetorical function that is crucial for making sense of both the character and the plot. It is this sense of idiolectal meaning which will preoccupy us in the remainder of this discussion. But a brief summary of our position regarding the scope of idiolectal usage may now be in order. We assume that, to attain the status of genuine idiolectal variation, and thus become a noteworthy object of the translator's attention, idiosyncracies must first display systematic recurrence in the speech behaviour of a given individual or group. Impermanence renders this kind of variation a one-off aberration and diminishes the returns which language users hope to obtain from a closer scrutiny of texts. An important corollary to this principle of recurrence is that it is only when shown to be employed for a specific purpose that idiolects become truly functional and, therefore, an essential part of the repertoire of meanings at the disposal of the text user.

THE FLOWER GIRL AND FUNCTIONALLY-MOTIVATED IDIOLECTAL MEANING

We begin our illustration by presenting (Sample 6.1) some representative examples of the use of 'tagging' in the linguistic performance of Shaw's Eliza Dolittle.

Sample 6.1

(a) THE FLOWER GIRL (*subsiding into a brooding melancholy over her basket, and talking very low-spiritedly to herself*) I'm a good girl, **I am**. [p. 24]

(b) THE FLOWER GIRL (*still nursing her sense of injury*) Ain't no call to meddle with me, **he ain't**. [p. 24]

(c) THE FLOWER GIRL (*resenting the reaction*) He's no gentleman, **he ain't**, to interfere with a poor girl. [p. 25]

(d) THE FLOWER GIRL (*rising in desperation*) You ought to be stuffed with nails, **you ought**. [p. 28]

(e) ELIZA (*protesting extremely*) Ah-ah-ah-ah-ow-ow-oo-oo!!! I ain't dirty: I washed my face and hands afore I come, **I did**. [p. 41]

(emphasis added throughout to highlight tagging forms)

This particular form of pseudo-emphasis occurs regularly in the speech of Eliza on her way to becoming what Higgins wants her to be. Under the watchful eye of the Professor, however, the form tends to disappear gradually, reappearing infrequently and only when the reader needs to be reminded of Eliza's linguistic and social past. This rules out the possibility that the peculiar form of emphasis is merely an accidental feature of dialect and encourages us as audience or readers to enquire into the motivation behind its use. Of course, a number of critical theories could be put forward in an attempt to account for this occurrence. But whatever theory one is to subscribe to, it must be able to explain the tagging, its emergence and disappearance in terms of Shaw's attempt subtly to transform Eliza and shift the power dynamic between her and others. In this kind of explanation, it is important to note, from the perspective of translation, that we have not remained prisoners of core register theory but have gone beyond this into the pragmatics of the communicative act as something intended and not as a mere dialectal reflex.

THE PRAGMATICS OF IDIOLECT

Judging by mainstream solutions to problems of idiolectal meaning in translation, we are inclined to think that, in comparison to other communicative variables, features of idiolect are given fairly low priority by translators when dealing with utterances such as those in Sample 6.1. As noted earlier, idiolectal meanings have always been located on the periphery of language variation and domains such as geographical or historical variation in language use have always proved somehow more worthy of attention by dialectologists, linguists and, for that matter, translators.

In the analysis and translation of variation in language use, the three aspects of field, mode and tenor are usually given careful attention. Sometimes, however, this may be based on a rather superficial conception of what, say, field of discourse implies. Thus, notions such as subject matter, casual speech and so on, which hardly capture the intricacies involved, tend to be at the top of the register analyst's checklist. The utterances in Sample 6.1 above would be classified along these lines and some vernacular form would be selected by the translator in the hope that, not being a standard form of language use, the vernacular would take care of the user and use dimensions of the source text (dialect, informality, etc.)

In looking at actual versions of *Pygmalion* in various languages, we soon discover that our criticisms of translations which adopt monolithic solutions such as Standard English = high variety and cockney = low variety are not justified in all respects. In the case of the Arabic version, for example, the translator has perceived the functionality of the tags, as can be seen from the following summary of our findings in the case of the Arabic version as in Figure 6.1. Figure 6.2 shows solutions adopted in some other translations of the play for the problem represented by *Ain't no call to meddle with me, **he ain't.***

Two points may be made about the translator's attempt to preserve in Arabic Eliza's peculiar use of emphasis. First, although

Form	Variety	Function
(a) *ummal* (Lit. 'or what!')	Egypt. Ar.	defiant
(b) *inta malak* ('what's wrong with you')	Egypt. Ar.	defiant
(c) *abadan* ('never')	Egypt. Ar.	defiant
(d) *tihish hash* ('stuffed fully')	Egypt. Ar.	defiant
(e) *waalahi ghasalthum kuwayyis khalis* ('By God, I washed them thoroughly')	Egypt. Ar.	defiant

Figure 6.1 Idiolect in the Arabic version

	Form	**Variety**	**Function**
FRENCH	Il n'a pas le droit de se mêler de mes affaires, il n'a pas le droit.	standard	emphatic
CAT	Pro això no és motiu per fer-me la llesca.	low social dialect[1]	defiant
PORT	No tinha nada que se meter na'nha bida!	geographical	defiant

Figure 6.2 Idiolect in French, Catalan and Portuguese versions

easy to overlook, the minutiae of Eliza's idiolectal use of tags have all been noticed and relayed. Second, some form of dialect is opted for in rendering the entire performance of Eliza, a decision which is not altogether inappropriate. The success of the translations under study remains relative, however. A number of questions can be posed at this stage regarding the translator's text strategy. For example, did the translator make a serious attempt at formally preserving the sense of recurrence by opting for one and the same form to translate each instance (a)–(e) in Sample 6.1 or were variants preferred? And, whatever the option taken, is the ultimate effect which cumulatively builds up through Eliza's performance properly relayed?

Judgements of this kind involve issues that are semiotic in essence. Utterances need to be seen as signs in constant interaction with each other and governed by intertextual conventions. Register membership and pragmatic purposes remain dormant unless and until they are placed within a wider socio-cultural perspective, involving sign systems as means of signification.

To proceed, we need to clear up a matter we have so far taken for granted. This is the literary-critical issue of what Shaw actually intended to say (or do with his words) through Eliza's use of the tags. As we have pointed out above, defiance is the reading which generally comes through in the translations consulted, a reading which we find not altogether inappropriate. However, going by the textual evidence, we would suggest that, if it is 'defiance', then this must be the kind of defiance that emanates from utter frustration; that is, it is ultimately reducible to a cry from someone trapped.

Consider, for example, Shaw's directions when introducing the various utterances where tagging occurs: *subsiding into a brooding melancholy over her basket, and talking very low-spiritedly to herself; still nursing her sense of injury,* and so on.

Contextually, on the other hand, Eliza cannot plausibly be seen as 'defiant', given that this form of tagging emerges in the early stages of her linguistic development only to disappear altogether as she 'matures' linguistically and ideologically. Rather, what Eliza is more likely to be doing is betraying a tremendous lack of self confidence, desperately seeking assurance for almost every statement she makes. It is this uncertainty, combined with an acute sense of failure that characterizes the power relations at work in her interaction with the outside world.

Here, the intentionality involved in the way Shaw willed Eliza to be has gone beyond the individual speech acts uttered in relative isolation from each other, in the same way as it has gone beyond the formal features of register attached to the various modes of use encountered. Complex systems of inference and presupposition, together with a variety of cultural assumptions and conventions are crucial to the intricate network of relations developed throughout the play. These surround what Eliza has to say and reflect the ways in which a given culture constructs and partitions reality.

Preserving the function of Eliza's idiolectal use may thus have to be informed by the 'human' or 'socio-geographical' criterion, rather than a purely 'locational' one (Catford 1965: 87–8). The translation of *Pygmalion* must therefore seek to bring out Eliza's socio-linguistic 'stigma', a communicative slant which, incidentally, should not necessarily entail opting for a particular regional variety and could as effectively be relayed through simply modifying the standard itself. By the same token, and remarking in general on the entire performance by Eliza, the user's status could adequately be reflected not primarily through phonological features but through a deliberate manipulation of the grammar or the lexis to relay the necessary ideological thrust.

We now have the beginnings of an answer to one of the two questions put earlier, concerning the cumulative values to be relayed. Rather than defiance, Eliza is more likely, from a position of weakness, to be displaying her powerlessness, albeit resentfully. Once this crucial value is identified, the remaining task for the translator is to ensure that consistency is established and maintained. We would suggest in the case of the Arabic version, for example, that *ummal* (which was chosen by the translator in one instance) will serve this purpose adequately throughout.

ATTITUDINAL MEANINGS IN THE FLOWER GIRL'S PERFORMANCE

In terms of genre analysis, Eliza may be said to operate within the constraints of a recognizable genre – a conventionalized 'form of text' which reflects the functions and goals involved in a particular 'social occasion', as well as the purposes of the participants in them (Kress 1985). To master the genre, Eliza could thus be presumed to have internalized a set of norms as part of her ability to communicate. Criteria for an adequate translation must therefore involve relaying the hurt feelings of a woman suspected unjustly of some social ill such as prostitution. Also relayed should be the agony of a woman protesting her innocence in such a situation, knowing full well that her voice is simply not loud enough to be heard or heeded either by a good-for-nothing father, or by those who perpetuate an inequitable social structure which has put her in the gutter in the first place. Emphatic tags relaying defiance, as in the Arabic translation, would simply fail to relay all of this and instead present an entirely different genre structure: it is not one of protesting one's innocence, but of protesting, full stop. Nor is it the cry of the downtrodden but of the powerful, the 'cocky', the 'cheeky'.

In all of this, attitudinal meanings are prominent. The ideological stance emanating from such a confident genre in the translation would not be the one intended in the source text: a different discourse to the one originally used emerges, a different mode of thinking and talking. Like the 'committed' discourse of the feminist, for example, what should be relayed is the subdued discourse of the powerless. This is the cultural code (Barthes 1970) or the ideological statement made by the likes of Eliza, expressing itself through a variety of key terms and syntactic devices. In short, hesitancy is a discoursal feature that characterizes Eliza's use of the tags. But, in the various translations consulted, this reading is consistently blurred by the use of the defiant or emphatic tagging. Instead, we are given a more self-assured tone, sparking off the wrong intertextuality.

Discourse and genre values, however, are too diffuse to be readily amenable to structured modes of expression. These various signals, which can give rise to sometimes conflicting readings, have to be accounted for by reference to a more stable framework. This is provided by the unit 'text', which imposes order on the open-endedness of discoursal meanings. Within the model of discourse processing advocated here, a textual structure is one in which communicative intentions are made mutually relevant in the service of a given rhetorical purpose (cf. Beaugrande and Dressler 1981; Werlich 1976). To illustrate how texts become units in which problems are resolved, let us consider one of the statements made by Eliza:

I'm a good girl, I am.

Here, the passage from *I'm a good girl* to the tag *I am* indicates that a problem is encountered. This problem may best be seen in terms of the tension between Eliza's past, her 'here and now' and her future aspirations. The conflict has to be resolved one way or another, and this may account for the style-switching from statement to tag syntagmatically and from a tag proper to the particular tag used here, paradigmatically. This configuration, together with intentionality, constitutes the mechanism by which texture is created and made to serve particular discoursal attitudes and particular genre structures.

In sum, the occurrence of tagging in *Pygmalion* is a textual phenomenon which has to be handled in translation by ensuring that the characteristics of use and user, intentionality and semiotic interaction are reflected. It is the latter characteristic of texts which is perhaps the most crucial. The use of tags by Eliza can be related intertextually to any one or all of the following:

(a) Similar tag occurrences in the immediate textual environment, for example:

> ELIZA (*rising reluctantly and suspiciously*) You're a great bully, you are . . . I never asked to go to Bucknam Palace, I didn't. I was never in trouble with the police, not me. I'm a good girl.

(b) Similar occurrences of tagging in the distant textual environment, for example, *I'm a good girl*, echoing the earlier occurrence *I'm a good girl, I am* (p. 24).

(c) Similar tag occurrences that lie completely outside the present textual environment (immediate or distant), as in the use of similar tagging in cockney.

(d) Utterances which in one form or another relay a similar meaning to that intended by The Flower Girl (e.g. by the 'oppressed' and the 'victimized', in the discourse of 'stigma' and 'hesitancy').

(e) Utterances which in one way or another point to the social occasion in question (e.g. the genre of feeble defiance and wounded feelings of someone who is unable to stand up to the bully).

(f) Utterances which in one way or another recall any of the above contexts only to contradict it, parody it, etc. For example:

ELIZA (*shaking hands with him*) Colonel Pickering, is it not?

In effect, Eliza's idiolect in *Pygmalion* acquires mythical dimensions almost akin to those of a fully-fledged persona. At one level of semiotic analysis, the entire performance of Eliza could be considered as one 'huge' sign that is made operational by the 'smaller' signs included within it. Like all semiotic constructs, emphatic tagging in Eliza's performance comes into being at an early stage in the play, acts on and interacts with the textual and extra-textual environment, changes and then dies away. Using a set of sign relationships (of the nature of (a)–(e) in Sample 6.1), Shaw intends idiolectal tagging to relay feelings of stigma. But this gradually gives way to a more defiant Eliza. When it fully comes to fruition, defiance no longer attracts the usual tag signs which were once the mode of expressing injured feelings, but becomes more forceful through the use of 'proper' tags and indeed tag-free English.

In conclusion, neither the Arabic version of *Pygmalion*, nor the other versions consulted, have fully upheld this dynamic fluctuation which builds on intended meanings and intertextual potential. Yet if communication in translation is to succeed, due heed must be paid to relaying intentional and intertextual diversity of the kind discussed here.

Chapter 7

Form and function in the translation of the sacred and sensitive text

We have so far discussed different kinds of demands made on the translator in a variety of professional settings. The nature of these demands has been shown to be essentially communicative. In their role as mediators, translators deal with elements of meaning that can and often will lie above the level of propositional content and beyond the level of the sentence. As we have seen, meanings of this kind emanate from a variety of sources including the register membership of the text, intentionality and intertextuality. Domains of contextual activity such as these have been shown to relate, in subtle and intricate ways, to aspects of text structure and texture.

In broaching the issue of how the various aspects of text-in-context relate to one another, we have pointed to the need to adopt a unified translation strategy which transcends professional or institutional barriers that have been artificially imposed. The ultimate goal of such an orientation is to promote an understanding of textuality that is, on the one hand, both rigorous and comprehensive, and on the other, not tied to specific tasks or situational requirements.

In this respect, we have also alluded to the fact that, with the communication explosion which the world is experiencing, the translator or interpreter is being called upon, more often than ever before, to work with texts which are remarkably creative and which display marked degrees of dynamism (i.e. interestingness). We have defined dynamism as the motivated removal of communicative stability. This element of manipulativeness often manifests itself in the way context, structure or texture defies our expectations and relays new meanings. These departures from established norms, we recall, are all part of 'informativity', a standard of textuality which relates to the unexpected and the new, in terms of the extra effects which they create. Informativity can permeate all aspects of text constitution, relaying in the process a variety of rhetorical effects which, as we shall see in the following discussion, make stringent demands on the translator as communicator.

THE PHENOMENON INVESTIGATED

Pursuing our predominant theme of the translator as communicator, and in an attempt to contribute to the form-meaning or expression-function debate which has been present in translation studies since antiquity, this chapter focuses on the translation of the sacred and sensitive text. With this global aim in mind, the textual phenomenon tackled here is one which is well-known in the rhetoric of a number of languages and which essentially involves a **reference switch** from one 'normal' (i.e. expected) syntactic, semantic or rhetorical mode to another. Within syntax, the switch may involve one of several linguistic systems, including pronominal reference, tense, definiteness, number and gender. We shall in this chapter take Qur'anic discourse in English translation as our main sample and supplement this with other examples drawn from the Bible and religious poetry. We have chosen this theme and the sample to be analysed in order to bring out the relevance to the translator of the way rules regulating patterns of usage may be systematically defied for rhetorical effect. When this happens, a translation problem invariably occurs.

In the rhetoric of a number of languages, including Arabic, switching involves a sudden and unexpected shift from the use of one form (a particular tense or pronominal reference) to another form within the same set. In the area of pronominal reference, this may be illustrated by the switch from the first person, which may be the norm and therefore the expected option in a given **co-text**, to the second person, which in that co-text constitutes a departure from the norm. Let us consider the following Qur'anic verse:

> For what cause should I not serve Him who has created me, and to whom you will be brought back?
>
> (*Yasin*, verse 22)

Expectations regarding the form of pronominal reference set up by the co-text in this utterance make the first person (*I*, *me*) a likely choice throughout. Suddenly, however, the pronominal reference is shifted to the second person in *you will be*. This constitutes a flouting of a norm or convention which expects that consistency of reference will be maintained almost by default. Similar shifts of reference can occur in the area of tenses (e.g. from an expected past tense to an unexpected present tense or vice-versa), in number (e.g. singular instead of plural), and/or in gender (e.g. masculine to feminine). From the perspective of the translator, what is perhaps particularly significant in this area of language use is the motivation behind such departures, the functions served by them and the compensation strategies which would have to be adopted in languages whose rhetorical systems do not share this phenomenon, in order to rectify the likely communicative loss.

INFORMATIVITY REVISITED

Informativity concerns the extent to which the occurrence of a given textual element is expected or unexpected, known or unknown (Beaugrande and Dressler 1981: 8–9). Highly informative utterances would be maximally unexpected and optimally dynamic, a processing complexity which nevertheless soon pays off since the more informative an utterance is, the more interesting it will be. Whatever the text, there will always be a certain element of unpredictability, a certain defiance of some expected norm, if only to enhance novelty and alleviate boredom.

At this juncture, it may be helpful to point out that the model of informativity, and indeed the theory underpinning the whole notion of textuality, are not exclusively a product of modern linguistic thinking.[1] Classical rhetoricians were always aware of the values attached to deviating from norms, or **foregrounding** and **defamiliarization** (to use the terms of modern stylistics). Deviations were explained most comprehensively in terms of rhetorical effects that go beyond the merely cosmetic. For example, Arab rhetoricians living and working some one thousand years ago had an entire vocabulary for notions such as norm and deviation, the marked and the unmarked and the motivation behind departures from the expected. While the grammarian was concerned almost exclusively with the 'virtual', abstract system, the rhetorician sought to describe both virtual and actual systems, searching for the whys and wherefores in the infinite creativity of meaning construction. The aim was to restore meaningfulness to what was at times dismissed as mere aberration.

Relying on such insights, together with those made available to us by modern text linguistics, we shall here explore the rhetorical thinking behind the textual phenomenon of reference switching. We hope to demonstrate how this line of inquiry can yield a useful set of insights into textuality itself and into the transfer of meanings from one language environment to another, particularly when working with the sacred text.

REFERENCE-SWITCHING: A MORE DETAILED STATEMENT

In rhetoric, the motivation behind reference-switching can generally be seen in terms of the need to break the monotony of speaking in one mode of reference; the switch is deemed to ensure variety and lend discourse a particular vitality. Along similar lines, the rhetorical function of reference switching may be viewed in terms of catching and holding the attention of the text receiver, and of arousing and renewing interest. To deal with this phenomenon, rhetoricians have sought to identify and classify the various functions performed by each type of occurrence. Within pronominal reference switching, the functions identified were said to:

1   relay a more supportive attitude and thus establish intimacy by, for example, involving the receiver in the communicative act;
2   underscore and specify certain concepts;
3   scold;
4   exaggerate the wonder of the situation in which the addressee finds himself.

From the perspective of translation, these rhetorical purposes and their linguistic realization, together with underlying motivations, are extremely important issues. Even if it were always possible, preserving source text form would be futile unless the function which the form is intended to serve were relayed at the same time. In cases of mismatch, intervention on the part of the translator becomes necessary, with the aim of explaining the discrepancy and communicating the added meanings. It is this need to communicate added meanings which will occupy us for the remainder of this chapter. As the first step in this investigation, we shall now consider the technique of compensation, proposed in translation studies as a means of recovering meanings potentially lost in translation.

COMPENSATION

The form-function mismatch is central to the discussion of compensation, which has been defined as a procedure for dealing with any source text meaning (ideational, interpersonal and/or textual) which cannot be reproduced directly in the target language (see for example Newmark 1988: 90; Baker 1992: 78). Hervey and Higgins (1992: 35–40) identify four categories of compensation:

1 Compensation in kind, where different linguistic devices are employed to recreate a similar effect to that of the source.
2 Compensation in place, where the effect is achieved at a different place from that in the source.
3 Compensation by merging, where source text features are condensed in the translation.
4 Compensation by splitting, where source meanings are expanded to ensure transfer of subtle effects.

Within typologies of compensation, it is generally agreed that, while phenomena such as puns and phonaesthetic effects would be included, instances of systemic transfer which do not have a specific stylistic or rhetorical function (such as grammatical transposition) would be excluded from the scope of compensation proper. But the overlap between the 'stylistic' and the 'systemic' is inevitable, a problem which has prompted the need to develop alternative typologies. Harvey (1995) distinguishes a stylistic and a stylistic-systemic component and various degrees of correspondence are identified (full, analogical and non-correspondence). Location in source and target texts of the effect to be reproduced is also posited as an important procedural axis and three categories, parallel, contiguous and displaced, are distinguished.

This theoretical account exemplified from real instances of language use in order to ensure that the typologies involved are usable by the translator in solving practical problems. To articulate a given stylistic effect, translators seek a method of disciplined appreciation of source text meanings, and an equally disciplined approach to text reproduction. Facility in this respect is acquired through working with sets of constraints governing different areas of text in context. Crucially, though, these must account not only for linguistic norms but also for the occasions when such norms are flouted.

To a certain extent, this has been included in approaches to translation such as those dealing with compensation. In practice, however, these approaches have tended to consider examples in isolation from their full context. Norm flouting, where the relationship of text to context is least straightforward, may be singled out as one area which has suffered from neglect. Problems in this domain, we suggest, can be meaningfully examined only when seen against the backdrop of the full range of contextual factors and the way these govern text development. As we have seen in earlier chapters, register, intentionality and semiotic meanings or signs are all involved. In the case of semiotic activity, categories such as genre, discourse and text, seen in terms of concrete structure formats and texture patterns, seem to us to be crucial. We shall now illustrate how these and similar resources of meaning are exploited in handling textual output belonging to the sacred text.

PRONOMINAL SWITCHING IN QUR'ANIC DISCOURSE

In dealing with reference-switching and the likely mismatch between form and function, we make the basic assumption that, underpinning a given switch from some expected norm, there are usually varying degrees of informativity that must be accounted for in the act of translation. Which type of compensation is used, however, is ultimately a matter of procedure which is dependent on the overall objective of identifying the rhetorical function and effect in a given source text. This concern with function, we suggest, is essentially an inter-semiotic matter. By this we mean the way the various standards of textuality outlined in Chapter 2 interact with each other to yield additional meanings within and across linguistic boundaries. In addition to the signs which we have referred to as socio-cultural objects (religious, social, political, etc.), we have also to cope with a fairly limited set of genre conventions, discoursal/attitudinal meanings and textual/rhetorical purposes.

Before considering alternative translations of the case of pronominal reference switching cited above as they appear in four published translations of the Qur'an, we want to suggest a plausible, context-sensitive reading of the switch involved. The verse in question needs to be seen as part of a larger sequence of mutually relevant elements or what we have been technically referring to as 'text'. Such a sequence must be long enough to allow for the emergence of a rhetorical purpose, and the analysis must seek to relate a text plan to a context of some kind. In the case we have before us, matching contextual parameters with actual linguistic realizations will prove useful in shedding some light on the interpretation of the segment under focus. Let us look at the sequence of elements within which the reference switching takes place, presented in Sample 7.1 with each element identified by a number.

Sample 7.1

1 Then there came running from the farthest part of the city, a man,

2 saying,

3 (a) 'O my people! Obey the apostles.

3 (b) 'Obey those who ask no reward of you and who have themselves received guidance.

3 (c) 'It would not be reasonable in me if I did not serve him who created me, and to whom you shall all be brought back.

3 (d) 'Shall I take other Gods beside him.

3 (e) 'If God most Gracious should intend some adversity for me, of no use whatever would be their intercession for me,

3 (f) 'nor can they deliver me.

3 (g) 'I would indeed if I were to do so, be in manifest error.

Dealing with the sequence in a bottom-up direction and focusing on the segment that displays reference switching (3c), we as readers normally react to what is being said in sequence (i.e. **syntagmatically**) and in terms of what could have been said but was not (i.e. **paradigmatically**). In the case of element (3c), the paradigmatic alternatives open to the speaker include:

(a) 'How is it possible for me to do otherwise than to serve him who created me, and to whom I shall ultimately be brought back.'

(b) 'How is it possible for you to do otherwise than to serve him who created you, and to whom you shall all be brought back.'

Had either of these been the actual words of the source text, choices (a) and (b) would certainly have failed in relaying the effect desired by the text producer. The relevant institutions and processes (field) may be described in terms of the stratification in Arabian society at the time. While the wealthy and influential men in the city (the addressees in the narrative) were doubtful of God's providence, the truth was seen by a man from the 'outskirts' (the addresser in the narrative), a man held in low esteem by the arrogant rich. It would not therefore be appropriate for someone in this position to engage in what is akin to a personal 'introspective' or internal monologue (choice (a)) nor to 'sermonize' or steer the receiver (choice (b)). Neither of these ideational structures would adequately achieve the desired effect. Something else had to be done and the utterance as actually produced, we suggest, came as close as possible to bringing together personal introspection and sermonizing, inimitably dealing with the social forces at work.

This brings us to the issue of social distance and the relations of **power** and **solidarity** (tenor) which will be crucial to the way the text is developed. For a man held in low esteem addressing the arrogant rich, choice (a) would have represented an almost total relinquishing of power (i.e. intensive introspection, of no concern to the addressees). Choice (b), on the other hand, would have relayed excessive power (basically telling people what to think by haranguing them). The requirements of the variable 'field' militate against the expression of either attitude. Examining the way the man said what he said from this interpersonal perspective, we once again observe an effective combination of power and solidarity, giving rise to a desirable degree of distance/intimacy followed by a remarkable degree of persuasive robustness.

Intimacy also influences the other factor of register membership, that of physical distance between the addresser and the addressees in the narrative (mode). Choice (a) relays remoteness, compromising the much-needed argumentative thrust. By the same token, choice (b) is too close in proxemic terms, running the risk of alienating the addressee. But in the actual text the arguer has won his audience over by initially putting them at their ease with non-**face threatening** introspection (maximal distance) only to turn the tables suddenly with the almost face-to-face admonition (minimal distance).

For the utterance in question to acquire its various ideational, interpersonal and textual values, however, intentionality must at some stage be involved and the purposes for which the utterance is used have to be borne in mind. As a speech act, the utterance relays a combined **illocutionary** force that defies easy categorization: is it a **representative**, a **verdictive**, an **expressive** or a **directive**? Probably, it is all these things. However, in opting for choice (a) (predominantly an expressive) or choice (b) (predominantly a directive), the speaker would have lost the intended ambivalence that is very much part of the discourse relayed through the reference-switch.

The communicative effect of the utterance also stems from the **implicature** yielded by defying the norm of uniformity and in the process flouting one of the **maxims** of 'cooperative linguistic behaviour', namely **manner**. This relates to the requirement that communication must be perspicuous and orderly. Choices (a) and (b) display these very features, but communicate them by explicit introspection and admonition, respectively. These rhetorical purposes and more besides are served much more subtly by 'implication' in the original utterance (3c), a persuasive tactic that is far more effective. The implicature yielded by the utterance in question may be glossed as 'as if you needed to be reminded! How reckless can one be!'

Had (3c) been made as explicit as (a) or (b), however, this would not only have compromised the overall persuasive appeal, but would also have created problems of **politeness**. Here, we take a broader view of politeness than that of the canonical theory, and deal with entire interactions, both written and spoken, as capable of being 'polite' or otherwise.[2] Thus, taking the interaction as a whole (Sample 7.1), choices (a) and (b) would each in its own way constitute a face-threatening act of a fairly serious kind.[3] The addressee's negative **face** (the basic claim to freedom of action and freedom from imposition) or positive **face** (the desire that self-image be approved of) would suffer if the addressee is excluded from involvement through the introspection of choice (a) or if harangued through admonition as in choice (b).

The utterance as actually produced (3c) also happens to encroach on both positive and negative face, but the threat to face is redressed skilfully by the sudden switch from distance to involvement and by reaching involvement via distance. As we have pointed out above, ideational values such as introspection, haranguing, sermonizing, all have a part to play in relaying overall polite or impolite effects. So do factors such as power and solidarity, and distance and involvement. It is this extensive coverage of the largest possible contextual area and the comprehensive mapping of this on to actual texts that seems to provide us with a framework within which pragmatic intention and action may most usefully be examined.

Tracing intentionality in this way inevitably leads us to social semiotics, which accounts for the way field, tenor and mode link up via intentionality with the socio-textual practices of given language communities. In terms of the semiotic macro-functions, it is primarily genre (e.g. the conventionally sanctioned 'admonition') which seems to be implicated when ideational meanings are apparent in actual instances of language use. Interpersonal meanings, on the other hand, are most naturally associated with attitudinal values yielded by given discourses. Finally, the textual resources of language are closely bound up with the notion of rhetorical purpose as the prime mover in the production and reception of actual texts. This network of relations may be represented schematically as in Figure 7.1.

Returning to the Qur'anic sequence in Sample 7.1, we can now see the success of the choice opted for (3c) in terms of socio-semiotic values. The switch from personal 'introspection' to 'sermonizing' is a genre-related matter which, given the intentionality involved, may be seen as part of the way we represent reality (ideation). Similarly, the switch from powerless reflection to powerful admonition is a discoursal matter, explainable in terms of the interpersonal relations intended. Finally, the change from a more subdued inner voice to a more vocal one is mode-related and is part of the textual resources of language. Thus, the dynamism of (3c) emanates from the gradual removal of stability and the way in which norms are flouted. Choices (a) and (b), on the other hand, would maintain a uniformity of generic, discoursal and textual values and in the process render them relatively impotent.

Incorporating the various contextual values yielded by the parameters discussed above, we can now offer the following translation of (3c):

How can I but serve Him who has created me and to whom you shall all be brought back?

field	>	social institutions/ processes	>	ideational meanings	> **genre** structures
tenor	>	power/ solidarity	>	interpersonal meanings	> **discourse** attitudinal meanings
mode	>	physical distance	>	textual meanings	> **text** rhetorical purposes

Figure 7.1 Register features as intended signs

Comparing our rendering with those opted for by the published translations could involve us in a full-scale translation assessment. In this chapter, however, our focus is much narrower since we are primarily interested in the way contextual factors constrain the translation of reference switching in actual texts. Let us first consider three of the translations of the Qur'anic verse:

1 *For what cause should I not serve Him who hath created me, and unto whom ye will be brought back?* (Pickthall)
2 *Why should I not serve him who has created me and to whom you shall all be recalled?* (Dawood)
3 *And why should I not serve him who originated me and unto whom you shall be returned?* (Arberry)

In these translations, we suggest that, while the reference switching is rendered formally, it is not preserved rhetorically. We recall that the switch is intended to tone down and make more acceptable the discoursal thrust of 'sermonizing' by juxtaposing it to an otherwise passive 'introspection'. Put differently, the powerful and yet intimate sermonizing now comes to be seen as a way of counterbalancing the tactical and temporary loss of power and distance in the preceding personal introspection. What we have in these translations does not quite tally with this overall picture. Our observations may be summarized as follows:

(a) In translation (1), the sermonizing clause (*and unto whom ye will be brought back*) is a weak 'representative' statement that is too distant even to serve as a 'reminder'. This is then placed against the background of an initial clause (the introspective *For what cause should I not serve Him who hath created me*) which relays self-serving defiance ('why shouldn't I? Give me a reason!'). Thus both clauses in the translation are inadequate in terms of the rhetorical contrast (powerless vs. powerful) which is crucial to the argument.

(b) In translations (2) and (3), the second clause features the modal *shall* which appropriately gives an edge to the intended sermonizing, but the contrast is still absent. The sermonizing is set against the background of the same self-seeking defiance as in translation (1).

The translation of the first clause in versions (1), (2) and (3) may now be compared with our suggested rendering ('How can I but serve Him who has created me') which relays less choice and more commitment on the part of the addresser in the narrative. In fact, it is this thematic focus which the fourth published translation reflects as closely as possible:

4 *It would not be reasonable in me if I did not serve him who created me, and to whom you shall all be brought back.* (Yusuf Ali)

Here, we note that, whereas the sermonizing in the second clause is rendered in a similar fashion to translations (2) and (3), the first clause adequately brings across the introspection intended, displaying the necessary minimal power and maximal distance. The function of the juxtaposition is thus both formally and rhetorically preserved. This becomes even clearer when we consider the translation of this segment in sequence:

Sample 7.2

Then there came running from the farthest part of the city, a man, saying, 'O my people! Obey the apostles. Obey those who ask no reward of you and who have themselves received guidance. It would not be reasonable in me if I did not serve him who created me, and to whom you shall all be brought back. Shall I take other Gods beside him. If God most Gracious should intend some adversity for me, of no use whatever would be their intercession for me, nor can they deliver me. I would indeed if I were to do so, be in manifest error.

But is it mandatory that stylistic devices such as reference switching always be preserved both formally and functionally? To embrace 'persuasive intimacy', the sermonizing clause in the Qur'anic verse under consideration could adequately be rendered as 'and to whom we shall all be brought back', or even 'and to whom you as well as I shall all be brought back'. Communicatively, even in the otherwise most adequate translation (4), the combination of 'you', 'shall' and 'all' may be slightly too abrasive even for the sermonizing tone normally required. A version incorporating 'we' or 'you as well as I' would recognize this in its attempt to enable the powerless man to argue convincingly with the rich and arrogant.

In actual practice, these considerations are likely to be over-ridden by the circumstantial factors which govern the translation of sacred and sensitive texts. In this domain, translating the letter of the source text is often considered to be of paramount importance and translators will be guided above all by this constraint.

TENSE SWITCHING AND BIBLICAL DISCOURSE

It will be recalled that reference switching is not necessarily a matter simply of personal pronouns. The phenomenon includes other deictic categories such as gender and tense. An example of switching tenses is to be found in the Qur'anic verse in Sample 7.3, presented in a formal back translation.

Sample 7.3

On that day the Tempest shall be sounded and all who dwell in heaven and earth *took fright*. (Ar. *faza'a*)

In the Arabic rhetorical tradition, the motivation behind such a tense switch is usually explained in terms of:

1 emphasizing the magnitude of the event referred to; and/or
2 showing certainty that the event will, in fact, happen.

It is perhaps worth pointing out that such values are comparable to the scale of power and distance discussed earlier in this chapter.

In one of the published translations, the above verse is rendered as in Sample 7.4.

Sample 7.4

On that day the Tempest shall be sounded and all who dwell in heaven and earth shall be seized with fear.

While not preserving the tense switch formally, this translation of the Qur'anic verse has certainly gone a long way towards preserving the rhetorical function involved. Operating within the constraints of English, which would not readily tolerate a shift in tense as drastic as this, the translator opted for the unmarked future tense. Interestingly, however, the translator selected *shall* (rather than the alternative 'will'). This lends the verse a certain resonance and authority which supports the notion of 'magnitude'. Furthermore, the use of 'shall' creates the impression of inevitability and thus promotes 'certainty' that the event will, no doubt, happen.[4]

In a similar fashion – and to show that rhetorical features such as those discussed above are not limited to Arabic or to Qur'anic discourse – let us consider an example from the Book of Jonah in the Old Testament.[5] The Prophet Jonah, having been held responsible for the storm in which his ship is engulfed, is thrown overboard and swallowed by a whale. From the belly of the whale, he prays to God as in Sample 7.5.

Sample 7.5

The Prophet's Prayer
Now the Lord had prepared a great fish to swallow up Jonah. And Jonah was in the belly of the fish three days and three nights.

Then Jonah prayed unto the Lord his God out of the fish's belly, and said,

> I cried by reason of mine affliction unto the Lord,
> And he heard me;
> Out of the belly of hell cried I,
> And thou heardst my voice.
> For thou hadst cast me into the deep, in the midst of the seas;
> (. . .)

It is at least superficially disconcerting to find Jonah referring to his present act of praying and his hoped-for delivery from distress in the past tense. Now, the prayer consists almost entirely of quotations from the Psalms which are in the past tense (intertextuality). The way they are incorporated into the currently developing text, however, suggests that the use of this tense is marked, expectation-defying and therefore highly dynamic. This dynamism is heightened by the striking incongruity of a man sitting inside a whale's belly employing the elevated and highly reflective discourse of the Psalms.[6] What then are the intended effects? One explanation may invoke the rich rhetorical tradition of the classical Semitic languages. It may be assumed that the tense switching in Sample 7.5 is similarly motivated to that encountered in Sample 7.3: it serves to under-score the earnest supplication from Jonah in his present position of powerlessness, and yet still express his confidence that God will in fact deliver him.

Contemporary theories of pragmatics also offer ways of accounting for such motivated departures from norms. Primarily, these relate to the interpersonal resources available to the language user. In dealing with a case like that of Sample 7.5, a Gricean account would focus on the implicature created by flouting the maxim of manner ('Be orderly'). Beyond this, there are the factors of power and distance which regulate how what we do with words relates to the social or ideological settings within which texts are naturally embedded.

Religious poetry and the prayer genre provide us with another example analysed in detail by Wadman (1983) and Sell (1992) within the framework of politeness theory. In *Longing*, a poem by George Herbert, it is observed that the speaker persists against all seemliness in his demands that his prayers be heard and even includes some complaints. In the beginning, however, these protestations are couched in 'polite' terms and relayed through devices such as hedging and questions. This is to emphasize both the speaker's distance from God and God's enormous power. Later, when Christ is introduced as an intermediary, the face-threatening protestations actually increase in strength, with the speaker asking not only to be heard but also to be healed. This is done in a much less self-effacing manner and in a way that eliminates much of the distance – 'My love, my sweetness, heare!'

To return to our biblical example, it is at least plausible that Jonah's use of tenses reflects his powerlessness and thus relays a distancing effect similar to the pronominal switch in the introspection clause of Sample 7.1 above ('For what cause should I not serve Him who has created me . . .'). It seems clear that, while in translating sacred texts translators will often wish to reflect the letter of the source text, they will also want to ensure as far as possible the retrievability by target text readers of what they perceive to be the intended effects of the source text. With the Jonah text in mind, we have consulted a number of published translations of the Old Testament into English, German, French, Spanish and Arabic and found that the translators invariably reflected the letter of the source text, perhaps at the expense of relaying intended effects to the modern reader. In cases where the brief is to enhance accessibility of the source text's intentionality, formal correspondence may have to take second place. The ultimate decision will depend on the brief (*skopos*) of the translation assignment. But decisions have to be taken in full knowledge of the range of possible options and their consequences. It is in this sense that discourse awareness is one of the essential skills of translators in negotiating meaning with a target reader.

Chapter 8

Cross-cultural communication

In this chapter, we shall focus on one particular text type – argumentation – and discuss it in relation to the way persuasive strategies may differ in different cultures. The term 'culture' should not be defined too restrictively. Differences in persuasive strategy, whether within the same language or between languages, must be seen in both social and linguistic terms. Cultural variation will be detected, on the one hand, in the way, say, a working class supporter of the British Labour Party and a Conservative British government minister argue and, on the other hand, in the way speakers of different languages use persuasive strategy. Furthermore, whether within the same language or between languages, cultural differences in argumentative style have been found to reflect deep divisions within society (Scollon and Scollon 1995). Texts may thus be seen as carriers of ideological meaning, a factor which makes them particularly vulnerable to changing socio-cultural norms.

In the text-type model adopted here, two basic forms of argumentation are distinguished: **through-argumentation** and **counter-argumentation**. The statement and subsequent substantiation of an initial thesis characterize through-argumentative texts. Citing an opponent's thesis, rebutting this and substantiating the point of the rebuttal characterize counter-argumentative texts. Within the latter prototypic format, two further structural formats may be distinguished: the **balance**, in which the text producer signals the contrastive shift between what may be viewed as a claim and a counter-claim either explicitly or implicitly (with the adversative signal suppressed), and the **lopsided argument**, in which the counter-proposition is anticipated by using an explicit concessive (e.g. *while*, *although*, *despite*). This argumentative typology may be represented schematically as in Figure 8.1.

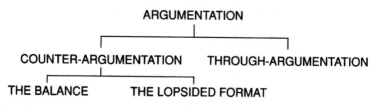

Figure 8.1 Typology of argumentation

When a text producer opts for this or that form, we suggest, the choice is not haphazard. Our primary aim in this chapter is to examine how the choice of argumentative strategy can and often does have serious implications in the pragmatics of language in social life and consequently for translation.

The question will be pursued first by enquiring into the plausibility of the view that choice of argumentative strategy is closely bound up with intercultural pragmatic factors such as politeness or power. There is also the suggestion that factors involved are not only pragmatic but also socio-political or even religious in nature. They include such matters as attitudes to truth, freedom of speech and so on. Furthermore, these interrelationships are thought to be behind the tendency, in certain languages and cultures, as well as in groups within them, to adopt a more direct through-argumentative style in preference to the more opaque counter-argumentative strategy. These are all issues which will occupy us in the following discussion, particularly when we approach the topic of translation from the perspective of cross-cultural communication.

TEXT TYPE: AN OVERVIEW

In the last 40 years or so, many attempts to set up a typology of texts have been made. Primarily due to the absence of a coherent description of context, however, many of these approaches have suffered from serious shortcomings in both substance and methodology. Classifying texts restrictively in terms of variables such as field of discourse, defined as involving only 'subject matter', has resulted in little more than a statement of the text's topic, with unhelpful categories such as 'journalistic' or 'scientific' texts. Similarly, categorizing texts in terms of an over-general notion of 'domain' has led to the recognition of so-called text types such as 'literary' or 'didactic'.

In the text type model advocated here,[1] shortcomings of this kind have by and large been rectified. This has been achieved by adopting a fairly comprehensive definition of context, in which categories such as register membership, intentionality and intertextuality culminate in the notion of a predominant rhetorical purpose. We also have to recognize that texts are multifunctional, normally displaying features of more than one type, and constantly shifting from one type to another. Given this inevitable hybridization, no categories, no matter how rigorously worked-out, can be expected to be definitive. The best we can hope to achieve is therefore an approximation to the reality of textual practice. One way of achieving this is to view text typologies on two basic levels – a static *langue* (a primarily systemic portrayal of some 'ideal' or prototype) and a dynamic *parole* (where the various actual departures from the norm may be accounted for – see Chapter 2). For example, the inclusion of argumentative features in an expository form would be an instance of a departure from the norm, which the translator can adequately reflect only if the added rhetorical effect created by the hybrid form is properly appreciated.

Consequently, if our aim is to describe norms as well as to account for exceptions, our model text typology must seek to encompass the diversity of rhetorical purposes normally involved in any act of communication. Communicative, pragmatic and semiotic values have to be seen within the static–dynamic continuum of text-in-context, introduced earlier in this book. This orientation encourages us to work within a system of constraints that ultimately regulate text types in use. Features of a given text type will be defined as elements in sequences of mutually relevant sentences, displaying the traces of a particular register membership, a particular intentionality and a particular domain of intertextual reference. The resulting contextual configuration constitutes the guidelines which text users instinctively refer to in adopting a given text strategy.

PREDOMINANT TEXT TYPE FOCUS

In the actual process of text production and reception, then, a focus cumulatively emerges and defines the type of the text. At a very general level, this may be identified in terms of a tendency to 'monitor' or to 'manage' a given communicative situation. Situation monitoring will be performed 'if the dominant function of the text is to provide a reasonably unmediated account'. Situation managing, on the other hand, takes place when 'the dominant function of the text is to guide the situation in a manner favourable to the text producer's goals' (Beaugrande and Dressler 1981: 162). Within these two general orientations, a more specific sense of text type focus may be identified. This has to do with a text producer's rhetorical purpose, which will determine the factors and circumstances in a communicative situation which are to be selected and made salient. Sample 8.1 is an example of how rhetorical purposes manifest themselves as monitoring or managing, sometimes in one and the same stretch of utterance. Here, the primary text type focus involves analysis or synthesis of concepts, a focus which characterizes exposition.

Sample 8.1

The explosion lighted every peak, crevasse and ridge of the nearby mountain range with an alacrity and beauty that cannot be described. It was the beauty the great poets dream about. Then came the strong, the sustained awesome roar that warned of Doomsday and made us feel that we puny things were blasphemous to dare to tamper with the forces heretofore reserved to the Almighty.

In working with this text, readers (and translators) perceive and respond to secondary values in addition to what may indeed be considered a primary contextual focus on exposition. The secondary values subtly serve an overall evaluative function. Sample 8.1 is taken from a report on the 'Trinity' test (the first tests of the atom bomb at Los Alamos). According to Lee (1992: 84), who analyses the text as an example of 'nukespeak', this kind of writing represents '. . . a more general process involving the application of religious discourses, as if the "awesome" power tapped by the new weapons was of divine origin'. The text remains expository but with a heavy admixture of evaluation.

As for texts which perform the rhetorical purpose 'argumentation', these primarily focus on the factors and circumstances involved in the evaluation of relations between concepts. Unlike exposition, which involves cognitive templates such as the 'frame' (establishing what things belong together in principle) and 'schemata' (establishing in what sequential order events may occur), argumentation has as its cognitive basis the notion of the 'plan'. As a global processing pattern exploited in argumentative texts, the plan regulates how events and states lead up to the attainment of a goal. All argumentative texts seek to promote or simply evaluate certain beliefs or ideas, with conceptual relations such as reason, significance or opposition becoming naturally meaningful and frequent.

To illustrate argumentation and at the same time demonstrate the inevitability of secondary rhetorical purposes making their presence felt at all times, let us consider Sample 8.2, drawn from a newspaper editorial.

Sample 8.2

Is the clubbing of seals humane?
The answer to that question is unequivocally *Yes*. Observers from humane organizations and veterinary pathologists visit the Canadian sealing operations each year, to observe killing techniques and perform autopsies on seals. Their reports are available to the public and indicate that the whitecoat harvest, which has attracted so much publicity, is conducted in a humane manner.

There is no aesthetically pleasant way to kill an animal, and it may be particularly unpleasant for those who have never seen the slaughter of animals. However, it is necessary to recognize that the East Coast seal hunt is a slaughtering operation, and there is no way that it can be made a pretty sight. It is however, neither cruel nor a massacre. Statements to that effect are false and misleading, designed to generate an emotional response to an otherwise normal operation.

In this sample, paragraph one is clearly a through-argument, paragraph two a counter-argument. This particular editorial, however, eschews the 'hortatory' tone which we normally associate with argumentation in general. Instead, an analytical orientation is deliberately adopted: reference to people is avoided as far as possible (e.g. *reports indicate*), nominalizations are preferred to straightforward agent-verb sequences (*a slaughtering operation*) and verbs of perception, feeling, etc. are rarely used. The overall effect is a world interpreted in new ways to accommodate an ideology under threat (Martin 1985).

In this regard, it is perhaps worth noting a striking similarity between argumentative texts and texts belonging to another 'operative' type, namely the **instructional**. The similarity, however, is to be viewed more in terms of the 'goals' aimed at rather than the 'means' adopted, including most importantly the use of appropriate linguistic devices to achieve such goals. That is, while argumentative and instructional text types both set out to 'manage' a given situation and thus focus on the shaping of future behaviour, the means of pursuing such goals are different. Instructional texts attempt to 'regulate' through 'instruction' (as in contracts and treaties); argumentative texts 'evaluate' through 'persuasion' (as in advertising and propaganda).

THE COUNTER-ARGUMENTATIVE TEXT

We recall that the counter-argumentative text is structured along the following lines: (1) the citation of a claim; (2) a counter-claim; (3) evidence; (4) conclusion. In this format, the degree of adversative, counter-claim explicitness may be related to the strength of the opposition to be voiced. The balance in some texts weighs heavily in favour of the counter-arguer's stance, in others in favour of a desire to be objective, whether genuine or not. Consider, for example, how the writer of the following text suppresses the adversative and in so doing enhances his own credibility and adheres to the conventions of academic writing:

Sample 8.3

Existing studies of development in the Gulf region have mostly restricted their concern to one aspect of development. A substantial number of surveys of mineral resources, studies on the feasibility of individual projects or the effectiveness of existing undertakings (especially in the oil industry), and studies of the functioning and development of individual economies have been undertaken. There have also been studies dealing with individual social or political aspects of the development process. What is lacking is an overall perspective of development, integrating the political, social and economic aspects, providing some conception of the nature of the economies, societies and policies which are emerging in the Gulf, and assessing the options and alternatives which lie ahead.

As we have pointed out previously, the suppressed adversative in languages like English but *what is lacking* must be made explicit in Arabic. This would inevitably entail some loss of source text rhetorical effect (e.g. subtlety), which must be compensated for by somehow preserving the general air of objectivity.

In this regard, it must be stressed that beyond the neat categories of any text typology, interaction is necessarily open-ended. To cope with this open-endedness, translators or interpreters need to be able constantly to relate actual words in texts to underlying motivations. For example, within a given language and across languages, the various forms of a given type may not be equally available to all users – a factor we may refer to as text type deficit. In these circumstances, the selection of a given text type becomes in itself imbued with socio-cultural significance, serving as a symbol of status, power, etc. As an example from this area of socio-textual practice, a genuine issue facing the court interpreter between certain languages may be whether to restructure a through-argument and present it as a counter-argument or vice versa.

Furthermore, when a particular choice of text type is made, it is normally done for a reason and preference for one or other of the forms will inevitably vary within, as well as across, languages and cultures. Since translators have a role to play in the way language ultimately evolves in social life (language planning, influence on lexical change, etc.), examining the multifaceted phenomenon of text type in communicative practice is something which translation theory cannot afford to ignore. Factors such as politeness, power and ideology have a role to play in the choices we make ranging from the smallest to the largest unit of linguistic expression. The use of texts is thus imbued with discoursal meaning, a phenomenon which will be at the centre of the following discussion.

ARGUMENTATION ACROSS CULTURES

Comparative research into argumentation from a cross-cultural perspective is still at a relatively embryonic stage. Nevertheless, work in this field points to a noticeable tendency in English towards counter-argumentation and, within this, towards the 'balance' (both explicit and implicit). In comparing this with Arabic, a language and culture which are fairly remote from English, we detect a preference for through-argumentation. Of course, through-argumentation is also found in English and counter-argumentation in Arabic, but these are significantly outranked by the other forms. In fact, when counter-argumentation occurs in Arabic, it is the 'although . . .' variety that is stylistically preferred.

ORDER OF PREFERENCE	ENGLISH	ARABIC
MOST FREQUENT	The balance counter-argument (both explicit and implicit)	Through-argumentation
↑	Through-argumentation	The lopsided argument
↓		
LEAST FREQUENT	The lopsided argument	The balance-argument (always explicit)

Figure 8.2 Argumentation across cultures

An order of preference can thus be identified and may be taken as indicative of certain general trends in English and Arabic. This is set out in Figure 8.2. Such rank scales are not merely statistical norms but are actually important indicators of psycho-cognitive predilections that underpin language use in activities as varied as translation and conversation. To illustrate this, let us consider Sample 8.4 as a text to be translated. The following analysis will primarily show how the textual resources of Arabic are stretched when handling counter-argumentation and how translation is likely to suffer as a result.

Sample 8.4

Mismanaged Algeria
The country's troubles are so glaring that it is easy to forget Algeria's strengths. At three o'clock in the afternoon in the poor over-crowded Casbah of Algiers, children leave school not to beg but to do their homework. Investment of some two-fifths of GDP a year during much of the 1960s and 1970s gave Algeria the strongest industrial base in Africa north of the Limpopo. The northern coastal bit of the country, where 96% of its 23m people live, is rich and fertile. It used to feed the Romans. It could feed Algerians if it were better farmed.

These strengths are being wasted. *Some 180,000 well-schooled Algerians enter the job market every year. Yet a hobbled economy adds only 100,000 new jobs a year, and some 45% of these involve working for the government. Algeria lacks the foreign currency it needs to import raw materials and spare parts to keep its factories running. The collective farms have routinely fallen short of their targets, leaving Algeria ever more reliant on imported food.*

For reasons already mentioned, we suggest that the overall balance (the entire text) is generally very difficult to handle in translation into Arabic. This is borne out by our own experience of working on this text with generations of advanced translator trainees. Some of the changes required by the textual systems of both English and Arabic and the difficulties involved in dealing with Sample 8.4 may be listed as follows:

1 The translator needs to make sure that the thesis cited to be opposed (the entire first paragraph) is rendered in a way that reflects the attitude of the source text producer towards what could be implied by the facts listed (i.e. less than whole-hearted commitment). This list of strengths is used here merely as the background against which weaknesses are shortly to be exposed. The procedure involved, which is alien to the way speakers of Arabic would normally argue, is thus a major obstacle to comprehending the source text and reproducing it in the target language.

2 The translator needs to to turn an implicit counter-argument into an explicit one, by retrieving the suppressed connector (*but, however*), and using this to initiate the counter-stance at the beginning of paragraph two: *These strengths are being wasted.* Ideally, this should be done without compromising source text subtlety, a process which makes the retrieval of pragmatic connectivity particularly onerous.

3 This is further compounded by another problem, namely, incongruity. The expectation which *These strengths are being wasted* invites will be that what follows must be a list of negative 'wastes'. However, what immediately follows (*Some 180,000 well-schooled Algerians . . .*) obviously defies this expectation. Within the text type conventions of English, this is not infelicitous. To substantiate a claim, the text producer can by all means opt for another counter-argument (text within text). In Arabic, however, coherence would most certainly be impaired by such a juxtaposition, and the translator would thus need to dispel this incongruity. This may be achieved by transforming the micro-balance (*Some 180,000 well-schooled Algerians . . ., Yet . . .*) into a lopsided format

in Arabic. Sample 8.5 is a formal back-translation of a suggested Arabic rendering of the relevant portion of Sample 8.4 above:

Sample 8.5

(. . .) But these strengths are being wasted. For, although some 180,000 well-schooled Algerians enter the job market every year, a hobbled economy adds only 100,000 new jobs a year, and some 45% of these involve work for the government. (. . .)

In the next chapter, we shall seek to identify and account for text-level errors which arise from ignoring processing strategies of this kind. But first let us look at the counter-argumentative text type from the standpoint of text structure and texture. This should provide us with a framework within which text type tendencies may best be explained in terms of notions such as power, politeness, attitude to truth and freedom of speech. It is here that cross-cultural differences will inevitably emerge, an issue which is relevant not only to the student of culture, but to translators and interpreters in general.

STRUCTURE, TEXTURE AND CULTURE

Typically, counter-argumentation involves two protagonists confronting each other: an 'absent' protagonist, who has his or her 'thesis' cited to be evaluated, and a 'present' protagonist, performing the function of orchestrating the debate and steering the receiver in a particular direction. In a language such as English, the text would be structured so as to make sure that a claim is cited and a counter claim is then presented and expanded. As Samples 8.3 and 8.4 have shown, reacting to such structural formats is essential when translating, say, from languages which take a fairly liberal attitude to text structure into languages that are more conventional in this regard. Consider now Sample 8.6. This is a formal back-translation of an Arabic source text and the way it is properly handled in the published English translation (Sample 8.7). The sample is presented in manageable chunks, numbered for ease of reference.

Sample 8.6

1 This has made clear that, regarding the tribal problems, the means of dealing with them and some of the transformations

which Iraq has undergone both before or during Medhet Pasha's era, there is a clear difference between the factors which govern the Iraqi tribal problem and those which govern such a problem in the heart of the Arabian Peninsula.

2 This is in spite of the fact that
    (a) the problems are similar in many of the manifestations of tribal life, and that
    (b) the Iraqi desert and the Nejdi desert merge into one another and are unseparated by any natural barrier such as mountains and rivers.

3 It therefore seems to us that despite the two problems being essentially tribal and desert-related, they should be seen as two separate problems in terms of the way they developed and the means proposed to combat and actually resolve them.

The various sections may now be labelled in structural terms: (1) is opposition; (2 (a) and (b)) are a thesis cited to be opposed; (3) is a conclusion. In the published translation the translator has renegotiated source text structure and opted for a plan schematically represented in Figure 8.3. Part of the target text is given as Sample 8.7.

Sample 8.7

No doubt, the Iraqi tribal problems and those which occurred in the heart of the Arabian Peninsula are similar in many of the manifestations of tribal life. There is similarly no doubt that the Iraqi desert and the Nejdi desert merge and are unseparated by any natural barrier such as mountains and rivers. However,

> No doubt . . . (2a)
> There is similarly no doubt . . . (2b)
>
> However . . . (1)
>
> Because . . . (1)
>
> Therefore . . . (3)

Figure 8.3 Target text counter-argumentative format

the factors which governed tribal problems in these two areas are different, as are the means of dealing with them ...

In addition to structural characteristics, argumentation normally displays predominantly evaluative texture. Evaluativeness is realized by the linguistic expression of emphasis (recurrence, parallelism, etc.), as well as by aspects of text constitution such as word order, the use of modality and so on. Cohesion is thus ensured. But coherence is established only when the various devices of cohesion are deployed in a motivated manner to reflect underlying connectivity and perceived as such. It is this establishment of coherence which may be problematic in intercultural communication.

The use of the **straw-man gambit** in English (relying on signals such as the text-initial, sentence-initial *of course, certainly, no doubt*) may at first glance give the impression that the views of the other side are being fairly represented. Essentially, however, such a representation is not always genuine. It is often slanted to steer the receiver in a particular direction. As Sample 8.4 has demonstrated, and as we shall make clear in Chapter 10 on error analysis, the textual meaning of signals such as 'of course ...' can be a source of difficulty for foreign users of English, with serious implications for the work of the translator.

THE PRAGMATICS OF COUNTER-ARGUMENTATION

As far as text type focus is concerned, then, it may safely be assumed that 'rebuttal' is a universal form of argumentation. However, in terms of the specific mechanisms involved (i.e. the variety of text forms, structures and patterns of texture associated with a given type), different languages and different cultures handle rebuttals differently. The general tendency in Arabic, for example, is to let the text hinge on the point of view of the person issuing the rebuttal. In English, the argumentative procedure of making the point of the rebuttal tends to be more explicitly oriented towards an accommodation of counter-claims.

To introduce a pragmatic component to our analysis of these tendencies, we propose to focus on English and the way the element 'thesis cited to be opposed' is handled. The analysis will be conducted from the standpoints of power and attitude to truth (as pragmatic variables), and of frank speaking and freedom of speech (as areas of language use seen more from a politico-cultural perspective). The rhetorical conventions at work in English in this domain will be compared with those operative in Arabic. In the course of the discussion, points relevant to translation will be underlined and illustrated.

Power

The concept of 'power' is a relevant factor in discussing the textual conventions governing the way counter-arguers orchestrate a text and cite the opponent's thesis. As a pragmatic variable within a theory of politeness, power may be defined as the degree to which the text producer can impose his own plans and self-evaluation at the expense of the text receiver's plans and self-evaluation (Brown and Levinson 1987). In this respect, the counter-arguer can be assumed to display slightly less power than the text receiver. To put it in terms of text type politeness, the counter-arguer appears to be making a concession in order to conform with the need to be 'polite' (not to harangue his receiver with foregone conclusions but to recognize the receiver's own plans).

From the perspective of power, we are therefore inclined to assume that to exclude the opponent (as in through-argumentation) is to exercise power, to include him or her (as in counter-argumentation) is to cede power. Here, it is interesting to note that, within the rhetorical and cultural conventions of English, to be seen to cede power, even if insincerely, enhances credibility. In Arabic, on the other hand, this relinquishing of power tends to be shunned as lacking in credibility and therefore unconvincing. Why should this be the case?

To answer this question, we can do no more than put forward a number of hypotheses. Let us start with one. It seems to us that the arguer in English is prepared to settle for this 'lesser' power because he or she knows that it is only a temporary condition. Often, the concession is not necessarily sincerely meant and certainly not binding; and the arguer will sooner or later have an opportunity to put forward an opposing view. In Arabic, on the other hand, counter-argumentation as a procedure tends to be avoided, unless it is explicitly signalled with concessives such as 'although'. This is perhaps because the arguer feels that, given the linguistic and the rhetorical conventions of the language, relinquishing power is bound to be perceived as irrevocable.

Attitude to truth

In English, the counter-arguer exercises power in another area of textual activity, namely that of being in sole charge of the way the opponent is to be represented. As we have pointed out, this is often done in a subtle and indirect way. To explain this, we need to invoke another pragmatic principle, namely that of 'truth'. Within what he called the 'cooperative principle', Grice (1975) defines truth under his maxim of 'quality' as follows: Try to make your contribution one that is true by not saying what you know to be false or that for which you lack evidence. This tends to be flouted by the counter-arguer when citing his or her opponent. What we have, then, is a statement of an opponent's position that is not sincerely represented. This is made possible by the particular use of certain intensifiers such as *of course, certainly, no doubt* and then by clues deliberately planted to curtail the scope of what the statement purports to say. For example, in *Of course, there are plays that justify a three-hour running time*, the statement could at face value be taken to relay an endorsement of the proposition in question. However, the subtle use of *there are* makes what is stated 'conditional' (i.e. 'there are some, but not many'). This is one way of undermining the authority of the claim cited.

Flouting any of the cooperative maxims is bound to yield an implicature. In the case of a counter-arguer flouting 'quality', the implicature could be assumed to be that 'everyone knows, including my opponent, that this is not the real point!'. In considering this fairly involved rhetorical manoeuvre and what can or cannot be accommodated by the rhetorical conventions of a language like Arabic, the peculiar use of emphasis and semantic indexing becomes particularly significant. These peculiarities of counter-argumentative style in English are alien to the rhetorical systems of a number of languages, something that could be explained in terms of socio-cultural factors such as the attitude to truth. To relay irony in Arabic, for example, it is the maxim of quantity (Do not say more than required ...) that is more often flouted and not quality, as is commonly the case in English. Consider this instance of irony in English (Sample 8.8) and its translation in Arabic (Sample 8.9).

Sample 8.8

(. . .) Since these facts are facts, Balfour must then go on to the next part of his argument . . .

Sample 8.9

(formal back-translation from Arabic)
Since these are flawless and totally unblemished facts, Balfour finds it incumbent upon himself to proceed and invite us to sample the next part of his argument . . .

ORAL AND VISUAL CULTURES

We conclude this discussion of cross-cultural communication with an attempt to explain not only how but also why the tendencies outlined above emerge and grow. A clue to this may lie in the ethno-methodological distinction between oral and visual cultures and texts. Here, the assumption entertained is that language communities have a number of possible modes of text development. An orally developed text is one characterized by repetition, redundancy, imprecise lexis and an additive **paratactic** syntax. Visual texts, on the other hand, are characterized by the elaborate organization of both content and expression, varied and precise lexis, complex **hypotactic** syntax and clearly signalled relations of contrast and causality.[2] The hierarchic organization of the counter-argument in a text such as Sample 8.4 above, for example, obviously caters for a situation in which, if something has been missed, the reader can always go back in the text and retrieve it. Now, while users of English and Arabic would no doubt have access to both the oral and the visual formats, we can assume that the tendency in English would be more towards the visual, with Arabic leaning towards the oral. This may explain why some of the problems we have discussed systematically recur in the work of translators dealing with these two languages. Contrastive rhetoric can play a vital role in helping us as language users to gain mastery over target modes of text development, to switch modes with ease and generally to appreciate the wider socio-cultural implications of thought patterns.

SUMMARY

In this chapter, we have discussed argumentation from the standpoint of persuasive strategy and the way this is differently handled in different cultures. The differences are considered to exist both within the same language and between different languages. Whatever the provenance, these differences have been found to reflect deep social divisions, with text type constantly functioning as a carrier of ideological meaning.

In the text type model adopted in this study, two basic forms of argumentation are distinguished: through-argumentation and counter-argumentation. Within the latter, two further forms are identified: the balance (a *however*-structure) and the lopsided (an *although*-structure). The aim of this analysis has been to examine how the use of one or the other argumentative strategy is closely bound up with pragmatic factors such as politeness, power and truth. Relating such tendencies to socio-textual norms and practices, and seeing these in terms of the distinction between oral and visual cultures, our conclusion is that these patterns can and often do have serious implications for the work of the translator. The insight should prove instructive not only in the study of the translation process but in domains as varied as contrastive rhetoric and communication theory.

Chapter 9

Ideology

Having appreciated the ways in which textual strategy is closely bound up with cultural beliefs, values and expectations, we now turn our attention to ideology and the ways in which it impinges upon the work of the translator. Such a concern is not new. Hermans (1985), Bassnett and Lefevere (1990) offer evidence of ideology at work in literary translating; Venuti (1995) shows the considerable consequences of translators' basic orientations – all reflecting concerns which have been part of the debate in literary translating for some time. Our perspective here is somewhat different. In recent decades, studies of ideology in language have achieved significant progress, through the work of Fowler and his colleagues (e.g. 1979), Hodge and Kress (1993), Fairclough (1989) and others. The insights provided by these studies advance our understanding of the way ideology shapes discourse and the way discourse practices help to maintain, reinforce or challenge ideologies. It is these insights which we seek to bring to bear on our study of the translator as communicator. In doing so, we hope to provide evidence of the ideological consequences of translators' choices and to show the linguistic minutiae of text-worlds in transition.

A fundamental distinction needs to be made from the outset. What follows is divided into (1) the ideology of translating and (2) the translation of ideology. That these two issues are closely related will be apparent to anyone who has, for example, reviewed the practice of (official) translators under totalitarian regimes. The extent of the translator's mediation is itself an ideological issue, affecting both (1) and (2). But whereas the major focus has hitherto been on the translator's basic orientations, we propose to pay more attention to charting the ways in which a text-world is or is not relayed to text receivers operating in a different cultural and linguistic environment, (whether the translator's intervention be consciously directed or unconsciously filtered).

DISCOURSE AND IDEOLOGY

We must begin with a working definition of the term '**ideology**'. In the Western world, it has become acceptable within the field of journalism and popular writing on politics to speak of ideologies in terms of deviations from some posited norm. Thus, communism, fascism, anarchism and so on would qualify as ideologies in this scheme of things while liberal democracy, presumably, would not. In a similar way, some political moves or measures are said to be 'ideologically motivated', as if others were not. Such an acceptation of the term is of no use to the linguist, from whose perspective *all* use of language reflects a set of users' assumptions which are closely bound up with attitudes, beliefs and value systems. Consequently, with Simpson (1993: 5), we shall define ideology as the tacit assumptions, beliefs and value systems which are shared collectively by social groups. Closely associated to this will be our use of the term 'discourse', as institutionalized modes of speaking and writing which give expression to particular attitudes towards areas of socio-cultural activity. The reference in these definitions to social groups and to institutions reflects the intertextual way in which discursive practices become established; it should not, on the other hand, be taken to imply that language use is wholly predetermined or that users exercise no control at all over their own discourse. Rather, we prefer to assume that a two-way process is involved, in which users are 'at one and the same time an active subject (agent) in the Discourse and passively subjected to its authority' (Gee 1990: 174).[1] In the same way, we shall not in our analysis make any powerful claim that there is a deterministic connection between the ideology – or 'world-view' – of a text producer and the actual linguistic structure of the resulting text. It is, after all, a commonplace to observe that a particular feature (say, agent deletion) may be used in a variety of contexts by different users for different purposes and to different effect. Nevertheless, observing the behaviour of text users (writers, readers, translators) and inferring the assumptions which underly expression leads to observation of patterns and trends; these may then be related to the assumptions made above concerning the mutual influences of individual text users, discourses, ideologies and society.

THE IDEOLOGY OF TRANSLATING

It has always been recognized that translating is not a neutral activity. Phrases such as *traduttore – traditore, les belles infidèles* and so on abound in the literature and polemic about the translator's latitude has always been fierce. Nabokov's (1964) famous tirade against 'free' translating is characteristic of the terms in which the debate has been set. Many writers have seen translators' options as lying between two polarities – 'free' versus 'literal', 'dynamic equivalence' versus 'formal equivalence' (Nida 1964); 'communicative' versus 'semantic' translating (Newmark 1981), dichotomies discussed in Chapter 1. Newmark (1981: 62) notes that the choice between communicative and semantic is partly determined by orientation towards the social or the individual, that is, towards mass readership or towards the individual voice of the text producer. The choice is implicitly presented as ideological. But it is above all Venuti (e.g. 1995) who brings out the ideological consequences of the choice. Distinguishing between 'domesticating' and 'foreignizing' translation, he shows how the predominant trend towards domestication in Anglo-American translating over the last three centuries has had a normalizing and neutralizing effect, depriving source text producers of their voice and re-expressing foreign cultural values in terms of what is familiar (and therefore unchallenging) to the dominant culture. A telling example is the homophobia apparent in Robert Graves's translation of Suetonius – convincingly documented by Venuti – reflecting dominant cultural values of the target language society at the time of translating (the United Kingdom in 1957) and 'creating an illusion of transparency in which linguistic and cultural differences are domesticated' (Venuti 1995: 34). Whether this domestication of foreign (i.e. source text) values is a conscious process or an unwitting one hardly matters: the effect is the same, namely to assimilate to a dominant – or even 'hegemonic' – culture all that is foreign to it. Thus, for Venuti, the translator cannot avoid a fundamental ideological choice and what had been presented by other writers as simply a personal preference comes to be seen as a commitment, no doubt often in spite of the translator, to reinforcing or challenging dominant cultural codes.[2]

It is important to appreciate that this view of domestication holds within a translation situation in which the target language, not the source language, is culturally dominant. Conversely, if a domesticating strategy is adopted in the case of translating from a culturally dominant source language to a minority-status target language, it may help to protect the latter against a prevailing tendency for it to absorb and thus be undermined by source language textual practice. One of the modes of translating in which this trend may most clearly be observed is the dubbing of imported English-language television serials into minority-status target languages. The constraints of this mode of translating are such that the default may in many instances be to relay source text structures and lexis as closely as possible, thus importing into a target language whose norms are less secure the discourse practices of a source language culture which in any case tends to dominate media output in the target language country in question.[3] Thus, it is not domestication or foreignization *as such* which is 'culturally imperialistic' or other-wise ideologically slanted; rather, it is the effect of a particular strategy employed in a particular socio-cultural situation which is likely to have ideological implications. The translator acts in a social context and is part of that context. It is in this sense that translating is, in itself, an ideological activity. Bearing all this in mind, we now turn to what happens to ideologies when they are translated, whether by a domesticating or a foreignizing method.

THE TRANSLATION OF IDEOLOGY

In order to concentrate now on what happens to text worlds in translation independently of situations of cultural hegemony, let us first consider an example in which the target language culture might be expected to share the cultural assumptions, beliefs and value systems discernible in the source text. One of the few existing studies of translation from the point of view of critical discourse analysis (Knowles and Malmkjaer 1989) analyses four translations into English of Hans Christian Andersen's fairytale *Den Standhaftige Tinsoldat* ('The Steadfast Tin Soldier'). The evaluative adjective *stand-haftige* which appears in the title appeals to values which are, at one and the same time, central to the moral import of Andersen's story (the tin soldier remains steadfast throughout many trials and tribu-lations caused by an unjust world) and shared by both Danish and English-language traditional value systems (the moral value of remaining steadfast in adversity). Yet the translation of this term is problematic. The toy dancer with whom the tin soldier falls in love is also at one point said to be *standhaftige* – but the term applies to the dancer only in the literal, physical sense that she remains frozen in the same posture. Ideally, both values need to be relayed in the target language term selected. 'Steadfast' is the English term which comes closest to relaying both the moral and the physical senses of the Danish term whereas two other translations offer 'staunch' and 'constant', which relay only the moral value. The analysis shows that variant translations at many points in the text reflect with varying degrees of explicitness the ideology of Andersen's text world, including such features as the use of transitivity to relay notions of power, control, responsibility ('they couldn't get the lid off' versus 'the lid would not open') and the use of recurrence (of the adjective *nydeligt* – 'pretty', with pejorative connotations of superficiality), retained throughout in one translation but variously translated as 'pretty', 'lovely', 'fine', 'charming', 'enchanting', 'graceful' in the others. The overall trend is clear. The range of available interpretations is reduced in translation (without there being any consistent evidence of an intention on the part of translators to domesticate or otherwise modify the range of potential meanings of the source text). Simply, the translator, as processor of texts, filters the text world of the source text through his/her own world-view/ideology, with differing results. Degrees of translator mediation may not always correspond to degrees of domestication.

It should be noted, however, that the decision, say, to translate all instances of the source text term *nydeligt* by the target language item 'pretty' may reflect either a concern to relay the ideological value implicit in the use of the cohesive device of recurrence or,[4] more simply, a general orientation towards literal translating, in the sense of selecting the nearest lexical 'equivalent' wherever possible. It is only when evidence of this kind is part of a discernible trend, reflected in the way a whole range of linguistic features are treated in a particular translation, that the analyst may claim to detect an underlying motivation or orientation on the part of the translator. In effect, the discernible trend may be seen in terms of degrees of **mediation**, that is, the extent to which translators intervene in the transfer process, feeding their own knowledge and beliefs into their processing of a text. The formal relaying of recurrence would thus be part of a global text strategy, characterized by greater or lesser degrees of mediation. With this in mind, we now propose to analyse three very different translations as illustrations of the translation of ideology and to discuss the likely effects of the consistent choices made in each case. Our analysis focuses on the constraints of genre, discourse and text, identified in Chapter 2 as intertextually established sign systems, together constituting the set of socio-textual practices within which communities of text users operate.

MINIMAL MEDIATION

Sample 9.1 is an extract from a translation of a message addressed by the late Ayatollah Khomeini to the instructors and students of religious seminaries in Iran.[5] As an exercise in translating from Farsi into English, it features problems of translating between languages which are, relatively speaking, culturally remote from each other (cf. Chapter 8). But our principal interest in this text sample lies in its exemplification of minimal translator mediation; the characteristics of the source text are made entirely visible and few concessions are made to the reader. It is what Venuti (1995) would call a 'foreignizing' translation.

Sample 9.1

In the name of God, the Compassionate, the Merciful.

Greetings to the trustees of inspiration, and to the martyred custodians of prophet-hood, who have carried the pillars of the greatness and pride of the Islamic Revolution upon the shoulders of their crimson and blood-stained commitment.

Salutations to the everlasting epic-makers from among the members of the clergy who have written their theoretical and practical epistles with the crimson of martyrdom and the ink of blood, and who, from the pulpit of guidance and preaching, have turned the candle of their existence into a luminous pearl.

Honour and pride on the martyrs from the clergy [. . .]

The genuine *ulema* of Islam have never given in to capitalists, money-worshippers and landlords, and they have always preserved this decency for themselves. It is a vulgar injustice for anyone to say that the hands of the genuine clergy siding with Mohammedan Islam are in this same pot and God does not forgive those who make publicity in this way or who think in this way. The committed clergy are thirsty for the blood of parasitical capitalists. They have never been in a state of conciliation with them – and never will be.

Of course this does not mean that we should defend all clergymen. Dependent, pseudo and ossified clergy have not been, and are not, few in number. There are even persons in the seminaries who are active against the Revolution and against pure Mohammedan Islam. There are some people, nowadays, who under the guise of piety, strike such heavy blows at the roots of religion, revolution and the system, that you would think they have no other duty than this. The danger of this inclination towards petrifaction, and of these stupid pseudo-pious people in the seminaries, should not be under-estimated. Our dear seminary students must not for a moment forget about the existence of these deceptive snakes with colourful spots on their skins [. . .]

In the opinion of some people, a clergyman was worthy of respect and honour only when stupidity engulfed all his being; otherwise there seemed to be something fishy about a clergyman who was honest, efficient and knowledgeable in what he was doing, and clever. [. . .]

It was through the war that we unveiled the deceitful face of the World Devourers. It was through the war that we recognized our enemies and friends. It was during the war that we concluded that we must stand on our own feet. It was through the war that we broke the back of both Eastern and Western superpowers. It was through the war that we consolidated the roots of our fruitful Islamic revolution. It was through the war that we nurtured a sense of fraternity and patriotism in the spirit of all the people. It was through the war that we showed the people of the world – in particular the people of the region – that one can fight against all the powers and superpowers for several years. [. . .]

What is perhaps most immediately conspicuous in this text sample is the unfamiliarity – to Western readers – of the mix of genres it displays. There are features here of at least three recognizable genres: the political tirade, the religious sermon and legal deontology. Statements of political policy (*It was through the war that we broke the back of both Eastern and Western superpowers . . .*) intermingle with the religious sermon (*God does not forgive those who . . .*) and points of Islamic law (references in passages of Khomeini's address, not reproduced above, to the 'cutting off of hands' and to 'the inner meaning of jurisprudence'). Such a combination of generic elements, however, although it is disconcerting for the average English-language reader, is entirely appropriate – and not necessarily perceived as hybrid – in the socio-textual practice of language cultures such as Farsi and Arabic. Although the scope of the translator for modifying genres in translation is limited, possibilities exist at the level of lexical selection (collocations, imagery and so on) for reducing the heterogeneity of the source text and rendering it more compatible with perceived reader expectations of what is appropriate to the occasion (of a head of state addressing a particular audience). What is significant in Sample 9.1, however, is that the translator's mediation appears to be minimal.

The translator's scope is perhaps most apparent in terms of discoursal features – as will be demonstrated in relation to Sample 9.2 later in this chapter. There are a host of textural devices which may serve as the vehicles for a discourse and provide evidence of the assumptions which compose an ideology. Among salient features in Sample 9.1, we shall comment on just a few: cohesion, transitivity, over-lexicalization and style-shifting.

Cohesion and transitivity

To begin with cohesion, the potential of recurrence to reinforce a point of view or display commitment or attitude was alluded to above in connection with the translations of Hans Christian Andersen. Here, the element *It was through the war that . . .* is repeated no fewer than six times in a short stretch of utterance (plus one instance of *It was during the war that . . .*), piling up evidence of the benefits to Islam of the war and reinforcing the source text producer's commitment to it. Faced with this unconventional (in a Western perspective) degree of recurrence, many translators might opt for varying lexicalization ('due to', 'on account of', etc.) or conflation of elements ('It was through the war that we unveiled . . . and recognized . . .'). Only the full recurrence of Sample 9.1, however, provides the target text reader with access to source text discourse. In a similar manner, the parallelism of the ritual greetings at the start of the text sample serves to tie together elements of meaning which are seen as being indissolubly linked but which without such parallelism might have appeared disparate.[6] Both cohesive devices – recurrence and parallelism – above all serve to introduce a pattern of transitivity in which a series of actors which are identified with each other (*trustees of inspiration, martyred custodians, epic-makers, martyrs from the clergy, we*) perform what are known as **intention process**es (*have carried, have written, cut off, unveiled, broke the back of . . .,* etc.),[7] thus relaying a powerful discourse of positive and decisive action. Finally, the sustained metaphor of blood creates a cohesive chain throughout the text in a series of doublets (*crimson and blood-stained commitment; crimson of martyrdom and the ink of blood; daubed in blood and martyrdom; soaked in blood on the pavements of bloody events* – these last two instances occurring in portions of the text not reproduced above). The concatenation of two terms in each instance and the sustained recurrence of the image are crucial to the construction of a text world between producer and receiver. Whatever the effect on target text receivers may be, the translator has preserved source text texture in these instances in order to relay a discourse as it stands in the source text.

Over-lexicalization

Over-lexicalization is a means of foregrounding (cf. Chapter 7) by drawing attention to prominent lexical choices.[8] Here, it is the heavy connotative values of a series of terms (*capitalists; money worshippers; landlords; parasitical capitalists; World Devourers*, etc.) which relay a discourse and create a text world in which external enemies are identified on both political and moral grounds. The over-lexicalization is an instance of markedness which gives dynamism to this source text and confronts the translator with a choice: either to seek target language terms of similar semantic import but which are relatively familiar to target language readers or, conversely, to calque the source text terms, however unfamiliar the resulting target language terms may appear. Clearly, the translation in Sample 9.1 has been carried out according to the second of these two principles.

Style-shifting

Within sociolinguistics, the phenomena of code-switching (the use of two separate languages or dialects in one speech event) and style-shifting (the use of distinct speech styles in one speech event) are amply documented and the hypothesis is advanced that such switching is never random.[9] Style-shifting enables speakers, among other things, to exploit the variables of power and distance, playing on aspects of their relationship with their addressees. In Sample 9.1, there are clear indications of variation of tenor, with colloquial expression intruding into an otherwise fairly sustained formal tenor. Compare for example the formal tenor implied by the use of: *turned the candle of their existence into a luminous pearl; denizens of paradise; ossified; petrifaction*, etc. with the markedly colloquial: . . . *that the hands of the genuine clergy . . . are in this same pot* and: *there seemed to be something fishy about a clergyman who . . . .* In this way, Khomeini is able to signal at one and the same time the authority of a head of state (power variable) and close identification with his addressees through the use of colloquialism (distance variable – cf. *our dear seminary students*). Whereas many translators might be tempted to opt for a more uniform target language tenor, this style-shifting has been relayed in the translation in Sample 9.1.

Having commented on genre and discourse features in Sample 9.1, let us briefly look at the signals which realize text, in the sense of a particular structural format serving a particular rhetorical purpose (narrating, arguing, etc.). Here, the emphasis is on evaluation and argumentation prevails. Now, in Chapter 8 it was seen that the norms of argumentation in Western languages such as English differ from those which are prevalent in such Eastern languages as Arabic and Farsi. The lexical token 'Of course' is conventionally associated with text-initial concession in English but its token-for-token equivalent in these other languages often introduces not a concession to be countered but a case to be argued through. Thus, for the English-language reader, the element: *Of course this does not mean that we should defend all clergymen . . .* sets up an expectation that a counter-argument will follow, along the lines of 'However, we should defend some of them . . .'. No such pattern is forthcoming in Sample 9.1 because what is involved here is a through-argument. The contrast between the 'genuine clergy' and the 'pseudo-clergy' is indeed present throughout the text but the signal to the reader indicated by *Of course* runs counter to expectations and sends target text readers down the wrong path in their construction of the text world. A signal which relays the intended format might be something like: 'Under no circumstances does this mean that we should defend . . .'

Thus, in Sample 9.1, the strategy of minimal mediation relays features of genre and discourse intact from source text to target text reader. In the case of text, however, the unmediated transfer of structural signals may, in fact, prove misleading and some adjustment proves to be necessary. Before commenting on the plausible purposes of the translator and the relay of intended effects, let us now, by way of contrast, look at an instance of maximal mediation to see the consequences of this opposite translation strategy.

MAXIMAL MEDIATION

In Chapter 2, we presented a text sample (2.1) in which the expectations of a particular genre of historical writing appeared to be borne out in a fairly static text. Towards the end of the chapter it was revealed that Sample 2.1 was in fact a translation of a Spanish source text marked by dynamic use of language. The translation constituted a radical departure from the source text in terms of register membership, intentionality, socio-cultural and socio-textual practices. Let us now take a close look at the actual translation procedures, to see how this different text world of the target text relays a different ideology.[10] Sample 2.1 is now reproduced here as part of Sample 9.2, together with the source text.

Sample 9.2

Tiene la historia un destino?

History or destiny?

Antiguos y prolongados esfuerzos por conservar la memoria de sucesos que afectaron a la comunidad integran el primer gran capítulo de la búsqueda del ser y del destino mexicanos. Así, ya en la época prehispánica se afirma una forma característica de interesarse por preservar la memoria de sí mismo y luchar contra el olvido. Esa memoria era indispensable a los viejos sacerdotes y sabios para prever los destinos en relación con sus cálculos calendáricos. Tal quehacer de elaboración y registro de una historia divina y humana perdura en miles de vestigios arqueológicos que abarcan más de veinte siglos antes de la llegada de los espanoles en 1519. Así, por

Mexicans have always exhibited an obstinate determination to safeguard the memory of the major events that have marked their society and this has coloured the way in which they view their identity and destiny. From pre-Columbian times they have been engaged in a continuous battle to save their history from oblivion. Knowledge of the past was the foundation on which their priests and diviners based their astronomic calculations and their predictions of the future. Countless archeological remains from the two thousand years before the arrival of the Spaniards in 1519 bear witness to the Mexican desire to interpret and record the history of gods and man. The stelae

ejemplo, las estelas de 'Los Danzantes' en Monte Albán, Oaxaca, fechadas entre 600 y 300 a.C., constituyen en el Nuevo Mundo el más antiguo registro de aconteceres, con sus años y días, nombres de lugares, de reyes y señores.

El destino – o los destinos – de los muchos pueblos que han vivido y viven en tierras mexicanas tuvo tiempos propicios y tiempos funestos. Hubo épocas de gran creatividad y otras de crisis y enfrentamientos, que llevaron a dramáticas desapariciones de hombres y de formas de existir. Los mitos y leyendas, la tradición oral y el gran conjunto de inscripciones perpetuaron la memoria de tales aconteceres.

Del más grande y trágico de los encuentros que experimentó el hombre indígena habrían de escribir personajes como el propio conquistador Hernán Cortés en sus *Cartas de Relación* y el soldado cronista Bernal Díaz del Castillo en su *Historia verdadera de la Nueva España*. Pero también los vencidos dejaron sus testimonios. Entre otros, un viejo manuscrito fechado en 1528, que se conserva ahora en la Biblioteca Nacional de París, consigna en lengua náhuatl (azteca) la memoria de lo que fue para los antiguos

known as danzantes ('dancers') at Monte Albán in the Oaxaca valley, on which are inscribed a record of the passing days and years, place-names and the names of kings and other notables, constitute the oldest known chronicle (600 to 300 BC) of the New World.

The people, or rather peoples, who succeeded one another on Mexican soil met with mixed fortunes. Bursts of creativity were punctuated by times of crisis and war which even led to the abrupt disappearance of entire populations and civilizations. The memory of these events lives on in the thousands of inscriptions and the legends of oral tradition.

The greatest and most tragic clash of cultures in pre-Columbian civilization was recorded by some of those who took part in the conquest of Mexico. Hernán Cortés himself sent five remarkable letters (*Cartas de relación*) back to Spain between 1519 and 1526; and the soldier-chronicler Bernal Díaz del Castillo (c. 1492–1580), who served under Cortés, fifty years after the event wrote his *Historia verdadera de la conquista de la Nueva España* ('True History of the Conquest of New Spain'). The vanquished peoples also left written records.

mexicanos el más grande de los traumas. (. . .)	A manuscript dated 1528, now in the Bibliothèque Nationale in Paris, recounts in Nahuatl, the language of the Aztecs, the traumatic fate of the Indians. (. . .)
	M. Léon Portilla

Sample 9.2 appeared concurrently in the Spanish- and English-language editions of the *UNESCO Courier*. This periodical reflects the aims of UNESCO as an institution, namely, the promotion of the cultures of the world and dissemination of knowledge and understanding of them. From the perspective of top-down analysis, both source text and target text thus have an identical generic specification (in terms of the social occasion constituted by their being written and the channel in which they are to appear) and are equally aimed at international readers with a moderately didactic intention. Yet, as outlined in Chapter 2, the genre of detached historical exposition which characterizes the target text, considered as a text in its own right, diverges from the history-as-commitment genre of the source text. In bottom-up analysis, the intertextual membership of an utterance (genre, discourse, text) is identified by text users on the basis of lexical choices and organization at the levels of texture and structure. It is to this micro-level of analysis that we now turn to observe the developing discourses of source text and target text.

The discourse features which we have chosen to present, as revealing the tacit assumptions which constitute ideologies, are once more lexical choice, cohesion and transitivity, together with, here and there, presupposition as an important component of intentionality (cf. the 'fourth assumption' in Chapter 2).

Lexical choice

The two texts in Sample 9.2 diverge so widely in terms of lexical choice that only some representative instances will be cited here. Source text items are presented on the left-hand side of the page, with a formal English version in square brackets; target text items appear on the right.

prolongados esfuerzos [prolonged   obstinate determination
efforts]

sabios [wise men]	diviners
encuentros [encounters]	clash of cultures
el hombre indígena [indigenous man]	pre-Colombian civilization
testimonios [testimonies]	written records
antiguos mexicanos [ancient Mexicans]	Indians

A clear trend is already discernible in these target text choices. The (Eurocentric) point of view presupposed in the choice of the items pre-Colombian and Indian were already alluded to in our earlier analysis; here, it will be seen that, in this respect, the source text adopts a more indigenous perspective. But when 'prolonged efforts' become *obstinate determination* and 'encounters' become *clashes*, the observer cannot avoid suspecting that the shift in point of view is much more than one of geographical and cultural perspective. At any rate, a completely different text world begins to develop. Above all, whereas the meaning potential of *sabios* covers both Western (i.e. purely rational) and non-Western forms of wisdom, the use of *diviners* tends to exclude the form of wisdom which is currently valued in the Western world. In this instance, it is the translator who opts for a marked term to represent an unmarked source text item. Crucially, the two terms presuppose diametrically opposed world views, one in which a group of historical actors is still valued and seen as relevant, another in which the same group is classified as no more than a historical curiosity.

Cohesion

That a more systematic shift is involved than that apparent in individual lexical choice becomes apparent when cohesive networks are examined. Even a cursory reading of source text Sample 9.2 would identify 'memory' and 'effort' as key concepts in the construction of the text world. In the case of *memoria*, there is multiple recurrence: five reiterations of the item in this short stretch of text. When this fact is linked to our earlier comments on recurrence in the case of the Hans Christian Andersen text, the target text representations of the item become significant. It is translated by *memory* (twice), *history*, *knowledge of the past* and, in one case, not represented at all. Thus the discoursal value of *memoria* – which has added meaning in societies in which oral tradition is valued – is lost or at least diluted. Meanwhile, *esfuerzos* ('efforts') collocates with a range of partly co-referring items such as *búsqueda* ('search'); *luchar* ('struggle'); *quehacer* ('task' – with the added connotation of 'duty'); *creatividad* ('creativity'), to promote a discourse of involvement and action. The notion of 'striving', of the active participation of the Mexicans in the creation of their own destiny, which is central to the source text, has become far more passive in translation:

esfuerzos [efforts]	obstinate determination
búsqueda [search]	the way in which they view . . .
luchar contra [to struggle against]	to save from
quehacer [task, duty]	desire
épocas de gran creatividad	bursts of creativity

Thus, active involvement in preserving memory has turned into passive 'viewing' and 'desiring' and 'knowledge of the past', while whole epochs of creativity have become occasional 'bursts'.

Transitivity

What is striking about sentence arrangement in the Spanish and English versions in Sample 9.2 is that, whereas the source text tends to place a series of inanimate actors in theme position, the target text opts for action processes involving human actors. Source text sentences 1, 2, 3, 4 and 6 constitute relational processes (X is Y; X has Y) in which the carrier is the effort/memory/destiny concept identified above as being at the heart of the discourse.[11] Target text sentences 1, 2 and 6 constitute action processes, with *Mexicans/they/the people or rather peoples* as actors. Whereas this human agency might at first seem to restore the indigenous peoples to an active role which we have seen them occupy in the discourse of the source text, we find on closer scrutiny that these action processes are in fact not **intention process**es (in which the actor performs the act voluntarily) but what are known as **supervention process**es (in which the process just happens). Thus:

Mexicans . . .	have always exhibited
They . . .	have been engaged
The people, or rather peoples . . .	met with mixed fortunes.

Here, the indigenous peoples, rather than being the creators of their destiny, appear as the hapless patients of what is visited upon them.

Cumulatively, all of these features relay discourses which point to two fundamentally opposed ideologies: destiny as personal commitment in the source text and history as passive observation in the target text.

Important differences in text structure between the Spanish and English versions were discussed in Chapter 2. They involved the suppression in translation of the counter-argument of the source text. The first instance is contained in the final paragraph of Sample 9.2. We reproduce the second of the two instances below as Sample 9.3 so that the ideological implications may be compared.

Sample 9.3

A un fraile extraordinario, Bernardino de Sahagún ... se debió el rescate de un gran tesoro de testimonios de la época prehispánica. Pero hubo también indígenas ... que siguieron escribiendo en su propia lengua náhuatl o azteca. (. . .)
[To an extraordinary monk, Bernardino de Sahagún (. . .) was owed the recovery of a great treasure of testimonies of the pre-Hispanic age. But there were also indigenous people who continued to write in their own languages.]

Target text
An extraordinary man, the Spanish Franciscan Bernardino de Sahagún, (. . .) gathered invaluable, first-hand information on the pre-Colombian era. Meanwhile, indigenous chroniclers were writing in their own languages.

In both cases, the rhetorical purpose of the source text is clear. While conceding that the official historical accounts have been based on the writings of the Conquistadors, the text producer strongly counter-argues that indigenous voices, hitherto neglected, are equally deserving of our attention. This rhetorical subordination of the official histories and corresponding promotion of Mexican versions is entirely missing in the target text.

Taken together, all of the features identified above converge in demonstrating that the translator's (maximal) mediation issues from and constructs a different ideology. In the English version, the producer of the source text, whose name appears underneath the published translation as the author of the text, is made to relay an ideology which downplays the agency – and the value – of indigenous Mexicans and dissociates (cf. the title of the article and its translation) history from destiny.

PARTIAL MEDIATION

We end with a further example of translator mediation – of a less extreme and more neutral kind than that exemplified in Samples 9.2 and 9.3. The work of the French historian E. Le Roy Ladurie is well known both within France and internationally and has become identified with a particular school of historical research. One of his most significant works, *Montaillou* (1975), appeared in English translation as a Penguin paperback in 1980, 'a shorter version of the French'. Its translator was an experienced and widely respected translator of literary and other texts, whose work could hardly be faulted on grounds of language competence or translation technique. Yet significant discoursal shifts occur between source text and target text throughout the work, of which the samples quoted below (9.4–6) are representative instances.

Sample 9.4[12]

Bernard Clergue (. . .) demande au prélat de bien vouloir lui communiquer les noms des mouchards qui l'ont mis dans le pétrin. [Bernard Clergue asks the prelate kindly to tell him the names of the grasses who have dropped him in it.]	Bernard Clergue (. . .) asked Jacques Fournier to tell him the names of those who had informed against him.

Sample 9.5

Arnaud Vital fit un jour à Vuissane Testanière (. . .) le 'coup de la poule': il lui donna une poule à tuer (acte qui, du point de vue catharo-métem-psychotique, constituait un crime). Vuissane essaya donc de tordre le cou à ce volatile,	One day (. . .) Arnaud played the 'hen trick' on Vuissane Testanière. He gave her a hen to kill – a deed which from the point of view of the Cathars, who believed in metempsycho-sis, was a crime. Vuissane tried to kill the fowl, but could

mais s'avéra incapable de l'occire.
[Arnaud Vital one day played on Vuissane Testanière the 'hen trick': he gave her a hen to kill (an act which, from the catharo-metempsychotic point of view, constituted a crime). So Vuissane tried to wring the neck of this feathered friend but proved incapable of slaying it.]

not bring herself to do it.

Sample 9.6

Quid de la mortalité en cette paroisse même?
Hélas. Dans le village aux croix jaunes, nous n'avons pas les registres de catholicité, inexistants à l'époque ...
[What (= Latin *quid*) of mortality in this parish itself? Alas. In the village of the yellow crosses, we have no Catholic records, inexistent at that time ...]

Unfortunately, no Catholic records were kept at that time ...

The use in Samples 9.4 and 9.5 of the marked items *mouchard, pétrin, volatile, occire,* carrying sign values such as colloquial, humorous or archaic, creates a second discourse, coexisting with that of more detached, authoritative historical analysis and narration, and in some ways similar to the style-shifting of Sample 9.1. Again, the variables of power and distance are involved, with the second discourse serving considerably to reduce the distance between text producer and subject and producer and receiver. Similarly, the internal dialogue of Sample 9.6, ('What of ...? Alas ...') by increasing reader involvement, reduces the power differential between producer and receiver. Such an unorthodox style of writing fits entirely with the innovatory approach to history championed by Le Roy Ladurie and his fellow historians of the *Annales* school and contrasts with the more elevated, authoritative discourse of more traditional historians.

The systematic way in which this second discourse is eliminated from the translation is all the more striking in that the translation is not a maximally mediated one in other respects. Apart from the selective reduction implied in the editor's brief, mentioned above, it interferes with the source text only as much as is compatible with easy intelligibility. The shift is clearly the result of a deliberate translator strategy. One possible motivation may be suggested. Sign values attaching to particular textural features in a source language intertextual environment may not necessarily be the same as those perceived by target text readers within their own intertextual environment. It is indeed possible that unintended effects will be relayed by an unmediated translation as readers seek to infer meaning from marked uses. In this way, Ladurie's second discourse may be interpreted in a target language-cultural environment as indicating laconic truculence, off-handedness or some other unintended attitude. For example, the use in Sample 9.5 above of the extremely unwieldy compound form *catharo-métempsychotique* is likely to be perceived by source text readers as having some satirical or debunking intention, given the predilection of French academic discourse for learned compounds of this kind. For a British readership which tends to shun such overt intellectualism in any case, the use here may simply have an alienating effect and appear pretentious. In other words the intended inference may not be drawn. Nevertheless, one might advance the view that the cumulative source text sign 'new historical writing' can and should be relayed in some manner, not necessarily at the level of the connotations attaching to particular lexical items. Heavily mediated and entirely unmediated translating are not the only alternatives.

SKOPOS, AUDIENCE DESIGN AND INTENDED EFFECTS

One could argue, following Venuti (1995), that our examples of maximal mediation and focused mediation both constitute wholesale domestication and that only the translation of the Khomeini text (Sample 9.1) provides access to the socio-textual practice of the source text producer operating within the socio-cultural norms of the source language community. There are, however, problems in adopting such a view. To begin, it is by no means self-evident that relaying the textural indices of Khomeini's discourse as they stand will enable target text receivers to infer meaning and construct a text world similar to that of source text receivers. Tokens take on values according to the environment in which they are used and the exchange value of Khomeini's discourse will be greater between members of the institutional environment shared by source text producer and receivers than they can be between source text producer and target text receivers, whatever the processing effort the latter are prepared to expend.[13] Let us remember that, if we accept even a weak version of the style-as-audience-design hypothesis outlined in Chapter 5, then we must concede that target text receivers are no more than eavesdroppers on Khomeini's address to his seminary instructors and students. In such cases, there will not even be initiative design between source text producer and target text receiver. Audience design, then, is an important component of *skopos* and crucial to translation as communication. The other component is task, that is, the translator's brief. The fact that Sample 9.1 was produced for the BBC Monitoring Service is probably the prime determinant of the translator's orientation; what would be required is a close representation of what the source text producer actually said.

Second, and more importantly, we would wish to distinguish between the kind of domestication involved in deleting a discourse for the sake of target text reader-acceptability (Samples 9.4–6) and the thoroughgoing but unacknowledged revision of an ideology , as in Samples 9.2 and 9.3. True, the translator or editor of Ladurie refers only to the need to produce 'a shorter version of the French' and the excision of Ladurie's discourse is unacknowledged as such. Yet it would be entirely plausible to argue that the motivation for the shift is to win greater acceptance for the text in a target language environment in which source text discoursal signals might not have the same exchange value. One does not have to accept such an argument to recognize that it does at least accept the need to relay intended meaning in the best possible way. The same could not be said of Samples 9.2 and 9.3, in which, deliberately or not, an author is made to promote an ideology fundamentally at variance with that of the source text. We perceive here a difference not only of degree but of kind. Yet if we accept that 'violence . . . resides in the very purpose and activity of translation' (Venuti 1995: 18), we are obliged to classify all of the translations reviewed in this chapter as instances of 'ethno-centric violence', separated only by a matter of degree. In terms of the position we have adopted as analysts (i.e. our own ideology), we would prefer to reserve our most extreme terms of condemnation for the kind of translating exemplified in Samples 9.2 and 9.3. One may debate whether the Ladurie text should have been relayed to target text readers in a more foreignizing fashion; our own view is that it should. But such a debate is hardly admissible in the case of Samples 9.2 and 9.3, which, we submit, fall far short of the accepted criteria for translating.

Chapter 10

Text-level errors

In this final section of the book (Chapters 10, 11 and 12), we address pedagogic issues, commencing with an exploration of translation 'errors'. So far in our discussion of the role of the translator as communicator, text-level errors have been mentioned often enough to justify a section of the book being devoted entirely to an examination of the topic. In this chapter, we shall leave aside mismatches of propositional meaning or breaches of the target language code (which may be due to inadequate *language* competence on the part of the translator) and focus on a number of problems in language use which can only be adequately accounted for as mismatches of text and context (which may be due to problems of *textual* competence). Although the term 'error' is not entirely appropriate (see further, Chapter 12), we shall, for the sake of convenience, refer to these as text-level errors, to be considered within a comprehensive model of discourse processing. The various components of the model have already been introduced, and only those aspects relevant to the analysis of errors beyond-the-sentence will be looked at more closely here. Categories belonging to register membership, pragmatics and semiotics will be invoked in an attempt to explain real cases of communication breakdown in both translation and interpreting.

While the various examples are, for practical reasons, presented in English, a number of other source or target languages are obviously involved. Reference will therefore be made to how these languages handle certain strands of textuality, particularly in the way they utilize texture to reflect compositional plans and comply with other higher-order contextual constraints. It is hoped that the identification of such linguistic features, which have so far received minimal attention in the existing grammars and lexicons of the various languages examined, will prompt further research into the discourse values of the features themselves and also into the adequacy of the model proposed here to account for text-level errors.

NEGOTIATING TEXT IN CONTEXT

The discourse processing model outlined in this book rests on the basic assumption that text users, producers and receivers alike, approach language in use by reacting to and interacting with a number of contextual factors. The text user attempts this task through a process of matching, seeking to establish links between text and context at every stage of the way. Let us try to relate this assumption to the analysis of a particular text sample (10.1). In the light of this analysis, we shall then discuss text-level errors detected in translations of this sample (Figure 10.2).

Sample 10.1

Letters
Checks and Balances
Sir – I note your criticisms of America's constitutional form of government (October 6th and 13th). Granted, our form of government may not be the most efficient in getting things done. Granted, the budget crisis was a disgrace and an embarrassment. But consider the alternative: I could be living in a country (1) without a written constitution which (2) is a unitary state in which a monopoly of state power is held by the national government . . .

What assumptions does an average, competent reader make in approaching a text such as this? Having merely glanced at the first sentence, the text user would most likely be thinking of correspondence with the press as the overall register provenance and would expect the evaluation of the proposition relayed in the initial sentence to be the overall pragmatic purpose. The reader would also have certain assumptions: that various socio-textual conditions have to be met for the letter to the editor to be appropriately handled as a genre; that commitment to a point of view would be the overall discourse; and that argumentation would be the predominant text type. This macro-analysis, however, is mere hunch, a set of hypotheses to be confirmed or disproved as micro-processing proper gets underway.

In dealing with the text at a micro-level of analysis, on the other hand, we may assume that the proposition in the initial sentence of the letter will provide our hypothetical reader with a basis on which to proceed in anticipating how the text will develop:

I note your criticisms of America's constitutional form of government.

In terms of English language and rhetoric, and journalistic conventions regulating correspondence with the press, the initial proposition sparks off a set of options in the reader's mind. Pragmatically, it can (1) invite an immediate rejection of what is implied ('the criticisms are noted but . . .') or (2) usher in an account which supports the proposition implied ('the criticisms are noted and . . .').

While it cannot be ruled out completely, the latter reading would be fairly implausible. Had the intention of the writer been to relay approval, he would probably have structured the text differently, perhaps opting for a different wording from the start. There are also textual conventions surrounding the act of writing to an authoritative and analytical national weekly. These militate against, say, the uncritical acceptance of what are essentially controversial points of view and instead generally encourage a more sceptical attitude, provocativeness and independent thinking. The more likely reading of *I note your criticisms* must therefore be something like 'but I find them unconvincing if not utterly groundless'.

With this still-hypothetical insight into the way the text might be developed, the reader would probably process the first sentence as one which sets the tone of the debate along these lines. Close reading for functional clues would confirm the 'rebuttal' hypothesis (option (1) above) and, in turn, would set in motion another system of options regarding what is to follow. The choices would be considered on the basis of evidence so far accumulated. Within its own intentionality (rejecting the proposition implied), intertextuality (the way argumentation works in English) and register (contentious correspondence with the press), the utterance in question could be followed either by (a) an immediate rebuttal, or (b) a development of the stance put forward before a rebuttal is issued.

There are two possible ways forward, then. The text producer could issue a rebuttal straight away or, more likely, would want to make further concessions, even if these were mere lipservice. The advantage of the first option is its directness, the disadvantage is its relative inflexibility. The advantage of the second option, on the other hand, is that it is credibility-enhancing, the disadvantage is its short-term failure to get to the point. As it turns out, the text producer opts for the second option but concurrently signals his real intentions by the use of the item *note*, whose formality alone often and conventionally flags a rebuttal in such contexts. The text producer makes an informal, temporary concession, appearing to recognize what the other side might say:

> *Granted, our form of government may not be the most efficient in getting things done.*

The intentionality of this 'thesis cited to be opposed', the signals it relays by occupying a preliminary position in the text and the register to which the text belongs begin now to interact with another area of textuality, that of structure. The overall structure of the text is determined by the context portrayed above, and in turn begins to determine the way the text hangs together. A further system of options is set up and the utterance which follows could, again, be either (a) a further concession or (b) a rebuttal. The utterance which follows implements option (a):

> *Granted, the budget crisis was a disgrace and an embarrassment.*

With this, concession-making seems to have reached saturation point and the text is now ready for the rebuttal proper:

> *But consider the alternative*

Here, the text producer is finally revealing his own position, namely that of arguing the point that the criticisms in question are not worth noting. But this is undertaken only after the writer has first enhanced his credibility by fair-mindedly reflecting the views of the opposition or at least appearing to do so.

It is perhaps worth remarking here that it is not only structure but also texture that is implicated in this process of negotiating context. Consider, for instance, the particular use of innocent-sounding lexico-grammatical features, and the glosses we provide in brackets for what we take these to imply (in Figure 10.1). In the course of the following discussion, we shall show how such curious 'false friends', which are planted deliberately and subtly, can be very misleading in translation. The underlying motive for this fairly ambiguous use of language, we recall, is essentially to curtail the

1	*note*	(but I do not accept)
2	*granted*	(but this is not sufficient)
3	*may not be the most*	(but it can be more efficient than others or simply efficient)
4	*in getting things done*	(but it is efficient in many other ways)
5	*crisis*	(just one instance, not a pattern)
6	*was*	(it is all behind us)

Figure 10.1 Ways of saying and ways of meaning

scope of emphasis generally relayed by the concession and, more specifically, by the use of conventional concessives such as 'granted', 'of course', etc. This so-called 'straw-man gambit' prepares the ground for the forthcoming rebuttal by making sure that a non-committal attitude is relayed.

To return to our sample, the text receiver is now better prepared for what to expect: the contextual configuration is becoming more transparent and both structure and texture more accessible. The text receiver must always be on the lookout for any last-minute change of plan, motivated by, for example, the need on the part of the text producer to be creative, interesting, etc. In the present case, however, there is only one way the text can go now, namely to substantiate the opposition and conclude the argument. A fully cohesive and coherent text emerges, displaying a texture and a structure that fit within a recognized contextual configuration.

THE MISHANDLING OF CONTEXT

The purpose of this rather lengthy demonstration has been primarily to open the discussion regarding what can go wrong with the way context is handled in translation and to show that errors of this kind can indeed be serious. We shall in the following sections analyse errors which translators and interpreters have actually made, relating to each of the contextual domains introduced so far. In this section, however, we shall take a broad view of the entire operation and show how, in an on-sight translation exercise, the mishandling of context by trainee translators resulted in a flawed performance in which all aspects of textuality suffered. Paradoxically, the output was fluent and almost faultless in terms of lexis and grammar.

The text used in this exercise was the letter to the editor analysed above, and those taking the test were all graduates in English from Middle Eastern universities, with considerable experience in either language teaching or translating or both. To give an idea of the gravity of the errors made before discussing them in some detail, it would be useful to consider the individual texts which were actually produced by the trainees. Limitations of space, however, make it difficult to produce a detailed analysis of each and every performance. We have thus chosen to concoct the text represented in Figure 10.2 by piecing together the evidence from a majority of student output texts.

I *note* your criticisms of America's constitutional form of government.	(formally and therefore sincerely intended in the sense of 'noteworthy')
You are absolutely right	(intended as 'there is absolutely no doubt')
in saying that our form of government *may*	(using the modal in its confirmative function)
not be *the most* efficient in getting things done.	(meant categorically)
You are absolutely right in saying that the budget *crisis*	(emphasized and made to sound momentous)
was	(a completed event)
a disgrace and an embarassment	(highly condemnatory)
BUT	[missed in 5 out of 12 renderings and, when incorporated, functioned as an extremely weak 'organizational' device]
consider the alternative	(with the list that followed, functioned as an invitation to experience what a haven of peace might genuinely be like)

Figure 10.2 Close back-translation from Arabic of Sample 10.1

Note: Glosses in brackets are provided to show the way a given text-element (italicized) was in all probability intended by the students.[1]

WHAT WENT WRONG AND WHY?

Let us start with a brief summary of what went wrong. The source of the erratic reading was essentially a failure to reconstruct context and appreciate text type properly. Given their linguistic and cultural background, those taking the test and making some of the errors discussed here most probably reacted to register merely in terms of a notion of journalistic writing that is on the whole supportive and not sceptical (e.g. Public Relations style). Within such modes of writing, cases to be made would invariably be executed by through-arguing and not counter-arguing a point, that is by stating an initial thesis and basically defending it (see Chapter 8).

Furthermore, we can safely assume that the initial proposition was seen by the readers in question as indicating that 'the failure of the American constitutional system is simply accepted'. In all probability, that is, the element *note* in the first sentence carried no dissonant connotations and could thus have simply been seen as equivalent to 'noteworthy'. Such a thesis needs to be substantiated – or so the majority of the students thought. The substantiation is initiated by the 'pseudo-emphatic' *granted* which once again was seen by most of the students as enhancing the initial reading they had opted for. Items such as *may not be the most efficient* were taken as statements of conviction and not distant probabilities. These were certainly not seen in terms of the 'straw-man gambit' which the text producer has deliberately used. The third sentence introducing further use of the *granted* device was no doubt understood along similar lines. So far, the students' reading would be an argument which might be glossed as:

> I wholeheartedly accept the criticisms and I think you are absolutely right in saying that ... and that ... (all sincerely meant, of course.)

By the time the 'opposition' was reached, it could not have made any impact on the students. Turned by most of those taking the test into an 'additive' ('and'), the adversative *but* simply came to provide another side to the unfolding argument. This would cover another, far more favourable alternative and not the actual flaws which the source text writer perceives in the British constitutional system. It is remarkable to what lengths readers will go in an attempt to make sense, to maintain sense constancy and to salvage originally constructed theories about what a text is likely to mean. To achieve this, the students had to ignore original texture signals and tease out meanings that further the translators' own goals (namely, to make their own readings work).

Now, we can put forward a number of hypotheses to explain all this in the terms of the discourse processing model we have adopted. In doing so, we are fully aware of the fact that verifiable evidence as to what goes on in the translator's mind is not readily obtainable. However, it is legitimate to make informed guesses and, in order to make these less haphazard, we shall seek support from contrastive rhetoric and, more specifically, from text-linguistic theories of cross-cultural communication.[2] As we saw in Chapter 8, these sources point to certain systematic tendencies among users of various languages towards certain rhetorical routines and not others. Within the rhetorical system of Arabic, for example, through-argumentation is by far the more favoured form. Without wishing to read too much into the effect which such mother tongue socio-textual conventions can have on the process of, say, reading in a foreign language, we suggest that the rhetorical norms governing source and target text organization in general certainly have a role to play.

A REGISTER ERROR

From this broad kind of analysis, we may now move on to consider more specific errors that implicate particular areas of textuality. It must be stressed, however, that error specificity is only a matter of what the analyst wishes to focus on for a particular purpose. That is, despite the fact that some errors may originate in one specific textual or contextual domain (e.g. register), the effect is inevitably wide-ranging, impinging on almost all of the other domains of textuality. To illustrate this, let us begin with an example from interpreting. In a simulation of part of the US Senate Watergate investigation in a liaison interpreting practice session with a group of postgraduate trainees, one aspect of the interaction was particularly interesting. This was to do with how the formality of the situation acted as an important constraint on the way the Chair challenged John Ehrlichman, one of President Nixon's most senior aides (Sample 10.2).

Sample 10.2

Q: Mr Ehrlichman, prior to the luncheon recess you stated that in your opinion, the entry into the Ellsberg psychiatrist's office

> was legal because of national security reasons. I think that
> was your testimony.
>
> A: Yes.

This is a case in which, according to Fairclough (1989),[3] formality both restricts access and generates awe. For example, the choice of *prior to the luncheon recess you stated* instead of 'before lunch you said' is highly formal. But this aspect of the interaction was not reflected by almost all of the students who took part in the interpreting session. The renderings in the target language were prosaic and the crucial level of source text formality was compromised. Of course, this is essentially a register problem, but it is not without pragmatic implications to do with power and politeness. The semiotic dimension of context is also involved, with genre-related as well as discoursal and textual values being necessarily glossed over.

A further example of inadequacy in negotiating register may this time be taken from literary translating. Like the interpreter, the literary translator needs to be aware of the rhetorical values yielded by the inevitable overlap between textual clues and factors of context. Sample 10.3 is the source text which presents us with a register problem.

Sample 10.3

Metamorphosis
The long project, its candling arm
Come over, shrinks into still-disparate darkness
Its *pleasuance an urn*. And for what term
Should I *elect* you, *O marauding* beast of
Self-consciousness? When it is you,
Around the clock, I stand next to and consult?
You without *breather*? Testimonials

To its not enduring crispness notwithstanding,
You can take that out. It needs to be shaken in the light.

To be delivered again to its shining arm –
O farewell grief and welcome joy! *Gosh*! . . .

                                                    (italics added)

This text was given as a translation assignment to a group of post-graduate trainees. For the sake of the experiment, the students were first introduced, albeit in very general terms, to the poem and the relevant text linguistic as well as literary-critical aspects.[4] Basically, the poem is stylistically schizophrenic: the first half (from which the above extract is taken) is characterized by a marked degree of hybridization with at least three registers present. The items in italics above point to: an 'archaic' register functioning as a marker of poetical language proper; American 'colloquialisms' introducing a dialectal dimension; and 'bureaucratese' providing a parody of academic discourse. The second half of the poem, in contrast, is characterized by total consistency of register membership. For example:

> The penchant for growing and giving
> Has left us bereft, and intrigued, for behind the screen
> Of whatever vanity . . .

Structurally and texturally, the two parts are thus deliberately made to confront one another. The aim of the exercise we undertook with our translator trainees was to see whether they were able to establish a link between text and context and incorporate insights yielded by such matching into their translation strategy. The results of the experiment were disappointing, with the majority of the renderings not adequately reflecting the motivations behind the deliberate hybridization that is the hallmark of the source text. Almost all of the students opted for one basic strategy, namely to neutralize and thus virtually immobilise the salient features in the first part. A crucial level of meaning was thus jettisoned, and the entire rationale behind the lexico-grammatical choices was all but irretrievably lost. Although the problem is one of register, failure to handle the rhetorical dynamism of the text has the effect of compromising both intentionality and intertextuality. Texture has also been shifted to relay neutral register values, a wholly unintended effect.

A PRAGMATIC ERROR

Moving now to a category of errors which are predominantly pragmatic, let us consider Sample 10.4, a fragment from another mock liaison interpreting session.

Sample 10.4

Journalist: Do you think that the Sudanese government has collected the price of its alliance with Iraq?

Sudanese government ex-minister (formal translation from Arabic):   These are questions which I find very difficult to answer. But there is evidence, some of it clear for all to see, and some about which inferences will have to be made. (. . .)

In discussing the background to this interview with the trainees prior to conducting the experiment, one or two crucial details were deliberately overlooked. These had to do with the fact that the Sudanese speaker is in fact an ex-government minister, that he is the leader of an influential group opposing the present regime, and that this group operates from Saudi Arabia, where the ex-minister now lives in exile. Also glossed over was the fact that the interview appeared in a London-based newspaper not sympathetic to the Iraqi regime. Such suppression of contextual information may be objected to as 'doctoring' the data to prove a point. But we felt that it was a valid research procedure and a useful way of controlling the relevant contextual variables. In fact, it is not uncommon in professional life for interpreters to operate in something of a contextual vacuum and, to cope, they often rely on the way the interaction develops as it gradually unfolds.

Before we turn to the actual interpreting and the erroneous assumptions relied on by some of the students, let us briefly present the way the journalist's question was intended: an invitation to engage in slandering some opponent (the Iraqi and the Sudanese regimes in this case). Pragmatically, this is all disguised as information-seeking. But the truth of the matter is that the Sudanese critic of the regime was being invited to embark on a virulent condemnation of what would be labelled by him as the hit-or-miss foreign policy of the generals in Khartoum, etc.

Now, if we look at the way the whole interaction was perceived and interpreted by some of the students, we see that this is totally at variance with the intentionality of the source text. Sample 10.5 is an example of one rendering:

Sample 10.5

Journalist: Do you think that the Sudanese government has collected the price of its alliance with Iraq?

Sudanese government ex-minister: I don't know how to answer questions like these. But proof will be available either in common sense terms or by inference if you like.

As we can see, the ex-minister in the way he is interpreted has taken offence to having 'his' government's integrity questioned. He is arguing along the following lines: 'If you must make accusations like these, I have news for you – we will be exonerated and the truth will be clear for all to see.'

One can easily imagine the kind of assumptions which must have been made for readings similar to the above to occur. It will be recalled that, in the wake of the Gulf War, the Sudanese government was generally assumed to be pro-Iraq. It is this important contextual factor which the students relied on in processing the text under consideration and consequently relaying different pragmatic meanings. At the same time, the students will have made the assumption that the interviewee is a current government minister.

In the light of this, the interaction was perceived by the students as a foolhardy attempt on the part of an impertinent journalist to provoke a government minister by asking him the liberal kind of questions we are familiar with in the Western media. The ex-minister's response was thus taken by the students pragmatically to be a rebuke in which the minister tells the journalist off for overstepping the mark. The actual reply is polite and restrained, but, to the students, this could only be the calm before the storm, and if the journalist persisted, he would perhaps be asked to leave.

A SEMIOTIC ERROR

A clear example of mishandling discourse, text and genre may be taken from an exchange (Sample 10.6) which took place in a mock liaison training session. A British journalist was using the familiar investigative kind of discourse, opening with a contentious, provocative statement. The text format of the question was a counter-argument in which after some lip-service endorsement, the journalist embarked on the rebuttal. In substantiating his stance, the journalist used expressions such as 'working for the government' which, given the general drift of the argument, can only be taken as pejorative. The genre in which all of this occurred was that of 'playing the devil's advocate', a familiar gambit in Western media interviews.

Sample 10.6

Journalist: Look at Tunisia. Despite democratic trappings, power remains concentrated and personalized. But perhaps more to the point, look at Algeria. Some 180,000 well-schooled Algerians enter the job market every year. Yet a hobbled economy adds only 10,000 new jobs a year, and some 45% of these involve working for the government.

The three trainees doing the interpreting in this mock session all happened to come from a country with an extremely rich economy and one in which the concepts of 'unemployment', 'looking for a job', and so on were by and large absent. Conversely, the notion of power being 'concentrated' and 'personalized' might not seem extraordinary. But most alien would be any sense in which 'working for the government' might be an expression used pejoratively. The interpreter trainees took turns to handle this situation. None of them was successful. The difficulty may essentially be ascribed to a failure to perceive the liberal discourse values attached to the concept of 'working for the government', which render it equivalent to saying 'not particularly valued'. But the problem is not only discoursal. Textually, the straw-man gambit is a potential blind spot for trainees from a different cultural background, as we have previously made clear. Furthermore, the genre of 'playing the devil's advocate' is equally baffling since it is not a common journalistic practice in the culture to which these students belonged.

A SUCCESS STORY

When context is misinterpreted, then, both structure and texture are invariably at risk. We end, however, with an example of what we consider to be a successful translation, in which principles of text structure are used as a means of refining what otherwise would have been misleading in English. Sample 10.7 is a formal translation from Arabic.

Sample 10.7

(. . .) 'We're locking up now.'
   Three men were smoking *kif* around one of the card tables. I asked Mr Abdullah if I could leave my bag with him till the

following day. He asked me to show him what was in it: two largish framed pictures, a pair of trousers, two shirts and a pair of socks.

If rendered without alteration, this narrative frame would relay a number of pragmatic meanings, including (a) Mr Abdullah's rudeness in encroaching on the narrator's negative face (cf. Chapter 5) by asking directly to see his private possessions, and (b) the oddness of the objects contained in the bag, a reading which is encouraged by the pragmatic values perceived in the preceding element (negative politeness). Yet neither of these inferences is intended in the source text, which is actually about Mr Abdullah's affable directness. Furthermore, there is nothing particularly face-threatening in the culture of the source language about asking to be shown the contents of a bag one is given to look after, nor is any stigma intended to be attached to the kind of objects revealed.

To facilitate retrieval of these and similar values, and to enable the reader to infer the right attitudes, the translator into English of Sample 10.7 had to negotiate the frame differently by introducing elements which in Arabic we do not seem to require but which are necessary in English (see the discussion of oral vs. visual texts in Chapter 8). Sample 10.8 is the published translation with the additional elements italicized.

Sample 10.8

(. . .) 'We're locking up now.'
   Three men were smoking *kif* around one of the card tables. I asked Mr Abdullah if I could leave my bag with him till the following day. *He said it would be alright, but he wanted to check what was in it, so I had to show him:* two largish framed pictures, a pair of trousers, two shirts and a pair of socks.

This particular instance of mediation by the translator for the purpose of relaying intended meanings may be usefully contrasted with those instances of mediation discussed in Chapter 9.

SUMMARY

In this chapter, we have identified a number of problems in the use of language and, from a translation perspective, argued that such departures from intended meaning can only be adequately accounted for by adopting a comprehensive view of context and its determining influence on text structure and texture. In the course of the discussion, aspects of our discourse processing model which are relevant to the orientation adopted in the analysis of errors beyond-the-sentence were more closely examined and applied to real cases of communication breakdown (as well as success), drawn from both translation and interpreting.

Both a broad kind of error analysis and an investigation of more specifically inappropriate renderings were attempted. The main conclusion is that, although errors and inappropriateness may originate in one textual or contextual domain and not in another, the effect is inevitably wide-ranging, impinging on almost all of the other domains of textuality. There is therefore an urgent need to broaden the discussion of translation errors and to invoke more context-sensitive models when identifying, classifying and remedying them. There is also a need to adopt an orientation which builds into teaching methods and materials selection the insights gained from an analysis of genuinely discoursal errors.

Chapter 11

Curriculum design

Along similar lines to Chapter 3, which focused on the training of interpreters, this chapter is intended to explore possible applications of text linguistics to the training of translators. As we have made clear in the course of the discussion so far, we take a fairly broad view of text linguistics and incorporate insights from various other disciplines such as stylistics, rhetoric, exegesis, discourse analysis, ethnomethodology, as well as from recent attempts at developing text grammars within a science of texts. In this chapter, we shall concentrate on syllabus design with the advanced translator trainee in mind. The question to be addressed is: on what basis could the selection, grading and presentation of materials for the training of translators be made more effective?

It will be argued that one way of tackling the issues involved in curriculum design for the training of translators is to adopt a text linguistic approach to the classification of texts. As we have already shown, central to such a text typology is the classification of language use in terms of rhetorical purpose (e.g. to argue), yielding in the process a set of text types (e.g. argumentation), a number of major sub-types (e.g. the counter-argument, the through-argument) and a variety of text forms illustrating a number of register variables such as technical/non-technical, subjective/objective, spoken/written. Thus, a particular text might be categorized as an objective (analytical) or subjective (hortatory) through-argument. In all cases, it is assumed that such a categorization is idealized and that, since all texts are hybrids, recognizing dominance of a given rhetorical purpose in a given text would be the best means of classification available.

RATIONALE FOR A TEXT TYPE APPROACH

As was pointed out in Chapter 10 which dealt with discourse errors, it is the inadequacy of sentential syntax and semantics to account for some of the problems encountered by the translator trainee that has prompted the search for an alternative. Furthermore, these difficulties are often experienced by students whose performance in terms of handling the grammar and the vocabulary of both source and target language, and whose awareness of socio-cultural issues in the two languages, are beyond reproach. Of course, what we have called text-level errors may in essence be syntactic, semantic or even morphological. But, the fact that those who commit these errors have a high level of language competence must surely point to the insufficiency of, say, mastering syntax without being aware of discoursal meanings (e.g. the ideological function of passivization). We are therefore inclined to conclude that training programmes need to address the area of language use where text meets context and is thereby structured and made to hang together (texture).

This is an area which has sometimes been neglected, not only in translator/interpreter training but also in the general field of foreign-language teaching. In the early 1960s, register analysis emerged to provide a framework that has exercised considerable influence on applied and socio-linguistics. Many studies with a theoretical bias, textbooks and manuals have been inspired by this rapidly developing discipline. In precise analytical terms, the procedures involved sizeable samples of language being delimited on the basis of broad contextual categories such as subject matter and then subjected to some form of qualitative, or more often quantitative, analysis.

In practice, however, such procedures have tended to ignore the rich range of textual activities which make up the communicative potential of, say, 'doing science' or 'practising law'. Also ignored are the discoursal values which the lexico-grammar relays in the process of communication. In short, important aspects of textuality are left unaccounted for, a weakness which stems from the erroneous assumption that the text is the sum total of its constituent parts, that the formality of a text, for example, is a function of a statistically determined predominance of certain lexical or grammatical features to the exclusion of all else.

Texts may be similar in their level of formality or their field of discourse and yet still display, in subtle ways, differences of some significance. Within tenor, for example, these differences move beyond the formal/informal distinction to include variables such as those of power and solidarity. Pragmatic meanings are relayed and texts begin to function as socio-cultural 'signs' within a system not merely of linguistic expression but also of socio-textual conventions.

It is the text type, as defined by overall rhetorical purpose, which provides the essential link between text and context. We consider it to be central to a comprehensive model of describing language in use. Viable text typologies promise a comprehensive framework which captures the symbiosis between textuality and the various levels of linguistic expression.

TEXT TYPE IN CURRICULUM DESIGN: A BASIC HYPOTHESIS

The basic hypothesis underlying our proposed curriculum design is one which relates the notion of text type to the actual process of translation and to the translator at work: *different text types seem to place different demands on the translator* (Gülich and Raible 1975). The notion of 'demand' may be usefully seen in terms of the kind of approach to translating which is felt to be most appropriate in dealing with a particular text type, meeting the criteria of adequacy it requires. To illustrate this briefly, we could suggest that, for example, the translation of a news report (which belongs to the expository text type) is likely to be less demanding than, say, the translation of an editorial (a text form subsumed under the text type argumentation).

The relative ease with which news reports can be handled, and the level of difficulty characteristic of translating editorials, may be explained in terms of aspects of text constitution such as the more straightforward compositional plan and the predominantly unmarked patterns of connectivity, theme-rheme development and so on which characterize exposition in general. Achieving adequacy in handling exposition is thus governed by a set of criteria that are appreciably different from and considerably easier than those involved in the translation of argumentation. In the latter text type, structure tends to be more complex and relatively more difficult to negotiate. Texture also tends to be opaque and to be manipulated for rhetorical effect. To respond to such different requirements, a choice of translation approach is clearly involved. Thus, while an approach which tends towards the 'literal' is likely to be appropriate and indeed sufficient for straightforward expository forms of texts (such as the news report), greater latitude may be needed in handling argumentation effectively.

THE RELATIVITY OF EVALUATIVENESS

The notion of 'varying demands' introduced above and explained in terms of criteria for adequacy and approach to translation is not a static, either/or concept, but a dynamic and variable one. Basic to the variability in question is text **evaluativeness**. This is a textual orientation which is established and maintained by means of a variety of linguistic devices that singly or collectively signal a move from what has been referred to as situation monitoring towards situation managing. In other words, text producers can opt either for a relatively detached account of a state of affairs or for steering the text receiver in a particular direction.

At a very general level of socio-textual activity, it is the degree of text evaluativeness that seems to be the single most important feature in distinguishing one text type from another. From this perspective, we may envisage texts as occupying different positions on a continuum of evaluativeness. The various forms of the argumentative text type, for example, tend towards the evaluative end of the continuum, while those of exposition will occupy the least evaluative end. Diagrammatically, this semiotic domain of text classification may be represented as in Figure 11.1.

VARYING DEGREES OF MARKEDNESS

Another scale of values can be superimposed on this continuum of evaluativeness. This represents the relative degree of markedness with which linguistic expression may be imbued (e.g. 'this matters' vs. 'it is this which matters', as unmarked and marked forms, respectively). At text level, the marked/unmarked distinction has already

+ Evaluative	− Evaluative
Argumentation	Exposition

Figure 11.1 Continuum of evaluativeness

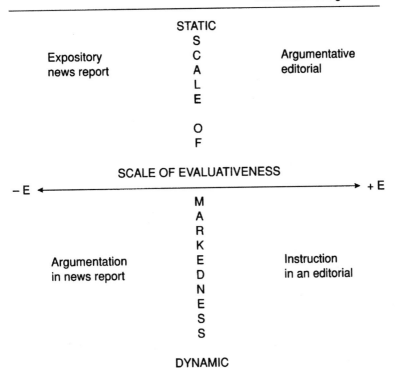

Figure 11.2 Scale of markedness

been introduced in Chapter 2 in terms of the static and the dynamic. An unmarked text fulfils expectations and thus renders a sequence of sentences somehow less dynamic than a marked text (which is unpredictable and expectation-defying). For example, an argumentative text encountered in an editorial will normally be expected and therefore less marked (and in a sense less dynamic) than an argumentative text purposefully intruding into a news report. This is represented in Figure 11.2, in which the scale of markedness is grafted onto the continuum of evaluativeness (Figure 11.1) and examples of text types are positioned in terms of their relative evaluativeness and markedness. Just as text type membership is determined by these parameters, so genres and discourses may either be used in an unmarked fashion (i.e. in a manner which fulfils expectations) or create dynamism through shifts which defy expectations. For example, the 'tests' section of the medical case history is generally located at the least evaluative and least dynamic end of both scales. The discourse encountered in such texts is one of detachment: it is expected and is therefore least marked/evaluative. When expectations are fulfilled, that is, we are in the predictable mode. However, when expectations are defied and the genre and discourse are shifted, we remain at the non-evaluative end of the scale (such a text will always be expository), but have to recognize slightly more dynamism than would otherwise be the case. In Chapter 2, the static/dynamic contrast was illustrated with the help of two fragments of texts cited by Frances and Kramer-Dahl (1992), reproduced here for ease of reference as Samples 11.1 and 11.2.

Sample 11.1

She [the patient] only recognized 4 out of 20 objects in this mode of presentation, but when the same objects were rotated in front of her immobile head, then 9 out of 20 were recognized.

Sample 11.2

For he [the patient] approached these faces – even of those near and dear – as if they were abstract puzzles or tests. He did not relate to them, he did not behold. No face was familiar to him, seen as a 'thou', being just identified as a set of features, an 'it'.

Sample 11.1 may be said to characterize the norm of the medical case history. But Sample 11.2, although it remains expository and covers a similar portion of reality to that of Sample 11.1, departs from the norm and somehow defies expectations of what medical case histories normally consist of. The departure may be identified not only in patterns of transitivity (e.g. four mental processes in Sample 11.2 for just one in Sample 11.1), but also in modality (e.g. compare the use of *just* in Sample 11.2 with the use of *only* in Sample 11.1) and in the way the text is developed (theme-rheme progression, etc.). Thus, to put it in text type terms, while both texts are expository in focus, Sample 11.2 is marked and is thus more dynamic than the unmarked Sample 11.1.

Following consideration of these semiotic structures (text, genre and discourse), we now incorporate the pragmatic domain of context into the scale of markedness presented above. Markedness in this respect occurs when intentionality in the use of language is opaque or indirect. This will occur independently of the degree of evaluativeness displayed by a given text. For example, the way *offspring* is used in the expository text fragment of Sample 11.3 shows considerable opaqueness of intention.

Sample 11.3

Let us take as our starting point the calculation of the General Register Office that by 1985 there would be in this country three-and-a-half million coloured immigrants and their offspring . . .

Terms such as *offspring*, habitually used in technical or legal discourses, are marked when used in a wholly different context and may relay non-straightforward intentionality.

Finally, a register continuum may be envisaged as running from one extreme where texts are markedly hybrid, to the other extreme where texts display consistency of register membership. Hybrid texts are by definition dynamic/marked, independently of the degree of evaluativeness they display. Sample 11.4 is an example of fluctuation in register membership from advertising to legalese in one and the same Woolwich Building Society advertisement.

Sample 11.4

If you're buying your first home, look no further than the Woolwich for your mortgage. Our new rates mean even better deals for first time buyers.

For friendly, practical advice about buying your first home, talk to our First Time Buyer Adviser at your local Woolwich branch. Or call us **It's good to be with the** free any time on **WOOLWICH** 0800 400 900 quoting ref GN7.

The First Timers first year discounts apply for the first year of the mortgage from the date interest is first charged on the mortgage. These rates apply only where a written offer of advance was issued on or after 26.7.93. Thereafter, our standard variable mortgage rate will apply. All rates are variable and APRs typical. A first charge over your property will be required as security for a First Timers mortgage . . .

YOUR HOME IS AT RISK IF YOU DO NOT KEEP UP REPAYMENTS ON A MORTGAGE OR OTHER LOAN SECURED ON IT

This fluctuation makes Sample 11.4 a hybrid, dynamic text. Variation of intentionality and register, as illustrated in Samples 11.3 and 11.4, are represented on the static/dynamic scale in Figure 11.3.

The 'varying demands' on the translator and the translation approach adopted in response to these are heavily influenced by the constant interaction between the two scales of evaluativeness and markedness. From the point of view of translator training, we can therefore advance the view that those tasks involving texts which are least evaluative and which, on a different level of abstraction, also happen to be unmarked, static, transparent in intent and consistent in register, will be the most straightforward to deal with. They tend to place the fewest contextual demands on the translator, and the translation approach is likely to be simply one of searching for appropriate terminology and grammatical arrangement.

DRAWING UP AND IMPLEMENTING A CURRICULUM DESIGN

Decisions which translators must take regarding choice of translation approach appropriate to different criteria of adequacy are, then, subject to text type, as defined in terms of overall rhetorical purpose. However, recognition of text type remains a heuristic procedure. The process involved is one of identifying in an exploratory fashion

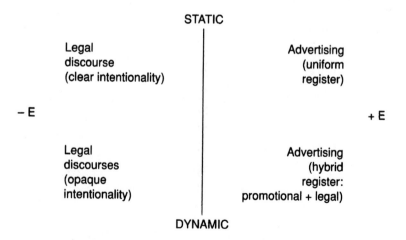

Figure 11.3 Intentionality and register on the static/dynamic scale

the principles which underlie the production and reception of texts and occurrences within texts.

Beyond text type, this heuristics taps more resources than just that of 'rhetorical purpose', identified so far to be the hallmark of all texts. There will be a discoursal element catering for attitudinal meaning and a genre element reflected in the conventional use of language appropriate to a given social occasion. Concurrently, intentionality, register membership, elements of structure and texture all contribute to the construction of meaning. Thus, in assigning an evaluative and unmarked status to Sample 11.5 below, we are not merely looking at 'counter-arguing' as the rhetorical purpose, but also at the discourse of contention as part of attitudinal meaning, the letter to the editor as genre, the claim/counter-claim as the structural plan of the text, and particular use of connectivity, to take but one example of the texture devices.

Sample 11.5

SIR – Dr Dugdale gives two assumptions on which he feels the WHO code for the marketing of breastmilk substitutes is based and states that these are testable – first, 'that breast-feeding is better than other forms of feeding', and, second, 'that mothers, especially those in developing countries, are so unable to distinguish the best interests of their infants that they can be deluded by advertising and commercial promotion'. He feels that the WHO code should be viewed by scientists with misgivings because they should test these assumptions, not merely state as axiomatic that 'breast is best'.

It clearly follows that governments should monitor the WHO code and should document the effects of its implementation on 'the mortality, health and growth of infants and children'. However, it is a fact that these data are outcome measurements reflecting many interrelated positive and negative factors, and it is obvious that infant feeding represents only one of these influences, as Dr Dugdale himself concedes. (. . .)

From the translator's point of view, the only potential difficulties encountered in dealing with such a text sample lie in the area of contrastive rhetoric (i.e. what is appropriate in different languages and cultures for the purposes mentioned above; cf. Chapter 10 on text-level errors and Chapter 8 on cross-cultural communication).

From the perspective of curriculum design, however, while the text veers towards the more evaluative end of the scale and will as such pose one or two problems, the complexity is nevertheless attenuated by the unmarked, static character of the text. Put differently, Sample 11.5 may be more demanding than, say, a less evaluative text (e.g. a straightforward news report), but less demanding than a text which is both evaluative and marked (e.g. the letter to the editor format borrowed and used in a satirical article with the aim of poking fun at something or other).

The next question to be addressed in a curriculum design based on text types is the position of **instructional** texts on the scale. This text type aims at the formation of future behaviour through both monitoring and managing a situation at one and the same time. Here, the kind of monitoring performed is unlike that of the majority of expository forms in that what is being monitored is not a pre-existing situation, but one that is currently being constructed and presented as a text world to be abided by in a performative fashion. Instructional managing is also unlike that performed in the majority of argumentative forms in that the act of managing is not seen in terms of evaluation-through-persuasion but in terms of regulation-through-instruction.

Instruction could thus conceivably be located either at the evaluative or the non-evaluative end of the scale. However, due to the largely formulaic nature of the structure and texture displayed by instructional texts, the contextual demands they make on the translator could safely be assumed to be of a straightforward nature, more akin to those imposed by any non-evaluative text. Put differently, the linguistic means adopted to achieve the instructional goal tend to veer towards the conventional and thus become a matter of whether or not one is familiar with the relevant conventions.

FROM TEXT TYPE TO TEXT FORMS

Naturally, extremes are artificial points on any scale. In reality, texts can never be so neatly categorized and are often found to display characteristics of more than one type and to veer from one point to another on the relevant scale. However, accepting polarity as a methodological convenience is always helpful in determining, as precisely as one needs to, the degree of evaluativeness or markedness possessed by a given text. This is important to the translator in the sense that judgement of the extent to which a particular text is evaluative or marked determines the translation strategy to be adopted, such as the more 'literal' or the more 'free' approaches which will be found to work better with certain types of texts than with others.

1 Instruction

With a general aim of reflecting in our teaching programmes a gradual increase in the degree of evaluativeness, and subsequently of markedness, we propose a design that begins with the instructional text type. The kind of instructional text we have in mind is exemplified by Sample 11.6. It is characteristic of the output which emanates from official bodies, ranging from international organizations to local governments, and which translators are often called upon to deal with. Responding to a context that is essentially non-evaluative, and with the intention to 'regulate' through 'instruction', texts of this particular type have conventionally developed a more or less finite set of structure formats that are highly formulaic. In terms of texture, instructional texts display features of a close-knit character, which the translator has to approach in a disciplined and methodical manner. In dealing with this highly constrained use of language, a more literal translation approach obviously presents itself as a workable solution: the instructional context is fairly circumscribed, text structure is generally formulaic, and cohesion is established by straightforward, stable means, with diction being generally unemotive and the overall tenor one of extreme detachment.

Sample 11.6

Preamble
The High Contracting Parties,
    Proclaiming their earnest wish to see peace prevail among peoples,
    Recalling that every State has the duty, in conformity with the Charter of the United Nations, to refrain in its international relations from the threat or use of force against the sovereignty, territorial integrity or political independence of any State, or in any other manner inconsistent with the purposes of the United Nations, (. . .)
    Have agreed on the following:

Article 1 – General principles and scope of application
1 The High Contracting Parties undertake to respect and to ensure respect for this Protocol in all circumstances. (. . .)

Once a given text type is identified and described, the next step is to identify the various text forms that are commonly encountered within it. In instruction, reliance on genre structure seems to be an ideal way of going about this. Taking certain types of legal documents such as the Resolution, the Treaty, or the Protocol (of which Sample 11.6 is an example) as the macro-genre, we find that these yield a set of micro-genres that are uniformly used. Thus, a treaty, for example, invariably has: (1) a signatory slot, (2) a preamble, (3) a verb of doing, (4) a set of articles. Sample 11.6 above illustrates the various segments thus:

The High Contracting Parties (1)
Proclaiming their earnest wish to see peace prevail among peoples (2)
Have agreed on the following (3)
The High Contracting Parties undertake to respect (4)

What makes this analysis particularly relevant is perhaps the fact that each of the above genre structures (e.g. the preambular paragraph) seems to have a 'language' of its own, which is essentially of a formulaic nature. Starting with these formats in a programme of translator training may seem odd, given the notorious difficulty of legal language in general. But, beyond problems of lexical equivalence, we suggest, this difficulty basically stems from lack of familiarity with the genre structures through which the legal institution conducts its affairs rather than through some instrinsic complication ascribable to legal language *per se*.

The various instructional forms are thus 'routines' which the translator either knows or simply does not know. But, if not known, these formats and terminologies are learnable with remarkable ease, since what is involved is essentially a finite set of conventional formats and a finite list of technical vocabulary. These inconveniences are outweighed by the fact that instructional text forms provide an ideal opportunity for introducing the trainee to a basic translation strategy which is to opt for the 'literal' unless there is a good reason to do otherwise (cf. Newmark 1988: xi and 68–9). Normally within the conventions of writing instructional material, the translator will find no such compelling rhetorical reason to justify deviating from the original. Consequently, the training session will not be occupied with prolonged discussion of matters other than those related to translation strategy.

2 Exposition

Next on the scale of evaluativeness is exposition. While the context of detachment encountered in legal language is also in evidence, expository prose tends to be less regulated. To reflect this, expository text structure, though still fairly tightly organized, is far less stringently formulaic than that of the instructional text. The same goes for texture which, though fairly stable, is far less constrained than that of legal language. Bearing in mind that a certain degree of evaluativeness is not uncommon in exposition, we usually find that diction can be fairly emotive, metaphoric expression is not a rarity and a general feel of semi-formality is allowed. In terms of translation strategy, an approach which permits lesser latitude works well with the more detached end of the spectrum, but has to be adjusted slightly to handle the freer, more evaluative forms.

In searching for the text forms common in this particular text type, the curriculum designer has to rely on an analysis of current practice in the field of expository writing. Like that conducted for the text type instruction, such a search will be primarily informed by genre criteria, and by one basic fact of language variation, namely, that to be distinctive, the various text forms identified must possess linguistic features that can be considered typical of the form in question. With these defining criteria, our own research into exposition has led us to the following list of forms that reflect a gradation from least to most evaluative.

1 **The abstract** (e.g. succinct statement of the content of an academic article)
2 **The synopsis** (e.g. as in a theatre programme)
3 **The summary** (e.g. summarized report of a set of events, etc.)
4 **The entity-oriented news report** (e.g. listing the aims of a new organization)
5 **The event-oriented/non-evaluative news report** (e.g. reporting the opening meeting of the new organization)
6 **The event-oriented/evaluative news report** (e.g. a critical review of the above meeting)

7 **The person-oriented news report** (e.g. report of a briefing given by the head of the new organization)
8 **The formulaic report** (e.g. the auditors' report)[1]
9 **The executive report** (e.g. Chairman's statement to the shareholders)
10 **The personalized report** (e.g. memoirs).

3 Argumentation

The various forms of argumentation within genres such as the Editorial, the Letter to the Editor and so on present us with the opportunity to apply our theoretical framework of evaluativeness to the more unconstrained kind of language use. Evaluativeness has already been allowed in the last two expository forms (e.g. the personalized report). But the context of argumentation proper is essentially one in which the need to persuade through evaluation is paramount. Text structure responds to this contextual requirement by encouraging creativity within formats which, though not entirely shapeless, are far less predictable and much more varied than the uniform organization of expository or instructional/legal texts.

The texture of argumentative texts is also fairly free, with a predominance of emotive diction, metaphoric expression and subtle uses of modality. In dealing with this kind of language variation, both the unit of translation (within the general notion of the criteria of adequacy) and the translation strategy involved have to be viewed differently. In the translation of argumentation, translators more often than not find themselves operating with greater degrees of latitude than that commonly offered by instruction or exposition. Of course, the procedures of working with the word or the phrase as a unit of translation and of adopting a literal approach cannot be ruled out completely. In practice, however, we find that such measures have to be constantly modified in the case of argumentative texts. Here, we find that larger stretches of text are usually tackled, with freer modes of translation sometimes becoming the only valid option.

In analyzing the kind of text forms which the text type argumentation can yield, a genre-based search similar to that conducted for exposition and instruction may be attempted. Similar criteria of selection can be adopted: text forms should have a specific character and the ordering must reflect a move from the less to the more evaluative. The following list of argumentative text forms is suggested:

1 **The analytical through-argument** (cf. Sample 8.2, paragraph 1)
2 **The hortatory through-argument** (cf. Sample 9.1, paragraph 5)
3 **The explicit (lopsided) counter-argument** (cf. Sample 8.5)
4 **The standard counter-argument** (the Balance) (cf. Sample 11.5)
5 **The suppressed counter-argument** (cf. Sample 8.3).

These forms were discussed fairly comprehensively from the perspective of cross-cultural communication in Chapter 8.

TEXT, DISCOURSE AND GENRE

In this chapter, text type has been assumed to be the single most important basis for the selection, grading and presentation of material. Now, while this may take care of aspects of text constitution such as the compositional plan and cohesion of texts, these do not exist in a vacuum.[2] A structural format or a cohesive pattern can only become operational by being appropriate to a given genre and even more significantly by being felicitous in relaying a given discoursal attitude. Thus, it becomes necessary at a second stage to refine our initial syllabus design by introducing discoursal and generic values. This second stage will be appropriate to a more advanced level of training.

Within the argumentation section, for example, the counter-argument may most naturally be seen to occur in the letter to the editor as a genre, and to display the committed discourse of, say, the monetarist or the Third World campaigner. Within exposition, the executive report may be presented in a Managing Director's Annual Statement (seen as a genre), in which a review of events (text) is subtly slanted to serve a particular set of attitudinal meanings (discourse). Finally, the individual articles in a legal document (a genre structure) could be selected from amongst those which adopt a diplomatic tone (discourse) in prohibiting, say, transgressions of human rights. This point can be put across most effectively by the choice of a particular mode of writing which may be classified as expository-instructional.

THE STATIC AND THE DYNAMIC

In putting together the kind of translator training materials described above, we have of necessity presented a somewhat idealized view of the rhetorical purpose of texts (e.g. counter-arguing), the attitudinal meanings of discourse (e.g. authoritativeness) and genre structures such as the 'preamble' in a legal document. To ensure that our categories reflect the reality of language use as consistently as possible, however, textual, discoursal and genre values should all be dealt with in a manner that captures the constant fluctuation of textual values within one and the same form, and the switching from one form to another.

These cases of marked and dynamic uses of language constitute stage three of our syllabus design and we have now to investigate the means to incorporate them into our scheme. Diagrammatically, the three stages of training may be represented as in Figure 11.4.

One way of introducing markedness in stage three would be to work with a checklist of departures from some norm. This list of situations giving rise to dynamic uses of language might include:

(a) hybridization of register
(b) opaqueness of intention
(c) shifts of genres
(d) competing discourses

STAGE 1

| Instructional | Expository | Argumentative |
| UNMARKED FORMS |

STAGE 2

Instructional   Expository   Argumentative   (Text)
Monetarist, Bureaucratic, etc.   (Discourse)
Letter To The Editor, Annual Report, etc.   (Genre)
UNMARKED FORMS

STAGE 3

Instructional   Expository   Argumentative   (Text)
Monetarist, Bureaucratic, etc.   (Discourse)
Letter To The Editor, Annual Report, etc.   (Genre)

Figure 11.4 A graded programme of presentation

(e) expectation-defying text structures
(f) marked texture.

For example, immediately after dealing with the instructional text type, or even in the course of presenting this component, a translation task involving register hybridization or marked texture may be helpful. Texts to use for this purpose could be drawn from the type of promotional literature which credit card companies or building societies, for instance, publish regularly (see Sample 11.4 above). These call for adjustment of strategy in mid-text and make the translator aware of the fact that uniformity of register may be an unattainable ideal and is often the exception rather than the rule. Within exposition, on the other hand, an example of how a report is made to serve at least two discourses other than the informative one may be helpful (see Sample 8.1). Finally, to 'dehumanize' by borrowing both legal and scientific discourse while engaging in a political argument about people's lives may be a good example of the way texts, discourses and genres can be hijacked and utilized outwith their natural habitat to relay all kinds of rhetorical effects (see Sample 11.3 or, for a different instance of competing discourse, Samples 9.4–9.6).

Here, we must stress that none of the stages or the categories within them should be assumed to be discrete, hermetic entities. Nor is the sequential order of the various stages static. Rather, what is involved in stages one, two and three should be viewed as a set of organizing principles which generally help us to avoid the randomness inherent in some approaches to curriculum design in translator training.

SUMMARY

In this chapter, we have explored possible applications of text linguistics to translator training. Syllabus design, with the advanced translator trainee in mind, was the main theme of the discussion and the basic question raised was: on what basis could the selection, grading and presentation of materials for the training of translators be carried out most effectively? It was argued that one way of tackling the issues involved in this area of translator training would be to adopt a text linguistic approach to the classification of texts.

The notion of 'rhetorical purpose' was used as the basis of a typology yielding a set of text types (e.g. argumentation), a number of major sub-types (e.g. the counter-argument) and a suggested list of text forms to illustrate the various categories and sub-categories (e.g. the objective counter-argument). To complement this primary categorization with a set of materials graded according to degree of evaluativeness, another scale was introduced to account for the degree of markedness envisaged primarily in terms of departures from norms.

This approach to curriculum design was essentially informed by a basic hypothesis, namely that different text types seem to place different demands on the translator, with certain types and forms being more demanding than others. The notion of 'demand' was defined in terms of the different translation procedures employed to meet different criteria of adequacy demanded by different text types.

Chapter 12

Assessing performance

The assessment of translator performance is an activity which, despite being widespread, is under-researched and under-discussed. Universities, specialized university schools of translating and interpreting, selectors of translators and interpreters for government service and international institutions, all set tests or competitions in which performance is measured in some way. Yet, in comparison with the proliferation of publications on the teaching of translating – and an emergent literature on interpreter training – little is published on the ubiquitous activity of testing and evaluation. Even within what has been published on the subject of evaluation, one must distinguish between the activities of assessing the quality of translations (e.g. House 1981), translation criticism and translation quality control on the one hand and those of assessing performance (e.g. Nord 1991: 160–3) on the other. But while all of these areas deserve greater attention, it is not helpful to treat them as being the same or even similar to each other since each has its own specific objectives (and consequences).

In this chapter, we shall concern ourselves only with issues relating to the evaluation of performance and, because of the vastness of the subject, we shall orientate our discussion mainly to the implications for performance evaluation of the hypotheses advanced in this book. For example, it will be apparent to the reader that some important issues in translating and interpreting, such as specialized terminology and documentation, have not been among our preoccupations. They are adequately covered in other publications. Correspondingly, we do not propose, in what follows, to consider methods for testing these particular translator/interpreter skills. But in each of Chapters 3 to 9 above, we have applied to some particular mode or field of translating activity an aspect or aspects of the model of communication presented in Chapter 2. In doing so, we have implicitly raised questions which are of relevance to the business of assessment. Moreover, Chapter 10 has shown how important it will be to incorporate beyond-the-sentence 'errors' into any scheme for assessment. Before we can consider these questions and make proposals in response to them, we need to have an appreciation of (1) what is unsatisfactory about the current situation of translator (and interpreter) testing; (2) what insights and principles from general theories of testing (including language testing in particular) need to be brought to bear on the design and implementation of tests; and (3) what proposals have been made from the perspective of translation studies for imposing some kind of order and systematicity on assessment procedures. In the light of these considerations, we shall then make some (necessarily tentative) suggestions for moving translator performance assessment in the direction of greater reliability and validity.[1]

WHAT'S WRONG NOW

We begin then with a brief expression of the unease felt by many at the unsystematic, hit-and-miss methods of performance evaluation which, it is assumed, are still in operation in many institutions. Nord (1991: 160–1) provides a challenging catalogue of what is unsatisfactory. She is critical of the practice of testing solely by means of the translation of an unseen written text and of selecting such texts on the basis of degree of difficulty alone.[2] Thus, all the skills involved in translating are tested at once and errors do not necessarily show which skill is deficient. Moreover, test-takers are often prevented from demonstrating one of their skills – their 'transfer competence' – simply because the source text is too difficult for them to analyse and understand properly. Meanwhile, if level of difficulty is the only criterion for text selection, then virtually any translation problem can occur in such texts. Thus, effectively, the test is uncoupled from the syllabus of what has been taught. (Attempts to link test to syllabus by the topic of the test text are invariably crude, given that topic is a poor predictor of the textural devices and structures which text producers actually use and of the rhetorical goals they pursue.) An additional criticism is that target texts produced by test takers give only a partial view of the thought processes and decision process they have gone through in arriving at their written response. It is consequently important to be clear about what any given test aims to assess.

To these points, several more may be added. It is still the case in some tests and competitions that no brief is given for the translation task to be accomplished. Thus, the purpose (*skopos*) remains unspecified and test takers are left to speculate what their examiner's goals might be. Meanwhile, testers have no agreed yardstick against which to judge performance of the task. It is perhaps partly because of this that 'error' becomes an all-or-nothing category, applied against some undefined absolute standard instead of responses being judged in terms of *degrees of acceptability for particular purposes*. We shall return below to the matter of what constitutes a translation error. At present, let us note the related tendency to assess by a 'points-off' system in which points are deducted from a total (presumably representing the worth of a perfect translation?) for each 'error' committed. This is at least an attempt to be systematic; but unfortunately, the tally resulting from such a calculation bears only a very indirect relation to the test taker's ability to translate. This is particularly so in that the estimation of what constitutes a 'grave error' (– 2 points?), a 'minor error' or a 'plus point' (+ 1? + 2?) remains very subjective, judged by some in terms of what the error reveals about language competence rather than about its consequences for a user of the translation.

Let us not pretend that there are easy solutions to problems such as these. As always, it is easier to diagnose than to suggest remedies. Nevertheless, the field of language testing has made considerable progress in recent decades – as have theories of testing and assessment in general – and it is surely time that some of the more basic insights from these disciplines be applied to the business of translator/interpreter performance assessment.

WHAT'S NEEDED

As Gipps (1994: 3) points out, the first question to be asked is: what is the assessment for? In any translator/interpreter training programme, an initial distinction needs to be made between **formative** and **summative assessment**. In formative assessment, the main aim is to provide a source of continuous feedback to teacher and learner concerning the progress of learning; that is, to support the learning process. Summative assessment, on the other hand, provides evidence for decision-making (fitness to proceed to next unit, to be awarded certification, a professional qualification, etc.) and takes place at the end of an instructional course (or course unit). What is important is that translation or interpreting exercises intended for the purpose of continuous feedback to trainees should not be conceived as a series of mini-examinations of a summative kind. In this way, a greater variety of exercise types can be introduced into the curriculum, providing for an heuristic approach to the development of skills.

Second, we need to distinguish between **proficiency testing** and **achievement testing** (see, e.g. Davies 1990: 6–7). In proficiency testing, one is concerned with judging the ability of the test taker to undertake a particular course of action, such as exercising as a professional interpreter or embarking on a translator training course. Achievement testing is based entirely on what has been taught in a particular curriculum. The relevance of this distinction is that, whereas an unseen written translation text of a particular level of difficulty might serve as a (kind of) proficiency test, its value as an achievement test is questionable in the terms of Nord's criticisms (see above). We believe that a greater role should be accorded to achievement testing, particularly at the intermediate stages of translator/interpreter training. After all, if the curriculum is not to be organized in a random fashion but designed on principles such as those advocated in Chapters 3 and 11, there is everything to be gained from increasing trainees' awareness of curriculum objectives and stages in skill development.

A further distinction concerns the way in which test performances are rated. **Norm-referenced assessment**, in which test takers are graded in relation to the performance of a given group or norm, may be seen as less useful for the purposes of translator/interpreter training than **criterion-referenced assessment**, in which test scores are interpreted with reference to a criterion level of ability. As Bachman (1990: 74) observes, criterion-referenced testing might typically mean that 'students are evaluated in terms of their relative degree of mastery of course content, rather than with respect to their relative ranking in the class'. One challenge in translation performance assessment, then, is to define levels of mastery of criteria in sufficiently objective terms for them to be usable by different testers in different situations. Some progress has been made in this direction.[3] This brings us to the notion of replicability; that is, the need to ensure that measurement of ability is based on procedures and rules that are sufficiently well defined to be replicable on different test occasions and/or by different testers. We are currently a long way from achieving this in translator performance assessment but initiatives which aim to increase the reliability of measurement should be encouraged.

To meet some of the criticisms noted above, one improvement might be to devise tests which seek to measure discrete skills (e.g. the ability to infer – cf. Chapter 5 – to handle idiolect – cf. Chapter 6) in the manner of objective tests.[4] This might counter some of the impressionism involved in judging translations. There is no reason why, particularly at formative stages, cloze tests, multiple-choice and other discrete-point testing methods should not be used for the purpose of assessing particular abilities and providing feedback to trainees. This would meet Hurtado's (1995) requirement that it should be learning objectives which provide the basis for test design. For example, one proposal has been to offer variant translations at discrete points in a complete target text, accompanied by its source text; candidates are asked to select the most appropriate formulation in terms of the purposes for which translation is required. In designing such a test, it would be necessary to ensure that (1) the variants offered are clearly and uncontroversially separated from each other in terms of appropriacy yet are not too obvious to present a challenge; (2) that the discrete points in the text are suitable for testing the particular ability (e.g. awareness of illocutionary force; ability to relay intertextual signals) to be measured; (3) that the discrete points are chosen to measure only that ability – i.e. that the test is valid; (4) that test takers are provided with all the extra-textual information necessary for making appropriate choices. This is of course no small task and, before investing the necessary effort in test design, testers would need to be convinced that the advantages in terms of feedback and skill development were sufficient. Moreover, the attempt to define and assess a uni-dimensional skill in isolation from other skills and other factors may to an extent be, as Gipps (1994: 71) suggests, artificial – especially in the case of translating if, as this book claims, texture is intimately bound up with the structure and indeed the entire context of texts. Prudence would suggest then that any objective testing of the kind outlined above should not replace but rather be complementary to the activity of translating whole texts.

'ERRORS' AND CATEGORIES OF ERROR

In translation studies, there is general agreement that a single, manageable set of categories for the classification of errors, transparent in use and diagnostic in relating an inadequacy to a translation procedure which may be learned, would be highly desirable. Several proposals have been made. Gouadec (1981), for example, provides an ambitious set of 'parameters', said to have an explanatory function and to measure the effect of an error in any particular text. With the entirely laudable aim of reducing the enormous element of subjectivity in translation performance assessment, he distinguishes and attaches a coded symbol to no fewer than 675 types of 'fault', allowing for a high degree of precision of analysis. To each parameter is then attributed a 'coefficient' corresponding to the gravity of the fault and set against a coefficient for the level of difficulty of the text. It is however doubtful that such a complex system is credible (i.e. likely to be used) or indeed that subjectivity can be eliminated in this mechanistic way. For example, the effect of an error has to be judged in terms of its incidence in the text in which it occurs and, text processing being a subjective and individual matter,[5] there is unlikely to be complete consistency between testers in the way the parameters are attributed and the gravity of an error is evaluated for a particular translation. Moreover, the system, for all its complexity, does not cater adequately for the assessment of semiotic and pragmatic values.

Sager (1983) proposes a much simpler grid, with a familiar classification by type of error:

- inversion of meaning
- omission
- addition
- deviation
- modification (unless justified by the translation specification).

This is similar to Gouadec's five categories within the parameter 'Nature of the fault' (*inversion, non-transfert, transfert partiel*, etc. – cf. Hurtado 1995, who also distinguishes source text comprehension from target text expression). But Sager's analysis by type is complemented by a three-way classification by effect of error:

- linguistic (does the error affect the main or a secondary part of sentence?)
- semantic (does the error affect the main argument or, e.g., an example?)
- pragmatic (does the error affect the intention in a significant or negligible way?)

This classification is useful in introducing a user dimension (Sager's whole analysis is concerned with quality and standards at a professional level) and in moving beyond the atomistic use of error categories at word or phrase level. Indeed, it is implicit in much of our analysis in this book (cf. Chapters 2 and 10) that judgements can only adequately be made when local occurrences are related to global requirements and global trends are seen to be reflected in local items. Perception of an ironic intention, for example, may not be assessable by attaching a symbol to an individual word or phrase in the test taker's target text since these local occurrences will merely support an overall pragmatic action. In such cases, it is beyond-the-sentence appropriateness which must be assessed (cf. Chapter 10). A crucial addition to the set of symbols used in marking scripts will therefore be a means of indicating the portion (item/phrase/sequence/text) of the entire response to which the symbol refers.

From our perspective, a flaw in each of the systems of assessment reviewed so far is their use of the term 'error' or (French) *faute*. As suggested earlier, this is not a helpful description for the majority of instances in which some measurable distinguishing feature might occur in a test response. For example, in judging the extent to which the source text values of reference-switching were or were not relayed in four published translations of Sample 7.1, there is no sense in which 'error' would have been an appropriate term to use. Rather, translators' choices may be seen as more or less appropriate for the particular purposes to be served.[6] The term error may then be reserved for two categories of actual mistake made by translators and referred to by House (1981) as 'overt errors', namely (1) significant (unmotivated) mismatches of denotational meaning between source and target text (subdivided into omissions, additions and substitutions); and (2) breaches of the target-language system (e.g. orthography, grammar). In all other cases, it is a matter of making judgements about the relative acceptability of the range of options from which the translator chooses.[7] Such judgements can, of course, never be completely objectivized. But those who are professionally involved in translating might expect to achieve a considerable degree of consensus in assessing the relative adequacy of variant translations – especially if, as suggested earlier, a well-defined focus is provided for each translation task set as a test. This might involve, for example, specifying an initiator and an end-use or status for the resulting translation.[8] Thus, in the case of text samples 9.4–6 quoted in Chapter 9, where significant divergence between source and target texts (Le Roy Ladurie's *Montaillou*) was noted, the translator's decisions can only be judged against whatever brief the translator was given, including the need to produce a selective reduction of the source text,[9] suitable for publication in paperback for the British market. In this sense, *skopos* (Reiss and Vermeer 1984) includes both specification of task and what we have referred to (cf. Chapters 4 and 5) as **audience design**.

DEFINING TRANSLATOR ABILITIES

It is perhaps appropriate at this stage to remind ourselves that we drew a clear line at the beginning of the chapter between translation quality assessment and translator performance assessment. The reminder is necessary because it is the quality of translations which is the subject of some of the works (Gouadec 1981; House 1981; Sager 1983) referred to in the previous section. Now, the ability to handle task specification and audience design, mentioned above, constitutes an important translator skill; it is teachable and should therefore also be testable. How then does this skill fit within the range of skills required of translators and how might we, for the purposes of testing, arrive at a workable taxonomy of translator abilities?

Hewson (1995) distinguishes translators' linguistic competence and their cultural competence, illustrating the latter by showing how cultural expectations for a particular genre (information for users accompanying medicines in the UK and in France) require considerable translator mediation. He proposes that positive points should be awarded in assessment for evidence that the test taker has correctly identified a translation problem of this order, before weighting is given to the particular solution adopted. In this way, cultural competence is always assessed and not obscured by any target language grammatical error, say, which happens to occur at the same juncture in the text. In addition to linguistic and cultural competences, Nord (1991) lists 'transfer' competence and 'factual and research' competence. These are, of course, important components of the translator's set of skills and it is an obvious (yet sometimes neglected) point that no amount of testing by means of an unseen written text without use of reference works will provide evidence of translators' research and reference skill.

An alternative approach provides some additions to and a different perspective upon the translator abilities so far identified.

Bachman's (1990) analysis of communicative language ability identifies three broad categories of knowledge and skills,[10] namely,
organizational competence (including grammatical competence and
textual competence); pragmatic competence (including illocutionary
competence and sociolinguistic competence, this latter including
register, dialect, etc.); strategic competence (judging relevance,
effectiveness and efficiency; forming plans for the achievement of
communicative goals). This analysis is comparable to aspects of
the model outlined in Chapter 2 and, drawing on both analyses
and incorporating the translation-specific points mentioned earlier,
we arrive at the set of translator abilities listed in Figure 12.1. The
division into a three-stage process (source text processing/
transfer/target text processing) is to some extent artificial, given that
these activities are at least partly concurrent. For example, knowledge of the task and notions of target text audience design may
well precede processing of the source text. Moreover, categories
overlap and the items listed are mutually influential. The rhetorical
purpose listed under transfer skills will have been determined during

source text PROCESSING SKILLS	TRANSFER SKILLS	target text PROCESSING SKILLS
Recognizing **intertextuality** (genre/discourse/text)	Strategic re-negotiation by adjusting:	Establishing **intertextuality** (genre/discourse/text)
Locating **situationality** (register, etc.)	**effectiveness** **efficiency** **relevance**	Establishing **situationality** (register, etc.)
Inferring **intentionality**		Creating **intentionality**
Organising **texture** (lex. choice synt. arrangement cohesion) and **structure**	to: **audience design** **task** (brief, initiator, etc.) in fulfilment of a:	Organising **texture** (lex. choice synt. arrangement cohesion) and **structure**
Judging **informativity** (static/dynamic)	**rhetorical purpose** (plan, goal)	Balancing **informativity** (static/dynamic)
in terms of estimated impact on: **source text readership**		in terms of estimated impact on: **target text readership**

Figure 12.1 Translator abilities

source text processing and will, in turn, determine target text processing. In short, each skill interacts with each other skill. Nevertheless, there is everything to be gained from a checklist such as Figure 12.1 from the point of view of designing tests and programmes of tests.

Much of what is involved in each of these categories has been discussed in earlier chapters. See, for example, the breakdown of requirements in relaying intertextuality at the end of Chapter 6 (Figure 6.2); the ability to reassess informativity in a target language cultural environment (Chapter 7). It is also interesting to compare the list of skills with the principles of a text-based syllabus design as outlined in Chapter 11 (or, in the case of interpreting, with the hypotheses in Chapter 3). Competent handling of mainly **static** texts, for example, constitutes a stage in the syllabus and a stage of proficiency to be tested. Ability to adjust for audience design and for task but still relay, say, an evaluative rhetorical purpose would likewise be a trainable and testable skill. In an achievement test, a table of specifications for the test (i.e. what we want to measure) should be devised before the test itself is set. A marking scheme based on these specifications would determine the weighting to be attached to the measurement of particular skills, as evidenced in the response to identified problems. A corollary of this is that, especially in formative testing, any shortcomings in a response which are not relatable to the skills specified for the test would not be penalized.[11] In essence, the test specification might single out translation problems identified in advance, including especially discourse/text-level problems of the kind discussed in Chapter 10.

TRANSLATORS' DECISIONS AS EVIDENCE OF KNOWLEDGE AND SKILLS

As soon as any checklist of the kind of Figure 12.1 is applied to the assessment of any translation submitted as a response in a test, problems will be encountered. These relate to the fact that the response itself, if it is a translated text, provides imperfect evidence of skills and deficiencies. This point can be illustrated from text Sample 12.1, in which selected trainee responses to a particular set of problems in translating an EU directive are exemplified.

Sample 12.1

Article 2	Article 2
Les Etats membres **prennent** toute mesure utile pour que ne soient distribués sur leur territoire que des médicaments pour lesquels une autorisation de mise sur le marché conforme au droit communautaire a été délivrée.	Member states **take** **are taking** **must take** **shall take** every necessary precaution to ensure that the only drugs distributed are those for which authorization subject to Community law has been granted.

Leaving aside other potential problems in this translated fragment, we shall focus on the form of the verb *take* in four test responses. Given the genre specification of the source text (a directive) and the brief (to produce a translation which might stand as an official translation with full legal status), it is apparent that only the response *shall take* may be regarded as adequate. Of the other responses, *must take* has at least the merit of relaying the appropriate illocutionary force (intentionality) but is inappropriate in terms of both genre and modality, while *take* and *are taking* are (informatively) misleading. It is in diagnosing the shortcoming, however, that the main problem is encountered. The inadequacy may be due to faulty source text processing (failure to recognize intertextuality, to locate situationality or to process texture, i.e. the particular use of the present tense in the source text) or it may be due to faulty target text processing (unawareness of the performative value of *shall take* in legal English) or, indeed, to a failure of strategic renegotiation at the transfer stage (insufficient appreciation of the brief). All those involved in translation teaching and testing are familiar with this kind of diagnostic problem. Still, certain points can be made with a fair degree of confidence. First, the source text set in the test includes a whole series of present tenses with the value of deontic modality so that only a complete failure in relating source text texture to source text intertextuality (instructional text type) would result in reiteration of the descriptive *are taking* form in the test response. Second, the response *must take* does show an awareness of the source text illocution and, if the form is reiterated in response to further source text tokens of the same kind, there is greater cumulative evidence of unawareness of target language intertextual norms than of faulty source text processing. Finally, responses to other source text tokens signalling performative speech acts may be matched to the responses *take/are taking/must take* to see whether source text intentionality is being perceived. For example, if a sequence in the same document:

> Aux fins de la présente directive, la définition du médicament **donnée** à l'article 1er ... est applicable.
> [For the purposes of this directive, the definition of the term drug shall be that **laid down** in Article 1.]

elicits the response:

> ... the definition ... is as **mentioned** in Article 1
> (emphasis added)

and this response co-occurs with a series of verbs of the form *take*, then there is evidence that the primarily deficient skill lies in the area of source text processing.

In other words, instead of underlining the item *take* and classifying it as an 'error in the use of tenses' or some such descriptor, it is important to relate items of evidence to each other in order to build a profile of the deployment of skills in the test response.

Nevertheless, it may be found more practical to create single testing categories of intertextuality, intentionality, etc., in order to avoid ascribing any given inadequate response to either source text or target text processing. There are definite advantages in formative testing to providing feedback which distinguishes between these two phases of processing; but in summative testing, where no feedback is to be given, it will not be strictly necessary to show that a shortcoming is due to one stage or the other – or to both.

DESCRIPTIVE PROFILES

Gipps (1994: 85) suggests that aggregate information (the collapsing of a set of individual test scores into a single figure) is less informative about an individual's level of performance than a descriptive profile of skill mastery. Thus, one might imagine that in translator/interpreter performance assessment, for each of the skill areas selected from the checklist (Figure 12.1) by the test designer, a mastery classification could be used. For example, on a five-point scale, a rating of five would indicate complete mastery, a rating of one total absence of mastery and a rating of three the minimal level of mastery consistent with, e.g., proceeding to the next course module without the need for remedial work. The major advantage of such profiles is that they provide far more usable feedback information than a numerical score for the whole translation, however arrived at.

CRITERION REFERENCING

The set of criteria devised for referencing test results would be similar to this. For the purposes of summative testing, the mastery criteria could relate to overall skills and the ratings could be determined by performance in a number of tests and continuous assessment tasks. The terms in which the criteria are couched would be closely related to curriculum objectives. For example, if the end-of-course objective is a level of proficiency compatible with exercising as a professional translator/interpreter, then criterion-referenced assessment would be devised in terms of degrees of mastery of that level of ability. If responding to, say, register variables is an intermediate curriculum objective, then mastery of this skill would be an explicit testing criterion. In practice, a five-point scale or something similar should suffice. Gipps (1994: 93) reports a current move away from over-specification in criterion-referenced testing, manageability being the operative factor.

Let us now look at a further example, to explore how some of the ideas put forward in this chapter might work in practice. In Chapter 4, we considered part of an EU parliamentary speech from the angle of simultaneous interpreting. Now, we shall imagine the same text being set as a written translation test, in which the situational circumstances of the source text are specified and the brief is to produce a translation to stand as an official record. For convenience, the text is reproduced below as Sample 12.2.

Sample 12.2

[. . .] Depuis lors, les administrateurs judiciaires – dans le cas de Leyland-Daf, *the receivers* – dirigent les sociétés et ont réussi, sur la base de financements à court terme, à relancer la production qui s'était arrêtée après l'effondrement financier de Daf.

Le lundi 8 février, la presse a publié un plan de restructuration qui aurait été préparé par les administrateurs judiciaires de Daf aux Pays-Bas, sur la base d'études effectuées par deux sociétés de conseil, l'une spécialisée en gestion et l'autre en comptabilité.

Sur base de ces études, un plan de restructuration a été élaboré, qui prévoit la création d'une nouvelle société anonyme qui absorberait la totalité des activités de Daf aux Pays-Bas et en Belgique dans le secteur de la construction des camions et des poids-lourds, ainsi que, peut-être, des opérations d'assemblage de Leyland-Daf à Leyland au Lancashire. Ce plan entraînerait également d'importantes suppressions d'emplois, estimées à plus de 5000 postes, ainsi que la fermeture de certains sites au Royaume-Uni. Les communiqués de presse indiquent qu'un financement de l'ordre de 1,5 milliard de florins serait nécessaire au cours de la période 1993–1995. A la suite d'une demande adressée par la Commission, les autorités néerlandaises ont précisé, le 10 février, que les parties concernées ne s'étaient pas encore complètement entendues sur le plan de restructuration, dont certains éléments doivent être examinés ultérieurement. Dans ces conditions, toute déclaration sur ce dossier présente pour le moment un caractère provisoire.

Déjà avant l'effondrement de Daf, la DG IV avait examiné deux cas d'aides non notifiées concernant un financement à court terme que les gouvernements néerlandais et flamand avaient accordé. Ces deux gouvernements ont annoncé qu'ils apporteraient encore leur soutien, à condition que toutes les parties arrivent à un accord sur un plan de restructuration complet. Etant donné que cela entraînerait certainement d'importantes aides d'Etat, la DG IV suit l'affaire avec attention. [. . .]

In designing the test, the first step will then be to draw up a table of specifications – i.e. what the tester proposes to assess. In addition to the broad macro-skills of source text processing, transfer and target text processing, the tester may wish to identify selected features corresponding to skills or knowledge which have figured in the (part of the) curriculum to which the test refers. Let us imagine that in our sample case, it is the processing of intentionality which is under particular scrutiny. What might then feature in the test specification is ability to relay the veiled remonstrance implicated in the source text by such elements as:

> *qui aurait été préparé . . . absorberait . . . entraînerait . . .* (conditionals of allegation)

with later collocations, jointly indicating a discourse of diplomatic complaint:

les communiqués de presse indiquent . . . [press communiqués suggest]
A la suite d'une demande adressée par la Commission . . . [following a request from the Commission]
Déjà . . . deux cas non notifiés . . . [two previous cases which had not been notified]
La DG IV suit l'affaire avec attention . . . [the DG IV is following the matter closely]

The marking grid for the test would then determine the credit to be given for competent handling of this intentionality, particularly in the case of the conditional of allegation which initiates this discourse, dynamically intruding into a more static narrative account. At the level of the text, the assessment grid might require testers, in respect of the selected criteria, to indicate as a response to the question: 'Has criterion X been met?' either 'Yes', 'Partly' or 'No'. Such forms of rating might accompany a more traditional numerical assessment and mitigate the relative unreliability of the latter.

SUMMARY

In this chapter various recommendations have been made which, although they are far from sufficient for the purpose of ensuring complete reliability and validity in translation testing, may assist in promoting a more systematic approach in which testing is less random. We have suggested (1) that as testers our first task is to determine what purpose a test is to serve and that formative assessment should generally be distinguished from summative assessment; (2) that in formative assessment, discrete-point testing (multiple-choice, cloze) and discrete-skill testing (e.g. via a commentary which the test taker submits with a translation) are feasible and can provide useful feedback; (3) that testing procedures be as explicit as possible; (4) that, for this purpose, useful tools are a table of translator skills (cf. Figure 12.1), a test specification indicating particular skills/features to be tested, an assessment grid closely geared to the specification and a set of criterion-related grades which avoid norm-referenced expression ('above average', 'outstanding') and define levels of mastery of criteria; (5) that for purposes of feedback a descriptive profile may be of greater assistance to the trainee than a numerical score; (6) that the term 'error' be restricted to significant mismatches of denotational meaning or breaches of the target language system and that all else in translations be judged in terms of adequacy for intended purposes.

Taken together, our three pedagogical chapters (10, 11, 12) make a plea for greater consideration to be afforded to text-level issues (genre, discourse, text type) in curriculum design, monitoring of trainees' output and in testing. We hope to have shown that organizing principles such as markedness (the static and the dynamic), evaluativeness (monitoring and managing) and the interrelatedness of context, structure and texture can be useful in avoiding hit-and-miss approaches to translator and/or interpreter training.

Glossary

absent discourse: a discourse of an absent individual or group which is invoked but not explicitly attributed. This rhetorical hijacking may serve a variety of purposes such as subtle appeal to authority or indeed irony. For example, an actual slogan once used by the Conservative party in Britain – 'power to the people' – invokes the discourse of an ideology the party abhors; in this case the absent discourse is that of Marxism invoked to be parodied.

achievement testing: the kind of testing which measures how much someone has learned with reference to a particular programme of instruction. **Proficiency testing**, on the other hand, posits no such reference to, say, a given course of study.

action process: see **transitivity**

actual: see **virtual**

addressee: see **audience design**

appropriateness: see **effectiveness**

argumentation: a text type in which concepts and/or beliefs are evaluated. Two basic forms of argumentation may be distinguished: **counter-argumentation** in which a thesis is cited, then opposed; and **through-argumentation** in which a thesis is cited, then extensively defended. Counter-arguments can be **lopsided** (the concession is explicitly signalled by the use of *although, while*, etc.), or can take the form of a **balance** (the opposition is introduced explicitly or implicitly by the use of adversatives such as *but, however*, etc.). The balance is also known as the **straw-man gambit**.

audience design: the adaptation of output by text producers to the perceived receiver group. Central to this notion is the extent to which speakers accommodate to their addressees and how speech style is affected. Four potential categories of text receiver have been identified: **addressee**s are known to the speaker and are directly addressed as ratified participants in the speech event (e.g. students of religious seminaries in Sample 9.1). **Auditor**s are both known to the speaker and ratified participants but they are not directly addressed (e.g. listeners to Tehran radio in Sample 9.1). **Overhearer**s are known by the speaker to be present but are neither ratified participants nor directly addressed (e.g. the Islamic nation). **Eavesdropper**s are those of whose presence the speaker is unaware (it could be suggested that the *Guardian* is an eavesdropper on Khomeini's address).

auditor: see **audience design**

aural text: see **visual text**

balance: see argumentation

bottom-up: see top-down

breaking a maxim: see the cooperative principle

coherence: see cohesion

cohesion: the requirement that a sequence of sentences realizing a >* **text** display grammatical and/or lexical relationships which ensure surface structure continuity. For example, in the exchange:

A: Where have you been?
B: To the Empire.

there is an implicit link between *have been* and *to the Empire* which accounts for the cohesiveness of the sequence. **Coherence**, on the other hand, requires that the grammatical and/or lexical relationships involve underlying conceptual relations and not only continuity of forms. Thus, the > **ellipsis** in the above exchange could conceivably be used to relay 'marital tension'. Coherence relations thus exist between co-communicants in a context of utterance.

communicative: see **context**

compensation: a set of translation procedures aimed at making up for the loss of relevant features of meaning in the source text by reproducing the overall effect in the target language.

connotation: additional meanings which a lexical item acquires beyond its primary, referential meaning, e.g. *notorious* means

---

* The symbol > stands for 'see the term indicated'. This is fully defined elsewhere in the Glossary.

'famous' but with negative connotations. **Denotations**, on the other hand, cover primary referential meanings of a given lexical item.

consecutive interpreting: see **liaison interpreting**

context: the extra-textual environment which exerts a determining influence on the language used. The subject matter of a given text is part of > **register** and can thus determine, say, the way the text presents who is doing what to whom (> **transitivity**). Three domains of context may be distinguished:

- a **communicative** domain, including > **register membership**;
- a **pragmatic** domain, covering > **intentionality**;
- a **semiotic** domain, accounting for > **intertextuality**.

the cooperative principle: the assumption that interlocutors cooperate with each other by observing certain so-called **conversational maxims**. These are:

- **quantity**:   give as much information as is needed;
- **quality**:   speak truthfully;
- **relevance**:   say what is relevant;
- **manner**:   avoid ambiguity.

However, these maxims may be **broken** (inadvertently) or apparently **violated** (when the > **deviation from the norm** of adhering to them is not communicated properly). In such cases, there would be no indirect meaning or **implicature** to be detected. Implicatures only arise when the maxims are **flouted** (i.e. not adhered to for a good reason). Thus, to say 'I am voting for Reagan because Carter is the evil of two lessers' could be

(a) a case of breaking the maxim of manner if uttered by someone who gets the idiomatic saying mixed up; or

(b) a case of violation if said to someone who is not aware of the original idiomatic saying; or

(c) a case of flouting giving rise to an implicature which might be something like 'it is all a charade and not worth talking about'.

co-text: the sounds, words or phrases preceding and/or following a particular linguistic item in an utterance. This may be compared with the > **context** enveloping that particular utterance.

counter-argument: see **argumentation**

criterion-referenced assessment: the kind of assessment which measures a candidate's performance according to a predetermined criterion or standard. A **norm-referenced** test, on the other hand, would measure how the performance of a particular candidate compares with that of (an)other candidate(s) whose score is taken as a norm.

cultural code: a system of ideas which conceptually enables > **denotative** meanings to take on extra > **connotative** meanings and thus become key terms in the thinking of a certain group of text users, ultimately contributing to the development of > **discourse**.

defamiliarization: the use of some strategy to make us pay attention to some peculiar use of certain modes of linguistic expression.

denotation: see **connotation**

deviation from the norm: norms subsume what is conventionally considered appropriate in speech or writing for a particular situation or purpose. These are sometimes deviated from for a 'good-reason' mostly to do with pursuing a particular rhetorical aim. For example, instead of an expected > **argument**, the text producer may opt for an > **expository** narrative. Such expectation-defying choice is normally more interesting and highly > **dynamic**. See > **the cooperative principle**, and > **informativity**.

directive: see **illocutionary act**

discourse: modes of speaking and writing which involve social groups in adopting a particular attitude towards areas of socio-cultural activity (e.g. racist discourse, bureaucratese, etc.).

distance: see **politeness**

double-accentuation: see **dynamic, deviation**

dynamic: a use of language that essentially involves a motivated > **deviation** from some norm. An unexpected form or textual convention is **hijacked** from its natural habitat and used in some less familiar textual environment. The latter would thus be **double accentuated** for rhetorical effect. For example, the satirical tone of Laurie Taylor on the back page of the *THES* stems primarily from borrowing the most unlikely genres, discourses and text formats for the occasion being addressed.

eavesdropper: see **audience design**

effectiveness: alongside standards which define and create textual communication (e.g. > **cohesion, coherence,**

intertextuality, etc.), a number of principles which control textual communication have been identified. These include **efficiency** (communicating with minimum expenditure of effort by participants), **effectiveness** (creating favourable conditions for the attainment of goals) and **appropriateness** (the compatibility of communication with setting and with the ways standards of textuality are generally upheld).

efficiency: see **effectiveness**

ellipsis: the omission (for reasons of rhetorically and/or linguistically motivated economy) of linguistic material whose sense is recoverable from > **context** or > **co-text**.

evaluativeness: the comparison or assessment of concepts, belief systems, etc. It is the determining factor in distinguishing > **argumentation** from > **exposition**.

event process: see **transitivity**

explication: in translation, the addition of extra material with an explanatory function. For example, the English word 'interference' in the following sentence used in a legal text is self-explanatory: 'Any person engaged in unauthorized broadcasting may be prosecuted before the court of any State where authorized radio communication is suffering interference.' In Arabic translation, the concept of 'interference' has to be explicated as follows: [. . . interference from such unauthorized broadcasting].

exposition: a text type in which concepts, objects or events are presented in a > **non-evaluative** manner. Three basic forms of exposition may be distinguished: **description** (focusing on objects spatially viewed), **narration** (focusing on events temporally viewed) and **conceptual exposition** (focusing on the detached analysis of concepts).

expressive: see **illocutionary act**

face: in the > **pragmatic** theory of > **politeness**, face involves the positive image which one shows or intends to show of oneself (positive politeness) and the desire to be unimpeded in achieving one's goals (negative politeness).

face threatening act (**FTA**): see **politeness**

field of discourse: see **metafunctions, register**

flouting a maxim: see **the cooperative principle**

foregrounding: the process of making an item or items prominent by manipulating word order, opting for overlexicalization, etc.

formative assessment: an activity in which the tests or other forms of assessment are used primarily as a teaching technique.

Feedback from the teacher enables students to learn from their mistakes and successes. **Summative assessment**, on the other hand, is an activity in which the tests or other forms of assessment are used solely to measure a student's abilities or potential capabilities.

free translation: see **literal translation**

functional sentence perspective: the assumption that a sentence is to be viewed within a particular communicative perspective, in which, in the unmarked form, what is mentioned first (> **theme**) is normally of less communicative importance than what follows (> **rheme**).

genre: conventional forms of texts associated with particular types of social occasion (e.g. the news report, the editorial, the cooking recipe). Within a given genre, subsidiary genres may be identified. For example, A Letter to the Editor may employ a number of sub-genres such as the 'auctioneer's falling gavel *going, going, gone*'.

heuristic: a set of analytic principles that rely on variable and not categorical rules, that help us to learn about and discover things in texts as we go along and that rely on hypotheses and options to be confirmed or disconfirmed in the light of unfolding textual evidence.

hijacking: see **dynamic**

hypotactic: see **paratactic**

ideational meaning: see **metafunctions**

ideology: a body of assumptions which reflects the beliefs and interests of an individual, a group of individuals, a societal institution, etc., and which ultimately finds expression in language. For example, the headline *Girl 7 killed while mum was drinking in pub* relays a particular ideological stance towards men and women which the newspaper in question adopts and propagates (see > **discourse**).

illocutionary act: using the sentence to perform a function which fulfils the **force** of an utterance. A **representative** act, for example, seeks to represent a state of affairs (stating, insisting); a **verdictive** evaluates and relays judgement (assessing, estimating); an **expressive** gives expression to the speaker's mental or emotional attitude (deploring, admiring); a **directive** seeks to influence text receivers' behaviour (ordering, requesting).

implicature: see **the cooperative principle**

imposition: see **politeness**

informativity: the degree of unexpectedness which an item or an utterance displays in some context. See > **deviation from the norm**.

instruction: a text type in which the focus is on the formation of future behaviour, either 'with option' as in advertising or 'without option' as in legal instruction (e.g. treaties, resolutions, contracts, etc.).

intention process: see **transitivity**

intentionality: a feature of context which determines the appropriateness of a linguistic form to the achievement of a > **pragmatic** purpose.

interpersonal meaning: see **metafunctions**

intertextuality: a precondition for the intelligibility of texts, involving the dependence of one text as a semiotic entity upon another, previously encountered, text. However, the intertextual reference, instead of evoking an image, can preclude it, parody it, or signify its exact opposite. This may be illustrated from the tactics of some political speakers using the opponent's terminology for their own ends.

langue: this refers to language as a system (e.g. grammar, vocabulary). When this is put to use, we are in the domain of *parole* which subsumes what we as speakers might say or understand.

liaison interpreting: a form of oral interpreting in which two speakers who do not know each other's language or know it imperfectly communicate through an interpreter, normally in spontaneous conversational settings. **Consecutive interpreting** involves the interpreter in taking notes of what is being said. At the end of each fairly large chunk of speech (or an entire speech), the interpreter gives an oral translation (normally in a reduced form) with or without the help of notes. **Simultaneous interpreting** is conducted in special booths where the interpreter listens through earphones and sometimes watches what is going on. As the speaker's statement proceeds, it is translated simultaneously into the other language. **On-sight translating** involves the immediate oral relay of the contents of a written source text.

literal translation: a rendering which preserves surface aspects of the message both semantically and syntactically, adhering closely to source text mode of expression. **Free translation**, on the other hand, modifies surface expression and keeps intact only deeper levels of meaning. The choice of either method of translation is determined by text properties to do with text type, purpose of translation, etc.

locutionary act: a distinction is made in > **speech act theory** between a **locutionary act** (the act of saying something – e.g. 'It is hot in here'), an **illocutionary act** (what is intended by the locutionary act – e.g. 'please open the window'), and a **perlocutionary act** (what the ultimate effect could be said to be – e.g. 'demonstrating who is the boss around here').

lopsided argument: see **argumentation**

macro-sign: see **sign**

managing: see **monitoring**

manner: see **the cooperative principle**

marked: see **unmarked**

material process: see **transitivity**

maxim: see **the cooperative principle**

mediation: the process of incorporating into the processing of utterances and texts one's own assumptions, beliefs, etc.

mental process: see **transitivity**

metafunctions: these are not to be seen as functions in the sense of 'uses of language', but as functional components of the semantic system. They are modes of meaning that are present in every use of language. Thus, the **ideational** function, which emanates from > **field of discourse**, represents the speaker's meaning potential as an observer: language is about something (e.g. *Ten Blacks Shot By Police* and *Police Shoot Ten Blacks* are two different ideational structures, one catering for a white perspective, the other for a black perspective). The **interpersonal** component, which emanates from > **tenor of discourse**, represents the speaker's meaning potential as an intruder: language as doing something (e.g. different uses of > **modality** relay different interpersonal meanings). Finally, the **textual** component, which emanates from > **mode of discourse**, represents the speaker's text-forming potential: how language is made both relevant and operational (e.g. choices of what occupies the slot > **theme** in the text is an orchestrating, textual consideration).

micro-sign: see **sign**

modality: expressing distinctions such as that between 'possibility' and 'actuality', and, in the process, indicating an attitude towards the state or event involved (e.g. 'may', 'must').

mode of discourse: see **metafunctions**, **register**

monitoring: expounding in a non-evaluative manner. This is in contrast with > **managing**, which involves steering the discourse towards speaker's goals.

mood: the basic choice we make between using a statement, a question or a command. This choice is not without significance in the analysis of > **ideology** and > **interpersonal meaning**.

motivatedness: the set of factors which rhetorically regulate text users' choices, whether conscious or unconscious.

negative politeness strategies: see **politeness**

nominalization: the condensed reformulation of a verbal process and the various participants involved as a noun phrase. This is an important grammatical resource for the expression of > **ideology**. For example, when saying *The net inflow is* . . ., the speaker can get round having to recognize the fact that it is 'immigrants who flow into this country in large numbers'.

non-evaluativeness: see **evaluativeness**

norm: see **deviation**

norm-referenced assessment: see **criterion-referenced assessment**

on-sight translation: see **liaison interpreting**

opposition: see **text structure**

overhearer: see **audience design**

paradigmatic: the 'vertical' relationship between forms which might occupy the same place in a structure (e.g. He walked *quickly / as fast as he could*). Syntagmatic relations, on the other hand, occupy the 'horizontal' axis and obtain between linguistic elements forming linear sequences (e.g. *come <> quickly*).

paratactic: pertaining to the joining together of sentences or clauses by juxtaposition. As used in this book, parataxis is extended to include cases where the links may be established with or without the use of connectives, but the dominant connectivity relationship is 'coordination' (e.g X and Y or X,Y). **Hypotactic** relations, on the other hand, restrict the connectivity to those links achieved through 'subordination' (X which is . . .).

parole: see *langue*

perlocutionary act: see **locutionary act**

physical proximity: see **register**, **mode**, **metafunction**

plan: a global pattern representing how events and states lead up to the attainment of a goal. Plans are predominantly utilized in putting together > **argumentative** texts.

politeness: a > **pragmatic** theory which is centered on the notion of > **face**, that is, the attempt to establish, maintain and save face during interaction with others. Two main factors regulate the degree of **imposition** which is ideally kept at a minimum: >

power and **distance**. In handling the latter, two basic sets of strategies are in use: **positive politeness strategies** (those which show intimacy between speaker and hearer) and **negative politeness strategies** (those which underline social distance between participants). Any irregularity in handling power and/or distance would result in compromising the degree of imposition in a wide range of what is known as **face threatening acts** (**FTAs**).

positive politeness strategies: see **politeness**

power: in the analysis of > **politeness**, > **tenor** or, more specifically > **interpersonal meaning**, two basic types of relationship may be distinguished: **power** and **solidarity**. Power emanates from the text producer's ability to impose his or her plans at the expense of the text receiver's plans. Solidarity, on the other hand, is the willingness of the text producer genuinely to relinquish power and work with his or her interlocutors as members of a team. Particular choices within > **mood** and > **modality** are relevant to the expression of either power or solidarity.

pragmatics: the domain of **intentionality** or the purposes for which utterances are used in real contexts.

presupposition: what the text producer assumes the receiver already knows.

proficiency testing: see **achievement testing**

pronominal switching: see **reference switching**

propositional content: the content involved in saying something that is meaningful and can be understood. Not included here is the function which the particular sentence performs in some specified context. For example, within propositional content analysis, *It is hot in here* would be analysed as a comment on the temperature of the room and not, say, an attempt to get someone to open the window.

quality: see **the cooperative principle**

quantity: see **the cooperative principle**

reference switching: the rhetorically-motivated change from use of an expected, norm-upholding linguistic form (pronoun, tense, gender or definiteness markers, etc.) to one which is expectation-defying. For example, *You delivered me* uttered as a prayer for deliverance.

register: the set of features which distinguishes one stretch of language from another in terms of variation in > **context** to do with the language user (geographical dialect, idiolect, etc.) and/or language use (> **field** or subject matter, > **tenor** or level of formality and > **mode** or speaking vs. writing).

relational process: see **transitivity**

relevance as a maxim: see **the cooperative principle**

representative: see **illocutionary act**

rheme: see **functional sentence perspective**

rhetorical purpose: see **text**

scenario: see **schema**

scene-setter: see **text structure**

schema: a global pattern representing the underlying structure of a text. A story schema or **scenario**, for example, may consist of a setting and a number of episodes, each of which would include events and reactions. Schema are predominantly utilized in putting together texts of the > **expository narrative** type.

script: a global pattern realized by units of meaning that consist of events and actions related to particular situations. For example, a text may be structured around the 'restaurant script' which represents our knowledge of how restaurants work: waitresses, cooks, tables where customers sit, peruse menus, order their meals and pay the bill at the end. Scripts are predominantly utilized in putting together texts of the > **expository descriptive** type.

semiotics: a dimension of context which regulates the relationship of texts or parts of texts to each other as signs. Semiotics thus relies on the interaction not only between speaker and hearer but also between speaker/hearer and their texts, and between text and text. This > **intertextuality** is governed by a variety of **socio-cultural** factors (e.g. > **politeness**), and > **rhetorical purpose**, yielding in the process a set of socio-cultural **objects** with which the social life of given linguistic communities are normally identified (e.g. the concept of 'honour' to an Argentinian). These factors and conventions are ultimately responsible for the way the **socio-textual** practices develop within a given community of text users (e.g. the norms of news reporting). (See > **genre**, > **text**, > **discourse**.)

sign: a unit of signification in which the linguistic form (signifier) stands for a concrete object or concept (**signified**). When the notion of sign is extended to include anything which means something to somebody in some respect or capacity, signs can then be said to refer to cultural objects such as *honour* (**micro-signs**), as well as to more global structures such as text, genre and discourse (**macro-signs**).

simultaneous interpreting: see **liaison interpreting**

situationality: see **register**

social distance: see **register, tenor, metafunction**

socio-cultural objects: see **semiotics**

socio-textual practices: see **semiotics**

solidarity: see **power**

speech act theory: see **locutionary act**

staging: see **thematic progression**

static: see **dynamic**

straw-man gambit: see **argumentation**

structure: see **text structure**

sub-genre: see **genre**

substantiation: see **text structure**

summative assessment: see **formative assessment**

supervention process: see **transitivity**

syntagmatic: see **paradigmatic**

tenor of discourse: see **metafunctions, register**

tense switching: see **reference switching**

text: a set of mutually relevant communicative functions that hang together (> **texture**) and are constructed (> **structure**) in such a way as to respond to a particular > **context** and thus achieve an overall > **rhetorical purpose**.

text hybridization: text types are rarely, if ever, pure. More than one text type focus is normally discernible. In such cases, one and only one focus will be predominant, the others being subsidiary or even marginal.

text structure: the compositional plan of a text. Different > **text types** exhibit different structure formats. Some of these are formulaic as in the structure of the **preamble**: *X and Y, having met . . ., Considering, Re-emphasizing, . . . have agreed . . .*.

text type: the way > **texts** > **structure** and > **texture** are made to respond to > **context** and to display a particular focus. Three basic text type focuses may be distinguished: > **exposition**, > **argumentation** and > **instruction**.

text type focus: see **text type**

text world: the model of coherence which gradually emerges as the internal relations within a text become clear through cohesion and other textual patterns. Cognitive templates such as the 'frame' and the 'schemata' facilitate the retrieval of text worlds.

textual meaning: see **metafunctions**

texture: aspects of > **text** organization which ensure that texts hang together and reflect the **coherence** of a > **structure** in a > **context**. Texture includes aspects of message construction such as > **cohesion**, > **theme-rheme** organization, as well as idiom and diction.

theme: that part of a sentence which, in the > **unmarked** case, occurs first and which normally has less communicative importance than the > **rheme**.

thematic progression (TP):   the tendency for > **themes** or > **rhemes** to concatenate in particular patterns, relating to > **text type focus**. In > **exposition**, for example, the tendency is for the discourse to display a pattern in which themes are redeployed as themes in the subsequent discourse (**uniform pattern**). In > **argumentation**, on the other hand, the tendency is for the discourse to have rhemes deployed as themes in the subsequent discourse (**zig-zag pattern**).

thesis cited to be opposed: see **text structure**

through-argument: see **argumentation**

top-down: in cognitive psychology and adjacent disciplines, two different ways in which humans analyse and process language are distinguished. Top-down processing involves the reliance by the text user on contextual information (higher-level knowledge) in actually dealing with the information received (words, sentences, etc.). In **bottom-up** processing, on the other hand, text users mostly utilize text-presented information as a point of departure towards the discovery of some contextual effect. Needless to say, both types of process are involved in any meaningful act of reading or translating.

transitivity: a linguistic system in which a small set of presumably universal categories characterize different kinds of events and process, different kinds of participants in these events, and the varying circumstances of place and time within which events occur. These variations in the structure of the clause are said to relate to different world-views and to relay different ideological slants. Thus, transitivity is a choice between three main processes that can be represented in a sentence:

(a) a physical or **material process** (e.g. 'John shaved his beard'). This category is further subdivided into: (1) **action process** (as above); (2) **intention process** (e.g. 'John aims to please'); and (3) **supervention process**, in which an action simply happens (e.g. 'John fell down');

(b) a **mental process** (e.g. 'John saw Jane');

(c) a **relational process** (e.g. 'Such a perspective is lacking').

Related to this choice of process is choice of participant and choice of circumstances.

uniform pattern: see **thematic progression**

unmarked: the state of certain lexical or grammatical items or structures which are considered to be more basic or common than other structures which are **marked** for particular effects. The cleft sentence *It was John who did it* is a marked form of *John did it.*

verdictive: see **illocutionary act**

violating a maxim: see **the cooperative principle**

virtual: a term used to refer to systemic aspects of language structure or *langue* before context is brought in to add another, deeper, dimension of meaning. When this happens, and linguistic structures are seen as part of *parole*, we are in the domain of the actual.

visual text: a text that is put together in such a way as to satisfy the requirements of literate (as opposed to orate) rhetorical conventions at work in societies characterized by literacy (as opposed to orality). In such societies, texts are normally heavily subordinated, possessing minimal unnecessary repetition and being generally tighter (or more complex) in terms of both > **structure** and > **texture**. Orate communities of language users, on the other hand, would be content with so-called aural texts that tend to be heavily coordinated, that exhibit a great deal of repetition and that are generally looser (or simpler) in terms of both > **structure** and > **texture**.

zig-zag pattern: see **thematic progression**

Notes

1 UNITY IN DIVERSITY

1 We also provide after each translation and between square brackets a formal, close back-translation into English. On this convention, see further note 7 to Chapter 2 and note 2 to Chapter 3.
2 For a clear account of transitivity and its role in signalling ideology and point of view, see Simpson (1993).
3 It could be argued that *mon être* (1.7) and *my grip* (1.8) are animate actors, in which case these processes would be classified as supervention processes. This would not affect the conclusions drawn here since, in both cases, processes are presented as just happening, independently of human volition.
4 See Hatim and Mason (1990), where there is a full discussion of each of these dimensions of context and the way in which they relate to the work of the translator.
5 Reiss and Vermeer (1984). See also on this notion Snell-Hornby (1988) and Nord (1991 and 1993).
6 Cf. Fletcher (1985).
7 Conversational implicatures: see Grice (1975). For a useful and straightforward account of Grice's Cooperative Principle, presupposition, implicature and related notions, see Brown and Yule (1983: 27–35).
8 Effectiveness and efficiency: cf. Beaugrande and Dressler (1981: 11). Cf. also Gutt's (1991) application of relevance theory to translating, which propounds a similar view.

2 FOUNDATIONS FOR A MODEL OF ANALYSING TEXTS

1 The foundation terms of reference in this are in the main provided by Beaugrande and Dressler (1981). Additional notions are drawn from a variety of approaches including Brown and Yule (1983), Fairclough (1989), Hatim and Mason (1990).
2 On 'sense constancy', see Hans Hörmann (1975), cited in Schmidt (1977).

3   The kind of intertextuality which involves the 'socio-cultural' may be likened to 'horizontal intertextuality' (Bakhtin 1986) or to 'manifest intertextuality' (Fairclough 1992). Similarly, the kind of intertextuality which involves the 'socio-textual' is akin to Bakhtin's 'vertical intertextuality' and Fairclough's 'constitutive intertextuality'.

4   The notion of register has seen a number of interesting modifications over the years. These attempts at extending register analysis include most of Halliday's later works (see bibliography), Martin (1990) and the work of others writing within the framework of systemic linguistics.

5   It is perhaps helpful to summarize with the help of a diagram how the Hallidayan system of 'semiotic macro-functions' fits within the original register categories:

> **Field** (social institutions and processes): observer ideational function: transitivity, etc.
> **Tenor** (social distance): intruder interpersonal function: mood, modality, etc.
> **Mode** (proxemic distance): the enabling textual function: theme-rheme progression, etc.

6   These examples are taken from Daniel Kies's (1992) detailed study of the uses of passivity and the suppression of agency in Orwell's *1984*.

7   In this book, we adopt the convention of producing what we will call 'formal' translations of texts originally not in English, and enclose these in square brackets. In this, we intend to translate literally only those features which are relevant to the particular point under discussion, leaving the rest in as idiomatic English as possible. In adopting such a procedure, there is a matter worth forewarning the reader about: the larger bulk of the text would be error-free which could distract the reader from attending to the point at issue. We have thus endeavoured systematically to highlight points of interest and gloss the nature of the problem.

3   INTERPRETING: A TEXT LINGUISTIC APPROACH

1   We are referring here to the essential components of context as outlined in the first sections of this chapter. It is of course the case that simultaneous interpreters are generally fully briefed in advance about such situational factors as the identity of the speaker and his or her likely views.

2   Another point related to the convention of using 'formal' translations for texts originally not in English (see note 7, Chapter 2) is to do with the segments that are at issue and are therefore rendered literally. These are bound to sound awkward in English (verbose, redundant, ungainly, etc.). Such oddness is deliberately retained in our formal renderings, but should not in any way be misconstrued as reflecting badly on the text producer or indeed the foreign language concerned. Speakers and the languages concerned could be and often are renowned for, say, an

extremely elegant oratorial style, but this inevitably gets distorted when literal rendering is opted for.
3 This is comparable to Bakhtin's (1986) use of the terms 'double voicing' or 'reaccentuation'.
4 Research in interpreting is vigorously pursued in a number of centres around the world: Gile (France), Candlin, Campbell, Gentile (Australia), Pöchacker (Austria), Shlesinger (Israel), etc. See next chapter.

4 TEXTURE IN SIMULTANEOUS INTERPRETING

1 In some cases, speakers do include the interpreter in their audience design if (a) they are aware that important addressees are relying on the interpreter and/or (b) they are aware of the role of the interpreter.
2 Several studies based on evidence from trainee output are now being produced. See, for example, Pöchhacker (1993), Shlesinger (1995).
3 For the purposes of this training exercise, the text of the speeches was delivered and video-recorded by a native speaker of French at an average rate of 100 words per minute.
4 The English gloss provided after each text sample is intended to assist comprehension of the ST only. It is in no way intended as a model interpreter version. It should also be noted that even the written presentation of what is in fact an oral ST is misleading in terms of the task which the interpreter actually faces; and further, that the interpreter output reproduced here is not, save in a rudimentary way, accompanied by the intonation patterns, stress and timing on which interpreters crucially rely in order to 'get their message across' in a coherent and cohesive fashion.
5 Cf. Halliday and Hasan (1976), who list intonation as a cohesive device in itself.
6 We have not attempted to provide full information on intonation since we wish to focus only on the question of whether or not a 'sentence-end' pattern is signalled.

5 POLITENESS IN SCREEN TRANSLATING

1 These norms appear to be generally observed in Europe and the Western world as a whole. It should be noted that, elsewhere, far greater intrusion of text on screen may be tolerated.
2 This is so because attention to face is what adds words to basic propositional meaning. As Brown and Levinson (1987: 57) observe, '. . . one recognizes what people are doing in verbal exchanges . . . not so much in what they overtly claim to be doing as in the fine linguistic detail of their utterances (together with kinesic clues)'.
3 Literal translations are provided in square brackets, simply as a guide to the form of the ST; the subtitles are reproduced on the right-hand side of the page.

4 Among the off-record strategies listed by Brown and Levinson (1987: 214) are: 'Do the FTA but be indirect ... *be incomplete*, use ellipsis' (emphasis added).

6 REGISTER MEMBERSHIP IN LITERARY TRANSLATING

1 In his introduction, the translator refers to a distinction between the 'bad Catalan' of the common people and the 'good Catalan' of the cultivated people of Barcelona.

7 FORM AND FUNCTION IN THE TRANSLATION OF THE SACRED AND SENSITIVE TEXT

1 It should be mentioned that Nida (1964) may be considered as one of the earlier translation theorists to broach the subject of stylistic unexpectedness or what is nowadays being discussed under informativity.
2 The basic theory of politeness as outlined in Brown and Levinson (1987) was summarised in Chapter 5. A number of useful modifications to the main theory include Myers (1989) and Sell (1992).
3 Indeed, choices (a) and (b) can usefully be compared to the last utterance analysed in Chapter 5 (3 Challenge), where the use of the pronoun *on*, with its ambiguity of references, serves the purpose of face-protection.
4 We are indebted to Anne Love (on the Masters course in Arabic at Heriot-Watt University) for this particular reading.
5 Ted Hope of the United Bible Societies was instrumental in bringing the Jonah text to our attention and in pointing out the problem of irony and how this is missed in a number of English translations.
6 We thank Gretel Qumsieh (on the Masters course in Arabic at Heriot-Watt University) for this insight into the motivation underlying the introduction of the Psalms.

8 CROSS-CULTURAL COMMUNICATION

1 For work on translation and text typologies that roughly falls within this orientation, see, for example, Emery (1989), Zyadatiss (1983). See also Hatim and Mason (1990), where this text typology is described.
2 This is seen from a translation perspective in Sa'adeddin (1989). The theoretical framework is explored in detail in the work of Prothro (1955) and Kaplan (1966).

9 IDEOLOGY

1 While accepting Fairclough's (1989: 17) view that discourse is 'social practice determined by social structures', we believe, with Pennycook

(1994) that a proper place has to be accorded to individual human agency.

2 Thus: 'foreignizing translation in English can be a form of resistance against ethnocentrism and racism, cultural narcissism and imperialism, in the interests of democratic geopolitical relations' (Venuti 1995: 20).

3 Zabalbeascoa (1993) comments on such a situation in Catalonia, where 'a number of intellectuals and politicians have acted as a mouthpiece for such reactions. Their argument is that a high percentage of foreign programmes (typically from the USA) is not only propagandistic regarding the themes, sociocultural values and messages contained in them, but also pernicious regarding the way in which they influence and change the forms and expressions of the vernacular.'

4 Cf. Chapter 2, p. 32, regarding the dynamism involved in repetition.

5 A fuller analysis of this translation, including the perspective of the Eastern rhetorical tradition, is to be found in Hatim and Mason (1991).

6 Parallelism: 'repeating a structure but filling it with new elements' (Beaugrande and Dressler 1981: 49).

7 Intention processes: 'Action processes may be . . . subdivided into intention processes (where the actor performs the act voluntarily) and supervention processes (where the process just happens)' (Simpson 1993: 89).

8 Over-lexicalization: 'the availability, or the use, of a profusion of terms for an object or concept' (Fowler 1986: 154).

9 See, for example, Gumperz (1982: 59–99).

10 A fuller analysis is provided in Mason (1994).

11 The terminology employed here is that used by Simpson (1993: 91–2), who defines relational processes as processes of being; and lists the participant roles in such processes as carrier ('roughly, the "topic" of the clause') and attribute ('a description or comment about the topic').

12 For the purposes of this text sample, the translation provided in square brackets attempts to represent the dynamic force of the ST expression; it is, in Newmark's terms, a communicative translation. The published translation appears, as usual, on the right-hand side of the page.

13 Cf. also Muñoz Martín (1995), whose critique of Venuti (1995) includes the point that a foreignizing translation is in itself an attempt to re-educate and adopt a position of authority, i.e. power, over the reader of the target text.

10 TEXT-LEVEL ERRORS

1 After the test and the transcription of the taped material of the session, the students were met individually and informally questioned as to how they perceived the intentionality of the source text and the meanings of the various elements tackled.

2 Important cross-cultural communication studies include the work of Gumperz (1977, 1982), Scollon and Scollon (1995).

3 For a detailed analysis of this and other examples from the perspective of power and ideology, see Fairclough (1989, 1992, 1995).

4 In dealing with this sample, both the literary-critical and the text-linguistic angles were provided by McHale (1992).

11 CURRICULUM DESIGN

1 It is perhaps worth nothing that the Formulaic Report, although highly constrained, has been placed after the more evaluative varieties of the News Report. For reasons of convenience, it was considered helpful to deal with the category Report separately from news reporting, and to consider it as consisting of the three basic variants: the Formulaic, the Executive and the Personalized.
2 On the distinction between text and discourse, see Candlin's preface to Coulthard (1975).

12 ASSESSING PERFORMANCE

1 Reliability: 'the extent to which an assessment would produce the same, or similar, score on two occasions or if given by two assessors'. Validity: 'the extent to which an assessment measures what it purports to measure' (Gipps 1994: vii).
2 'At universities which run courses for training professional translators, the only method of monitoring learning progress appears at present to be the translation of a text. The source-text material used for exams is selected almost exclusively according to the degree of text-specific difficulty' (Nord 1991: 160-1).
3 See, e.g., Languages Lead Body, *National Standards for Interpreting and Translating*, Crown copyright (forthcoming).
4 'In an *objective test* the correctness of the test taker's response is determined entirely by predetermined criteria so that no judgement is required on the part of scorers. In a *subjective test*, on the other hand, the scorer must make a judgement about the correctness of the response based on her subjective interpretation of the scoring criteria' (Bachman 1990: 76).
5 Conversely, for a translation test to be valid, it must allow a reasonable consensus among testers as to the text world it constructs or as to the range of possible interpretations. Accepting that no two readings of a text are ever identical need not entail a view that it is impossible to measure the accuracy of a translation.
6 Cf. Sager (1983: 121): 'There are no absolute standards of translation quality but only more or less appropriate translations for the purpose for which they are intended.'
7 Cf. Hewson and Martin (1991), whose variational approach aims to encompass the *range* of options available to the translator.
8 For example, Sager (1983) lists as uses: scanning and discard; reading for information; detailed information and storage for future reference; draft for other texts; publication, for prestige or for public record; legal validity.
9 Likewise, it would be pointless to evaluate a consecutive interpreter's performance by measuring it against a full translation, given the general

expectation that the consecutive interpreter should seek to be efficient, i.e. occupy less time than the ST.

10 Cf. Canale (1983), who distinguishes grammatical competence (including knowledge of lexis), socio-linguistic competence (appropriateness to context), discourse competence (combining forms and meanings into texts) and strategic competence (compensating for breakdown and enhancing the effectiveness of communication); cf. also Canale and Swain (1980), and R. Bell (1991) who adopts this framework for describing translator communicative competence.

11 Cf. Nord (1991: 162), who suggests that, in achievement testing, new or unfamiliar translation problems which occur in an examination text should not be included in the evaluation.

References

Abu Libdeh, A. (1991) *Metaphoric Expression in Literary Discourse with Special Reference to English–Arabic Translation.* Unpublished PhD thesis, Heriot-Watt University, Edinburgh.

Bachman, L. (1990) *Fundamental Considerations in Language Testing.* Oxford: Oxford University Press.

Baker, M. (1992) *In Other Words.* London: Routledge.

Bakhtin, M. (1986) *Speech Genres and Other Late Essays* (eds C. Emerson and M. Holquist, trans. V. McGee). Austin: University of Texas Press.

Barthes, R. (1970) *S/Z.* Paris: Seuil.

Bassnett, S. and Lefevere, A. (eds) (1990) *Translation, History and Culture.* London: Pinter.

Beaugrande, R. de and Dressler, W. (1981) *Introduction to Text Linguistics.* London: Longman.

Bédard, C. (1986) *La Traduction technique: principes et pratique.* Montreal: Linguatech.

Bell, A. (1984) 'Language style as audience design'. *Language in Society* 13: 145–204.

Bell, R. (1991) *Translation and Translating.* London: Longman.

Berk-Seligson, S. (1990) *The Bilingual Courtroom. Court Interpreters in the Judicial Process.* Chicago: University of Chicago Press.

Brown, G. and Yule, G. (1983) *Discourse Analysis.* Cambridge: Cambridge University Press.

Brown, P. and Levinson, S. (1987) *Politeness. Some Universals in Language Usage.* Cambridge: Cambridge University Press.

Canale, M. (1983) 'From communicative competence to communicative language pedagogy', in J. Richards and R. Schmidt (eds) *Language and Communication.* London: Longman, 2–27.

Canale, M. and Swain, M. (1980) 'Theoretical bases of communicative approaches to second language teaching and testing'. *Applied Linguistics* 1 (1): 1–47.

Catford, J. (1965) *A Linguistic Theory of Translation.* Oxford: Oxford University Press.

Chaume, F. (forthcoming) 'Textual constraints and the translator's creativity in dubbing', in B. Moser-Mercer (ed.) *Proceedings of IX International*

Conference on Translators' Strategies and Creativity. Prague, 1995.

Coulthard, M. (1975) *Discourse Analysis.* London: Longman.

Darò, V. and Fabbro, F. (1994) 'Verbal memory during simultaneous interpretation: effects of phonological interference'. *Applied Linguistics* 15 (4): 365–81.

Davies, A. (1990) *Principles of Language Testing.* Oxford: Basil Blackwell.

Emery, P. (1991) 'Text classification and text analysis in advanced translation teaching'. *Meta* XXXVI (4): 567–77.

Fairclough, N. (1989) *Language and Power.* London: Longman.

—— (1992) *Discourse and Social Change.* Cambridge: Polity Press.

—— (1995) *Critical Discourse Analysis: The Critical Study of Language.* London: Longman.

Fletcher, C. (1985) 'The functional role of markedness in topic identification'. *Text* 5: 23–37.

Fowler, R. (1986) *Linguistic Criticism.* Oxford: Oxford University Press.

Fowler, R., Hodge, R., Kress, G., Trew, T. (1979) *Language and Control.* London: Routledge and Kegan Paul.

Francis, G. and Kramer-Dahl, A. (1992) 'Grammaticalizing the medical case history', in M. Toolan (ed.) *Language, Text and Context: Essays in Stylistics.* London: Routledge, 56–92.

Gee, J. (1990) *Social Linguistics and Literacies: Ideology in Discourses.* London: Falmer Press.

Gerver, D. (1976) 'Empirical studies of simultaneous interpretation: a review and a model', in R. Brislin (ed.) *Translation. Applications and Research.* New York: Gardner, 165–207.

Gile, D. (1995) *Basic Concepts and Models for Interpreter and Translator Training.* Amsterdam: John Benjamins.

Gipps, C. (1994) *Beyond Testing. Towards a Theory of Educational Assessment.* London: Falmer Press.

Gouadec, D. (1981) 'Paramètres pour l'évaluation des traductions'. *Meta* XXVI (2): 99–116.

Goldman-Eisler, F. (1980) 'Psychological mechanisms of speech production as studied through the analysis of simultaneous translation', in B. Butterworth (ed.) *Language Production 1: Speech and Talk.* New York: Academic Press, 143–54.

Goris, O. (1993) 'The question of French dubbing: towards a frame for systematic investigation'. *Target* 5 (2): 169–90.

Grice, H. (1975) 'Logic and conversation', in P. Cole and J. Morgan (eds) *Syntax and Semantics 3: Speech Acts.* New York: Academic Press, 41–58.

Gülich, E. and Raible, W. (eds) (1975) 'Textsorten-Probleme', in *Linguistische Problemen der Textanalyse.* Jahrbuch des Instituts für Deutschesprache in Mannheim. Dusseldorf: Pädagogischer Verlag Schwann, 144–97.

Gumperz, J. (1977) 'Sociocultural knowledge in conversation inference', in M. Saville-Troike (ed.) *28th Annual Round Table Monograph Series on Language and Linguistics.* Washington DC: Georgetown University Press.

—— (1982) *Discourse Strategies.* Cambridge: Cambridge University Press.

Gutt, E.-A. (1991) *Translation and Relevance. Cognition and Context.* Oxford: Basil Blackwell.

Halliday, M. (1978) *Language as Social Semiotic*. London: Edward Arnold.

Harvey, K. (1995) 'A descriptive framework for compensation'. *The Translator* 1 (1): 65-86.

Hatim, B. and Mason, I. (1990) *Discourse and the Translator*. London: Longman.

—— (1991) 'Coping with ideology in professional translating'. *Interface: Journal of Applied Linguistics* 6 (1): 23-32.

Hermans, T. (1985) *The Manipulation of Literature: Studies in Literary Translation*. London: Croom Helm.

Hervey, S. and Higgins, I. (1992) *Thinking Translation. A Course in Translation Method: French-English*. London: Routledge.

Hewson, L. (1995) 'Detecting cultural shifts: some notes on translation assessment', in I. Mason and C. Pagnoulle (eds) *Cross-Words. Issues and Debates in Literary and Non-literary Translating*. Liège: L3 – Liège Language and Literature, 101-8.

Hewson, L. and Martin, J. (1991) *Redefining Translation: The Variational Approach*. London: Routledge.

Hodge, R. and Kress, G. (1993) *Language as Ideology* (2nd edn). London: Routledge.

Hörmann, H. (1975) *The Concept of Sense Constancy*. Mimeo: University of Bochum.

House, J. (1981) *A Model for Translation Quality Assessment*. Tübingen: Narr.

Hurtado, A. (1995) 'La didáctica de la traducción. Evolución y estado actual', in P. Fernández and J-.M. Bravo (eds) *Perspectivas de la Traducción*. Valladolid: Universidad de Valladolid, 49–74.

Knowles, M. and Malmkjær, K. (1989) 'Translating ideology: language, power and the world of the Tin Soldier', in *Language and Ideology. ELR Journal 3*. Birmingham: University of Birmingham, 205-41.

Kress, G. (1985) *Linguistic Processes in Sociocultural Practice*. Victoria: Deakin University Press.

Lambert, J. (1990) 'Le sous-titrage et la question des traductions: rapport sur une enquête', in R. Arntz and G. Thome (eds) *Übersetzungwissenschaft: Ergebnisse und Perspektiven. Festschrift für W. Wilss zum 65. Geburtstag*. Tübingen: Narr, 228-38.

Lee, D. (1992) *Competing Discourses*. London: Longman.

McHale, B. (1992) 'Making (non)sense of postmodernist poetry', in M. Toolan (ed.) *Language, Text and Context: Essays in Stylistics*. London: Routledge, 6–38.

Martin, J. R. (1985) *Factual Writing: Exploring and Challenging Social Reality*. Victoria: Deakin University Press.

—— (1992) *English Text: System and Structure*. Amsterdam: John Benjamins.

Mason, I. (1989) 'Speaker meaning and reader meaning: preserving coherence in screen translating', in R. Kölmel and J. Payne (eds) *Babel. The Cultural and Linguistic Barriers between Nations*. Aberdeen: Aberdeen University Press, 13–24.

—— (1994) 'Discourse, ideology and translation', in R. de Beaugrande, A. Shunnaq and M. Heliel (eds) *Language, Discourse and Translation in the West and Middle East*. Amsterdam: Benjamins, 23–34.

Muñoz Martín, R. (1995) 'La visibilidad, al "trasluz"'. *Sendebar* 5, University of Granada, 5–21.

Myers, G. (1989) 'The pragmatics of politeness in scientific articles'. *Applied Linguistics* 10 (1):1–35.

Nabokov, V. (1964) 'Translator's introduction', in A. Pushkin, *Eugene Onegin, Translated from the Russian, with a Commentary, by Vladimir Nabokov*. New York: Bollingen Foundation.

Newmark, P. (1981) *Approaches to Translation*. Oxford: Pergamon Press.

—— (1988) *A Textbook of Translation*. London: Prentice Hall.

Nida, E. (1964) *Towards a Science of Translation*. Leiden: Brill.

Nord, C. (1991) *Text Analysis in Translation*. Amsterdam: Rodopi.

—— (1993) *Einführung in das funktionale Übersetzen*. Tübingen: Francke Verlag.

Peirce, C. (1931–58) *Collected Papers* (ed. C. Hartshone). Cambridge, Mass.: Harvard University Press.

Pennycook, A. (1994) 'Incommensurable discourses'. *Applied Linguistics* 15 (2): 115–38.

Pöchhacker, F. (1993) 'From knowledge to text: coherence in simultaneous interpreting', in Y. Gambier and J. Tommola (eds) *Translation and Knowledge*. Turku: University of Turku, 87–100.

Reiss, K. and Vermeer, H. (1984) *Grundlagen einer allgemeinen Translationstheorie*. Tübingen: Quelle and Meyer.

Sa'adeddin, M. (1989) 'Text development and Arabic–English negative interference'. *Applied Linguistics* 10 (1): 36–51.

Sager (1983) 'Quality and standards – the evaluation of translations', in C. Picken (ed.) *The Translator's Handbook*. London: Aslib, 121–8.

Schmidt, S. (1977) 'Some problems of communicative text theories', in W. Dressler (ed.) *Current Trends in Textlinguistics*. Berlin: de Gruyter, 47–60.

Scollon, R. and Scollon, S. (1995) *Intercultural Communication. A Discourse Approach*. Oxford: Basil Blackwell.

Sell, R. (1992) *Literary Pragmatics*. London: Routledge.

Shlesinger, M. (1995) 'Shifts in cohesion in simultaneous interpreting'. *The Translator* 1 (2): 193–214.

Simpson, P. (1993) *Language, Ideology and Point of View*. London: Routledge.

Snell-Hornby, M. (1988) *Translation Studies. An Integrated Approach*. Amsterdam: Benjamins.

Stewart, M. (1992) *Personal Reference and Politeness Strategies in French and Spanish: A Corpus-based Approach*. Unpublished PhD thesis, Heriot-Watt University, Edinburgh.

—— (1995) 'Personally speaking . . . or not?: the strategic value of *on* in face-to-face negotiation'. *Journal of French Language Studies* 5 (2): 203–23.

Sykes, M. (1985) 'Discrimination in discourse', in T. Van Dijk (ed.) *Handbook of Discourse Analysis 4: Discourse Analysis in Society*. New York: Academic Press, 83–101.

Titford, C. (1982) 'Subtitling, constrained translation'. *Lebende Sprachen* 27 (3): 113–16.

Venuti, L. (1995) *The Translator's Invisibility. A History of Translation*. London: Routledge.

Vöge, H. (1977) 'The translation of films: subtitling versus dubbing'. *Babel* 23: 120–25.

Wadman, K. (1983) ' "Private Ejaculations": politeness strategies in George Herbert's poems directed to God'. *Language and Style* 16: 87–106.

Werlich, E. (1976) *A Text Grammar of English*. Heidelberg: Quelle and Meyer.

Zabalbeascoa, P. (1993) *Developing Translation Studies to Better Account for Audiovisual Texts and Other New Forms of Text Production*. Unpublished doctoral thesis, University of Lleida.

Zyadatiss, W. (1983) 'Text typologies and translation'. *The Incorporated Linguist* 22 (4): 212–21.

Index